Bill W.

Bill W.

A Biography of Alcoholics Anonymous Cofounder Bill Wilson

FRANCIS HARTIGAN

Thomas Dunne Books
St. Martin's Griffin
New York

THOMAS DUNNE BOOKS.
An imprint of St. Martin's Press.

BILL W.: A BIOGRAPHY OF ALCOHOLICS ANONYMOUS COFOUNDER BILL WIL-
SON. Copyright © 2000 by Francis Hartigan. All rights reserved. Printed in
the United States of America. No part of this book may be used or reproduced in any manner whatsoever without written permission except in the
case of brief quotations embodied in critical articles or reviews. For information, address St. Martin's Press, 175 Fifth Avenue, New York, N.Y. 10010.

Book design by Diane Hobbing of Snap-Haus Graphics

www.stmartins.com

Library of Congress Cataloging-in-Publication Data

Hartigan, Francis.
    Bill W.: a biography of Alcoholics Anonymous cofounder Bill Wilson /
Francis Hartigan.
            p. cm.
    Includes bibliographical references and index.
    ISBN: 978-0-312-28391-9
    ISBN: 0-312-28391-1
    1. W., Bill. 2. Alcoholics—United States—Biography. 3. Alcoholics
Anonymous.
    I. Title.
HV5032.W19 H37 2001
362.292'86'092—dc21
    [B]   99-055856

P 1

For Ernie Kurtz and Mel B.,
with gratitude and affection

CONTENTS

ACKNOWLEDGMENTS

If any book can be written in isolation, it certainly isn't a biography, and this one has benefited from the generosity of many people. First among them would have to be Lois Wilson. She freely shared with me her unparalleled knowledge of AA and her husband, and she granted me complete access to all the material in her possession pertaining to both. Lois also made sure that I met the important historical figures among her many visitors. I have sometimes disagreed with her here (as I did when I knew her) and discussed issues I know she would have found intolerable, but my admiration, respect, and affection for this most remarkable woman remain undimmed.

Second would be Nell Wing, who shared unstintingly her vast knowledge of Bill Wilson and Alcoholics Anonymous. Both women's assessment of Bill Wilson as a great man was unqualified, and in this respect, I share their view of him completely.

It is much harder to rank the contributions of so many others, and I will not try. Charlie Bishop, Jr., the "Bishop of Books," prodded me to take on this project and supported me in every possible way during the years it took to complete it. I am also grateful for the many books Charlie has published on AA-related topics that otherwise would never have seen the light of day.

Ernie Kurtz and Mel B., old friends who had plowed this ground before me, were breathtakingly generous with their time and knowledge. Each was consistently encouraging, and their genuine desire to see this project further our understanding of Bill and his relationship to AA has meant more to me than I can say. Both Ernie and Mel read the manuscript at various stages and offered sound criticism. Mel actually read it twice, and in doing so saved me from a number of factual errors. Their combined helpfulness provided me with a working example of the spirit of fellowship that I will always remember.

This project also owes a large debt of gratitude to the Center for Alcoholism and Addiction at Brown University. At a critical point, the Center hosted the Chester H. Kirk Collection on Alcoholism and Alcoholics Anonymous Information Researches Conference. The conference provided me with the opportunity to meet or become reacquainted with many people who had written about and/or researched a great many of the topics I wanted to cover. Everyone was encouraging and supportive, and, besides Ernie, Mel, and Charlie, several other attendees subsequently provided me with invaluable assistance.

Bill White, whom I first came to know at the conference, became a good friend and a reader of the manuscript who provided valuable commentary. Bill also shared with me his knowledge about the founding of Charles B. Towns Hospital, which he acquired in the course of preparing his landmark history of addiction treatment. Ron Roizen, another new friend made at the conference, became a reader and a provider of insightful commentary and enthusiastic support. Others whom I either met or re-met at the Brown conference who provided help and support include Mitchell Klein, L. Earl Husband, Wally Paton, and Andrea Mitchell.

The Reverend Stephen S. Garmy, Vicar of Calvary Church in New York, was very generous with his knowledge and insights about the Oxford Group in New York. Lynn Harbaugh graciously shared her master's thesis on High Watch Farms and her thoughts about what life was like for New York–area AA members in the 1940s and 1950s. Sheila Gibbons, the archivist at Riverside Church, was most helpful, as were the archivists at the Midwest Jesuit Archives and the Archives of the Episcopal Church. The librarians of the Kreitzbergh Library at Norwich University, at Burr and Burton Academy, and Brooklyn Law School also provided able assistance.

Frank Drollinger and John Robinson, two very old friends, served as lay readers, thereby helping to ensure that I wasn't preaching to the choir. Frank and his wife, Carol, also graciously lent me their beach home during the several "working vacations" the project encompassed, and friends Paul and Joanne Dolan did the same with their mountain retreat.

David C. Lewis, M.D., Director of the Brown Center for Alcohol and Addiction Studies, was supportive and encouraging, and Tovah Reis from the university's medical library provided research assistance. Mary-Jo Kline of the Hay Library at Brown shepherded me through the Chester H. Kirk Collection on Alcoholism and Alcoholics. Anke Voss-Hubbard provided the same service in my researches at the Rockefeller Archive Center. The staffs of the New York Library Mid-Manhattan branch and the Library for the Performing Arts were unfailingly helpful and courteous, as was the staff at the AA Grapevine, Inc., the New York Academy of Medicine, and the libraries of Temple University.

Leslie Goat, a good friend at Dartmouth College's Baker Library, was very diligent in tracking down certain articles for me. In Vermont, the archivists at the Dorset Historical Society and the Manchester Historical Society were extremely helpful, as were Ozzie, Bonnie, and the entire staff at the Wilson House.

I gratefully acknowledge the contribution made by the many other people who generously shared with me their knowledge of Bill Wilson, including Barry Leach; Bryan Lynch and Anne Lynch; Clarence Snyder; Dorothy Strong; Leonard Strong, D.O.; "Bud" Strong; and Harold U. Others who shared their insights include Steve Schutte; Nan Robertson; Sue Windows; Robert "Smitty" Smith; Jack Norris; Tom P.; LeClair Bissell, M.D.; Dennis Manders, Lib. S.; Shepperd Strudwick, Jr.; Anne M.; Merton M.; Donald D.; Kerry O.; Abram Hoffer, M.D.; Humphrey Osmund, M.D.; Ellen Huxley; and Adele Smithers.

There are literally hundreds of others to be thanked. People who, at one time or another during the twenty years I spent asking myself the question, "What was Bill Wilson really like?" provided helpful clues. Most were AA members, but many were not. Among this latter group were the Mario at the post office where Bill picked up his mail; the neighbor who shared with me something of his conversations with Bill when he was out for his walks; and the Mario at the service station that took care of Bill's cars. All three thought he was a great man, saw themselves as guardians of his privacy, and counted him among their friends, which I'm sure he was.

My agent, Susan Zeckendorf, believed in this project from the moment that she laid eyes on it. She was wonderful during the tribulations of seeking a publisher, and a calm and reassuring presence throughout the tortuous and often anxiety-provoking publication process. Tom Dunne, my editor and publisher, saw its value when few others did, and his enthusiasm and support seemed to increase in pace with the project's development. As an editor, he seems to have perfect pitch: every note he questioned was a false one or at least off-key. Anne Savarese also provided keen and insightful editorial commentary, Juli Barbato assiduous copyediting, and Melissa Jacobs diligent assistance in seeing the manuscript through to the printed page.

However much I may have benefited from the assistance of others, the opinions herein are mine alone, and I alone am responsible for any errors, factual or otherwise.

Finally, I will be forever grateful for the indulgence of my children, Louisa and Willie, and Phoebe Kaylor, my dearest friend and companion. They had to compete with this project for my time and attention, then put up with the fatigue and grumpiness my work on it often engendered.

A WORD ON ANONYMITY

Always, it would seem, a touchy subject in AA circles and perhaps never more so than today. In this project, I have adhered to what I concluded was the consensus opinion among the researchers, archivists, and librarians assembled at the Chester H. Kirk Collection on Alcoholism and Alcoholics Anonymous Information Researches Conference referred to previously. In identifying deceased members of AA and Al-Anon, unless I had reason to believe that either they or their surviving family members would object, I have provided both first and last names. In all other instances, members of AA or Al-Anon have been identified as such using their first name and the first letter of their last name only.

Bill
W.

INTRODUCTION

THE POSTER BOY

That AA was never the "Bill Wilson Movement" is probably the biggest reason it's not just another in the line of failed personality cults dedicated to helping alcoholics that preceded it. Wilson had researched these earlier efforts, and he was aware of the contribution their cultic aspects made to their ultimate failure. That AA has never strayed from its primary purpose, helping alcoholics to stop drinking, is a tribute to his insight and his skills as a "social engineer." It is also why, more than twenty-five years after his death, Alcoholics Anonymous continues to grow and to prosper.

Bill Wilson's personal popularity in AA circles was enormous. People would wait in line at large AA gatherings just to touch his sleeve. Many treated him like the Messiah or, in today's world, a rock star. He could not ride an elevator or walk down a hallway without being accosted. People strained to hear anything he might say even in casual conversation. Most often, members wanted just to meet him and thank him for what he had done for them. Others would seize any opportunity to tell him what was wrong with AA or with Bill Wilson himself. Wilson also had his enemies, many of them people who were previously among his staunchest allies. They accused him of betrayal, of power mongering, of lacking principle, of trying to ruin the organization he had dedicated his life to, of personal immorality, and even of insanity. Some even imagined that he was siphoning off enormous sums of money from a fellowship that had taken vows of corporate poverty.

With the exception of his womanizing, none of these charges were true, and many of them flew in the face of the facts. Instead of power mongering, almost from the beginning of AA, Wilson engaged in a process of devolving power to the fellowship at large. At the point where the charges of profiteering were most flagrant, he and his wife were dependent on the often-scant charity of friends for a place to sleep and the very clothes on their backs. Perhaps most ironically, Bill was most likely to be charged with being unprincipled and double-crossing when he took stands based on a desire to ensure that Alcoholics Anonymous would always be open and welcoming to the alcoholic who was still suffering. Judging from the guilt and remorse he suffered over his inability to control his sexual impulses, even his infidelities seem to be evidence not of a lack of standards but of a failure to live up to them.

Wilson was probably the most available leader any movement has ever had. He listened, absorbing the criticism or the praise, often beyond the limits of his endurance. While at least some of a rock star's fans might be reluctant to approach him, Bill wanted AA members to feel as though AA belonged to them, and they often assumed that he belonged to them, too. This made it almost inevitable that people would believe that he shared their own aspirations for AA. When it would become clear that he did not, their sense of betrayal could be enormous.

The attention Bill received from the membership at large made his appearances at AA events an exhausting ordeal. Anyone might have found them hard to take, but it was especially so for Bill, for reasons those who accused him of hogging the spotlight could never appreciate. The truth was that Bill never felt worthy of the praise, and the criticism only served to reinforce his already low opinion of himself.

Bill in a good mood was a hale and hearty fellow. In the early years of his recovery, his buoyancy seemed capable of overcoming all obstacles. It carried him through the struggle to turn into a reality his vision of being able to give alcoholics everywhere the help he had found in the middle of the night, in December 1934, just a few weeks before Christmas. It was the night Bill Wilson knew that he had had his last drink.

Five years later, with *Alcoholics Anonymous*, also known as the *Big Book*, published but not yet selling, the joyous energy he had come to think of as a birthright reclaimed had begun to wane. By the early 1940s, with the book selling like hotcakes and AA fast becoming a household word, Bill was experiencing periods when he simply could not summon the energy to get out of bed.

Even after he stopped drinking, Wilson had a number of personal problems, and he regarded as moral failings his inability to deal with them successfully. His financial situation never truly righted itself, his womanizing continued, and no matter how severely it was affecting his health, he could never manage to quit smoking. There was also the fact that he could not find any effective means of dealing with his crippling depressions.

More than anything, Bill wanted AA to have a governing structure that would keep it on course and safeguard it against the personal failings of someone like himself. He devoted his life to this task. From AA's earliest beginnings, he had voluntarily submitted his own desires to the will of the forty or so alcoholics staying sober in Akron and New York. Bill believed in the wisdom of this approach, and he felt sure that, no matter how large AA became, the direction of the organization should ultimately reside in its "group conscience." It was a vague term, at best, and while the concept might seem workable when there were only forty members or even a few hundred, as the hundreds became thousands and then tens of thousands, it seemed to many like a prescription for chaos. There were times when his effort to, as Bill put it, "turn the fellowship over to the fellowship," seems to have been opposed by the entire membership.

That AA is governed as a laissez-faire representative democracy is in some sense reflective of Wilson's lifelong political conservatism. It is also an expression of his deep concern for the spiritual health of humankind. Bill Wilson believed that the struggle for money, power, and position was threatening to destroy the world. It was typical for him to see things on such a grand scale and lay his plans accordingly. Wilson believed that AA would one day be able to help alcoholics everywhere. He also thought that AA was itself the world's best hope for avoiding the cataclysm he saw as the ultimate consequence of blind materialism.

Wilson could have indulged in the most blatant megalomania. Instead, he worked for thirty years to create a uniquely "unorganized" organization that would be capable of surviving him. More than twenty-nine years after his death, alcoholism is still very much with us, but AA has helped millions recover from what once was regarded as a hopeless affliction. Alcoholics Anonymous groups can now be found in more than 140 countries.

Bill had been dead twelve years when I met his wife, Lois, in February 1983. It was my first time at Stepping Stones, the summerhouse in northern Westchester County that had been the Wilson's only home since 1941. As part of the festivities surrounding AA's fiftieth anniversary in 1985, Stepping Stones was declared a New York State Historic Site.

It is a large house, brown-shingled, with a mansard roof pierced by dormers. The windows, doors, and porches are painted a striking blue; "Wilson blue," Lois called it. When approached from the driveway, the house sits somewhat below grade level, as though partly tucked into the surrounding gardens, lawns, and woods. The land in the back and to the side away from the drive drops off steeply. The house was originally approached from this side, along a nearly vertical path secured by big flat stones.

On the day I met her, Lois was recovering from a bout of bronchitis. She was in the large bedroom downstairs, which is painted a darker, softer blue, sitting up in bed and coughing violently. When the coughing stopped, the way she threw her tissue into the nearby wastebasket let me know what she thought of being sick; it was a great nuisance. She was just weeks away from her ninety-third birthday, and the way she watched me take her in told me how she felt about being old; another nuisance. Beginning some two weeks after that first meeting, I would work for Lois until her death in October 1988. I spent many hours a day with her, five and sometimes six or seven days a week. Bill Wilson was her most frequent topic of conversation.

During that time and for several years thereafter, I had the opportunity to review Bill's papers, including hundreds of letters and manuscripts of the books and the many articles he wrote for AA. I also came to know virtually everyone still alive who had known him well, and many others who knew him casually. All of them had something to say about Bill Wilson.

"Bill was a great man," Lois would say, nearly any time someone mentioned her husband in her presence. He was indeed. Aldous Huxley regarded Wilson as "the greatest social architect of the twentieth century." Next to providing Alcoholics Anonymous with its governing structure, perhaps the most important of Bill's many contributions to AA was the power of example he provided. After half a lifetime spent bobbing and weaving, this brilliant, talented, deeply flawed man reversed field. For more than thirty-five years he showed up, just as he was, and gave it his all.

In 1990, *Life* magazine named William Griffith Wilson among the one hundred most important figures of the twentieth century. It is hard to imagine the way things were before this hopeless drunk, and hopeless failure, became a "changed man." There is Alcoholics Anonymous, of course, and the Al-Anon Family Groups, Inc., and Alateen. There is also Narcotics Anonymous, Overeaters Anonymous, Gamblers Anonymous, Debtors Anonymous, and all of the other twelve-step-based programs. And there is the National Council on Alcoholism and Drug Dependencies, the schools of alcohol studies, and all the substance-abuse treatment programs. It may not be too much to say that we would have none of this without him.

AA traces its beginnings to the day that Wilson, a washed-up stock analyst from Brooklyn, succeeded in convincing Robert Holbrook Smith, a trembling proctologist from Akron, Ohio, to stop drinking. AA is considered to have been "cofounded" by these two men. As AA's "one anonymous drunk helping another" approach caught on, they would come to be known the world over as "Bill" and "Dr. Bob."

Their respective contributions to AA seem to be parallel to the depths to which they had fallen. Robert Smith had a very serious drinking problem. It made him notorious in Akron as the rectal surgeon whose patients truly "put their ass on the line." By the time Wilson got to him in the spring of 1935, Smith was fifty-six years old. In spite of his best efforts to stop, he was drinking nearly constantly, and his medical practice was virtually nonexistent.

Eight months earlier, Bill Wilson had been in far worse shape. Although he had had a successful career on Wall Street, by the fall of 1934, Wilson was unemployable and $50,000 in debt ($600,000 in year 2000 dollars). He was living in his wife's family home, a row house on Clinton Street in Brooklyn Heights, but his father-in-law had defaulted on the mortgage, and he and Lois had a place to live only by the grace of the mortgage moratorium declared by President Roosevelt. Wilson was drinking gin around the clock. Lois was still with him, but their beds were on different floors. Lest he jump out a window in a fit of drunken despair, Bill was sleeping on a mattress that had been dragged down to the ground floor.

Lois had been by his side for more than half of his thirty-nine years. She had helped him recover from the sudden death of his high school sweetheart and she had stood by him when, after his army service in World War I, he had failed repeatedly to find a place for himself in civilian life. In 1925, she had joined him in throwing over what little they had accomplished together to spend a year hoboing up and down the eastern seaboard, gathering the information and developing the techniques that would form the basis of his Wall Street success.

From the time he joined the army and had his very first drink, Wilson's alcoholism had progressed relentlessly. Lois had done everything in her power to help. At first her efforts centered on controlling his drinking. Later, she sought ways in which they could live with it. Finally, when it was clear that Bill's drinking was destroying them both, she tried frantically to get him to stop.

By the fall of 1934, she, too, was at the end of her rope. Bill's doctor, an expert on alcoholism, had told her that he thought her husband's case was hopeless. There were even signs that his drinking had caused irreversible brain damage. Lois could do little more than leave her husband a few dollars in the morning, so that he would have enough booze to keep himself from going into withdrawal while she was off clerking in a department store. When she wasn't working or cleaning up after Bill, she was looking for sanitariums, in preparation for the seemingly inevitable day when she would have to commit him.

That anyone could help a man whose alcoholism had progressed to the point Robert Smith's had in 1935 was unusual and unexpected. But that someone as sick as Bill Wilson was in 1934 could recover at all, let alone spontaneously, virtually on his own, is nothing less than a miracle.

From the day of his last drink in June 1935, Robert Smith would live another fifteen years, during which he would personally help thousands of alcoholics, retrieve his good name in the community, and establish a life of relative contentment. Bill Wilson lived thirty-six years after he stopped drinking. Lois always said that she knew, from the moment she first saw him after his "miracle," that he would never drink again, and he never did. But in some ways, her life with Bill after he stopped drinking was filled with as many difficulties as it had been before. "Serenity" was not a state anyone ever attributed to the sober Bill Wilson.

For precisely this reason, the circumstances of his recovery became a double-edged sword. A major source of the awe in which Bill was held had to do with his having been struck sober through what could be seen as some kind of divine intervention. The gap between how Bill saw himself in this area and the way others perceived him could hardly have been greater.

As someone God was thought to have touched, he was presumed to have a moral authority that trumped what others might think in this "society of equals." No matter how frequently he reiterated his belief that AA was itself a "spiritual kindergarten" and that, far from being a spiritual giant, he was someone who seemed doomed for perpetuity to repeat the course, it did little to diminish the awe in which he was held. While this could be useful in helping him to have his way in disputes over policy matters, being regarded as spiritually superior could certainly have its downside.

When his depressions became severe and he sought relief from them through psychotherapy, many AA members were outraged. Bill was castigated for not working his own program. He was accused of never having taken the AA Steps, and the primary evidence offered for this was that he had stopped drinking as a result of a spiritual conversion experience.

Bill's greater influence in AA is also a consequence of his having outlived Robert Smith by so many years. Yet there could hardly have been an alcoholic whose despair Bill was not equipped to appreciate. Because an enduring emotional balance seems always to have eluded him, Bill was never far removed from the struggles of the newcomer. Coupled with his essential goodness, Wilson's lifelong personal intimacy with suffering was no doubt a major factor in AA's spectacular success.

Bill Wilson was always interested in widening the AA franchise. AA might have started out as a men's club for white, middle-aged upper-middle-class men who had lost nearly everything, but it was never Bill's idea that it should remain that way. He wanted AA to reach *every* alcoholic, and long before anyone had to experience the devastation he had known. Even before working for Lois, I knew a man who had joined AA in New York in 1946, when he was only twenty-eight years old. "I was quite desperate," he told me, "but many members thought I was too young, that I couldn't possibly have suffered enough to be a 'real' alcoholic. Bill's attitude was, 'If he's here, he belongs here.' " From all reports, Bill felt this way about women, blacks, homosexuals, and even hippies.

The symbolism of Bill and Dr. Bob as cofounders emphasizes the importance of fellowship in the AA approach: the alcoholic alone can do nothing about his or her drinking. However, by accepting help from other alcoholics and by working to help other alcoholics oneself, the battle against alcoholism can be won.

The AA approach is also moral, nearly religious. Alcoholics find that being around other alcoholics who are not drinking can make it possible for them to stop drinking themselves. But admission of personal failings and the defects of character that lie behind them are an integral part of the step-by-step process through which alcoholics effect a "spiritual transformation." This personal change for the better is thought necessary in order to keep from returning to drinking.

Wilson's influence on this moral aspect of AA was complex and profound. AA's "moral angle" also helped to make the years of his greatest achievements and acclaim torture for him.

Many of Bill's failings centered on his arrogance. There were also, more devastatingly, his losing battles with depression, his compulsive womanizing, and a deep, and ultimately insatiable, need for approval. Even at the height of his success, Bill could be both certain that people were against him and determined to win them over. Once he succeeded in doing so, though, he seemed to lose interest. Soon, the quest for something or someone else he could not have would begin again.

Bill was hardly a poster boy for the joys of living a sober life the AA way, yet AA's poster boy was exactly what he was supposed to be. It was the role he was expected to play both in AA and in his many public appearances before distinguished medical, academic, and governmental bodies; not once or twice, but again and again, for more than thirty-five years. He played the part because it was expected of him and because, although he might not feel worthy of it, he liked the attention. Like most seducers, Bill was far from immune to the siren song of fame.

He also played the part for another reason. We have come to take AA's preeminent place in society for granted, but when Bill died in 1971, the establishment of a substance-abuse treatment industry based on AA principles was still more than a decade away. During Bill's lifetime, the AA approach was still on trial despite its successes. If AA's "head man" had not been up to the challenge of fronting AA, it would not have spoken well for its effectiveness. Bill played the role of a model of recovery, and he kept playing it even when he knew from past experience how the praise heaped on him would leave him feeling. He did it because he loved AA, although he often felt trapped and miscast as its spokesperson. He did it because as long as there was anything he could possibly do to keep another human being from having to suffer the way he had, he felt he had no choice.

Whatever else Bill Wilson was, he seems essentially to have been a good and an honest man. In the 1950s he was still working to pay off the debts he had incurred when the stock market crashed in 1929, yet he refused a sixty thousand dollar gift from a wealthy AA member. In the 1960s, when he went back to investing in earnest, on at least one occasion he reimbursed someone who had fared poorly by taking his advice. While he sometimes enjoyed the attention and prominence accorded him as AA's head man, he first tried to move out of this role in 1936, even before AA's *Big Book* had been written.

Bill Wilson was politically conservative; he railed against Roosevelt, and he opposed the welfare state all his life. But his opposition was based on spiritual grounds rather than on any zeal for a "survival of the fittest" elitism. He saw society at large as being in the grip of a power struggle that was tearing it apart, and he worked assiduously to keep the same thing from happening to AA. He was also personally generous to a fault; he never turned away someone in need.

Bill certainly had his male chauvinist side, yet he worked to open the AA franchise to women virtually from AA's inception, and he encouraged women to hold executive positions in AA. The first and, to date, only female manager of the AA office in New York was appointed in 1947 at his urging. Bill also struggled to open the fellowship to African Americans as early as 1940. As far as he was concerned, gay men and lesbians were always welcome. Marty Mann, the first woman to stay sober in AA, was a lesbian and a close friend of the Wilsons', who regularly socialized with Marty and her partner. As early as 1945, Bill even encouraged an AA clubhouse in New York to take in a black man who showed up with bleached-blond hair and wearing makeup. That the man was also a drug addict meant as little to Wilson as his cross-dressing. Twenty years later, when Bill was in his seventies, he was taking hippies to lunch, praising their grasp of the AA program, and lobbying the fellowship at large to be more welcoming and tolerant toward these young people who looked and acted so different.

Bill Wilson's life is full of paradoxes and ironies, but perhaps none is more central to AA's success than the difference between the smiling picture of health and stability he projected and the driven and depressed man he often was. The public Bill may have attracted thousands to the AA way of life, but once inside the tent, it was the struggles of the private Bill that made his fellow alcoholics feel truly welcome, warts and all.

1

IN THIS CORNER

The thing people who knew Bill Wilson seem to admire the most about him was his mind. Bill was a highly intelligent and talented individual with an eclectic approach to problem solving. He was unhesitant about taking what already existed and adapting it to suit his purpose. He was also capable of engaging in an extended process of profound, original thinking. When something interested him, he was a prodigiously hard worker, but he had a seemingly constitutional inability to behave like other people. If you needed someone who could show up every day and do what needed to be done, Bill Wilson was not your man. Whenever this was required of him, he failed.

Lois was in many ways Bill's opposite. He was well over six feet tall, while she barely topped five. Bill was all length and lean, while Lois, always more filled out than he was, in her middle years tended to be stout. Both had brilliant, iconoclastic minds and a quick and original sense of humor. Both were very good people. Bill was born November 26, 1895, Lois March 4, 1891, and in some ways they were products more of the nineteenth century than of the twentieth. They were fiercely ambitious, but for them, doing well had little to do with material success. For Bill Wilson and for Lois Burnham Wilson, the doing well that truly mattered was the result of good works.

Bill was compulsive, given to emotional extremes. Even after he stopped drinking, he was still a heavy consumer of cigarettes and coffee. He had a sweet tooth, a large appetite for sex, a major enthusiasm for LSD, and, later, for niacin, a B-complex vitamin. Lois was, by nature, abstentious. Although no one would accuse her of being plodding, she was nothing if not steady. She never smoked, had virtually no interest in sweets, drank two cups of coffee a day, never slept with any man except Bill, and gave up sex altogether with menopause.

When Bill joined with Gerald Heard, Aldous Huxley, and others in their early experiments with LSD, Lois didn't have the slightest curiosity about it. When at Bill's urging she finally took LSD herself, she claimed not to have felt a thing. Of those who witnessed her one attempt at tripping, only Bill, who desperately wanted her to experience what he was, ever contradicted her version of the event.

Lois drank, but her idea of drinking was to have a scotch and water, or in the summer months a gin and tonic, before dinner. The only time she or anyone else could recall her ever getting drunk was when she did so deliberately, in an attempt to show Bill how ridiculous he looked when he was. When, at the age of ninety-five, her doctor told her that she would be better off if she did not drink at all, she stopped completely and never looked back. Lois's steadiness did not keep her from being an interesting and engaging woman, with a willingness to flout convention that was every bit a match for her husband's. She had her enthusiasms, but they were as unvarying as her devotion to Bill.

Perhaps the biggest way in which Bill and Lois differed had to do with their backgrounds. Anyone who cared to could justifiably accuse Lois of marrying below her class. Bill was always very much aware of this, but he was neither as lowborn nor as uncultured as he felt himself to be. Lois's family never regarded him as their inferior. On the contrary, they welcomed him into the fold and treated him like one of their own.

Bill came from a long line of "real" Vermonters, Vermont born and bred. His father's family had for generations worked in the marble quarries of Mount Aeolus as foremen and managers. His father's father, William Wilson, Bill's namesake, had married into another old Vermont family, the Barrows. Several generations earlier, a Barrows had built the largest house in East Dorset, a small town halfway between Rutland and Bennington in southwestern Vermont. Bill's great-grandfather Barrows converted the house to an inn that functioned as the community's social center.

The Wilson family was known to produce great "public" people. Wilsons were pleasant and sociable, great storytellers, and widely admired, but they were not good at more intimate relationships. The same alcohol that made them outgoing with strangers or casual acquaintances seemed to leave them incapable of admitting the need for, let alone sustaining, deeper human contacts. Bill's paternal grandfather renamed the Barrows House the Wilson House, now famous in AA circles as the birthplace of Bill W. Bill saw a lot of his paternal grandfather, William Wilson, and his paternal grandmother, Helen Wilson. In time, Bill would have more in common with his grandfather Wilson than his name.

As the highest point visible from East Dorset, Mount Aeolus had great symbolic value. Bill said one of his early recollections was of looking up from his crib, seeing the "vast and mysterious" mountain, and wondering whether he would ever climb that high. Many years later, in attempting to describe the spiritual conversion he had experienced in December 1934, Bill said he "felt lifted up, as though the great clean wind of a mountain top blew through and through."

Bill's grandfather Wilson also linked Mount Aeolus to a profound spiritual experience. William Wilson may have preferred inn keeping to quarrying, but inn keeping is seldom the right occupation for a hard-drinking man. His attempts to control his drinking led him to try Temperance pledges and the services of revival-tent preachers. Then, in a desperate state one Sunday morning, he climbed to the top of Mount Aeolus. There, after beseeching God to help him, he saw a blinding light and felt the wind of the Spirit. It was a conversion experience that left him feeling so transformed that he practically ran down the mountain and into town.

When he reached the East Dorset Congregational Church, which is across the street from the Wilson House, the Sunday service was in progress. Bill's grandfather stormed into the church and demanded that the minister get down from the pulpit. Then, taking his place, he proceeded to relate his experience to the shocked congregation. Wilson's grandfather never drank again. He was to live another eight years, sober.

Bill's mother's family included doctors, lawyers, teachers, and storekeepers. At the turn of the century, about three hundred people lived in East Dorset, many of them in houses owned by Gardiner Fayette Griffith, Bill's maternal grandfather, who was known as Fayette. Fayette's cousin, Silas Griffith, made his fortune in lumbering and was Vermont's first millionaire. Fayette himself had gone into lumbering, importing lumberjacks from Canada to harvest hardwoods in the mountains near East Dorset. His other interests included farming and real estate. He even owned East Dorset's water supply. Bill's grandmother Ella Griffith was a much less forceful personality than her husband, but she was kind and loving toward Bill. Clarence Griffith, Bill's uncle, had died the year before Bill was born, and Bill seems to have played a surrogate role for the senior Griffiths. Fayette doted on Bill's every accomplishment and saw to it that he had everything a boy could possibly desire, including his own horse and, unusual for the time, a motorcycle. Fayette also provided Bill with a kit from which he built one of the first crystal radio sets in Vermont.

Fayette was a great reader, and he encouraged his grandson's interest in reading. Bill would later recall going on "reading jags" at an early age, during which he would go to bed more to read than to sleep. Fayette also tried to impart to Bill his own strong work ethic. Bill worked on his grandfather's dairy farm, made maple syrup every spring, and became skilled enough in woodworking to make his own bows and arrows, skis, and sleds. He also tried unsuccessfully to build a glider, in imitation of the Wright Brothers.

Bill's father, Gilman Wilson, and his mother, Emily Griffith, were widely liked and admired. They had known each other all their lives, and they had a lot in common, including exceptional intelligence and ambition. Given the limited extent of their acquaintance with the world beyond Dorset Township, their marriage seemed inevitable. But as uncommon as divorce was in that time and place, they found it as inevitable when their differences began to grate.

Some people can truthfully say of one of their parents that he or she was not the sort of person who should have had children. In Bill's case, this seems to have been true of both his parents, for they seem always to have been more interested in their own lives than they were in Bill's or his sister's.

Their marriage was a stormy one. After their divorce when Bill was eleven, his father took a job in western Canada, and Bill did not see or hear from his father for nine years. His mother, who had been absent for extended periods, moved to Boston to study and practice medicine, leaving Bill and his sister, Dorothy, an intelligent and pretty girl several years his junior, with her parents. Bill saw very little of his mother after that. Understandably, both his parents' behavior toward him marked him in ways that would affect him the rest of his life.

Bill's family did not have the educational background Lois's did, but his father had been to college, and his mother was a teacher before she married. The Griffiths lived next door to the town library, and Bill had free run of it. Bill was exposed to music at an early age, and his family encouraged his aptitude for science and invention. While he began his education in the two-room schoolhouse in East Dorset, from age eight to age eleven, he also attended school in the nearby Vermont city of Rutland when his family lived there. He spent his high school years at Burr and Burton Seminary in Manchester, an old and well-established private school.

Fayette Griffith, Bill's grandfather, clearly loved his grandson, and he and Bill were close. Both of Bill's grandparents seem to have done their best to meet his emotional needs, and Bill was also close to his sister, Dorothy. He saw a lot of both the Griffith and the Wilson sides of his large and, by Vermont standards, rather prosperous extended family. His mother returned to East Dorset several times a year, and they exchanged letters when she was in Boston.

Bill claimed always to have felt self-conscious about his small-town background, but given his parents' lack of interest in him, it may have been an advantage. In addition to Bill's maternal grandparents, other people also played a parental role. These included Bill and Rose Landon, the couple next door to the Griffiths who ran the town library out of their home, and Mark Whalon, a man ten years Bill's senior who was in college when he and Bill met.

Whalon made an important contribution to Bill's knowledge of the world of ideas and of the world itself beyond rural Vermont. In doing so, he was continuing an effort begun by Bill's father who, when drunk, had a penchant for waxing philosophical. Like his grandfather Wilson, Bill's father was a hard-drinking man. Whalon also did something else Bill's father surely would have done: he took the young Bill Wilson to one of the local taverns. Bill drank unfermented cider on this occasion, but he found the male camaraderie and egalitarian ease he encountered there as seductive as alcohol would be later, even when he was drinking alone.

Bill could not compete with Lois's social experience, but neither was he the rube he felt himself to be. He was very popular at Burr and Burton, where he was president of his senior class. Many of the "summer people" were in his circle of friends, including the Burnham boys from Brooklyn, with Lois's brother Rogers and Bill particularly close.

ACCEPTANCE

If Bill Wilson's background was not as modest as he liked to claim, neither was Lois Burnham's as high as she sometimes made it out to be. Her father, Clark, was a prominent physician in Brooklyn Heights, New York, and her father's father had been a physician, a lawyer, and a minister of the Swedenborgian Church. One of her father's cousins was Daniel Burnham, the famous Chicago architect. Her mother, Matilda Hoyt Spelman, was from an old aristocratic American family. A cousin of her maternal grandfather's was married to John D. Rockefeller, Sr., whom Lois would later recall meeting at a family gathering.

Lois's family lived in a row house in Brooklyn Heights, only blocks away from both sets of grandparents. The Burnhams had a cook, a maid, and a man to tend the fires, make the repairs, and take care of the horses and carriage. In the spring, the whole household would follow her father's patients to Manchester, Vermont, where her mother's family had a smaller version of the grand Victorian houses that line Manchester's Main Street. Lois's father was a champion amateur golfer and a founder of the exclusive Ekwanok Country Club. Robert Todd Lincoln, Abraham Lincoln's son, lived in Manchester and donated the land for the club. The Lincolns were social acquaintances of the Burnhams, and Lois played with their children. Lois went to Packer Collegiate, an exclusive girls school in Brooklyn, and her brothers and sisters also went to private schools. Her brothers went on to become physicians like her father.

It was all quite grand, but their life had a marginal quality, as well. The Brooklyn Heights house was on Clinton Street, which marked the easternmost boundary of the exclusive heights neighborhood, and barely a block from Atlantic Avenue, which is its southernmost boundary. The house was also a brick front rather than the more fashionable brownstone. Throughout Lois's childhood, it was rented, not owned. Some of the family furnishings were other people's discards that Lois's father had literally picked up off the curb. While her father eventually bought the house, he later defaulted on the mortgage.

Lois's childhood was marked by steadily diminishing expectations. She was the first of five children, three girls and two boys. As the family expanded, its fortunes contracted, for while her father's practice included many of his fellow Brooklyn–Manchester Victorians, there weren't enough of them. He also accepted patients so poor that he never bothered to send them a bill.

There was another aspect to the family's growing impoverishment. In spite of the many differences, Lois's family background may have been much more like Bill's than either of them ever acknowledged. Lois always characterized her family's annual migration to Manchester as something of a forced march, since staying in Brooklyn would have largely left her father without an income. The truth is that it was more a matter of keeping up appearances. They went to Vermont every spring because her mother's family had always done so.

Clark Burnham may have occasionally prescribed for some of his Brooklyn patients when they were in Vermont, but he was never accepted as a practicing member of the Manchester medical community. The reason for this had more to do with his personal reputation than his medical skills. Burnham was known as someone who liked a good time above all else. He could be loud and boisterous. He was also known as a hard drinker, a cardplayer, and a womanizer who was not very particular as to whether the object of his attentions was single or married. This lifestyle may have affected his medical career in Brooklyn, as well, for he was rumored to have been denied privileges at a New York hospital. It was certainly too much for the medical establishment in Manchester. Clark Burnham never had an office in Vermont, and he was never admitted to the local medical society.

During the six months a year the family spent in Vermont, her father's income seems to have been meager, at best. As the family expanded, what began as difficulty in keeping up appearances became a struggle to make ends meet. The family began to rent out the large Manchester house and a few years later, they sold it. Beginning when Lois was still a young child, her family did not live in Manchester at all but in a camp on Emerald Lake, near East Dorset. The carriage was maintained until cars came along, because it would not do for a doctor of his social class to make house calls on horseback. The size of the household staff diminished, with some servants kept on primarily out of loyalty. Silas, the last of their coachmen, stayed on to tend the fires, and he was still there long after the Wilsons could offer him nothing but a roof over his head. Lois has written that parting from him was one of the saddest things about having to leave the house on Clinton Street in 1939, six years after her father defaulted on the mortgage.

Lois's childhood may have been the envy of many, but it was also increasingly threadbare and anxiety filled. The gentility she knew was characterized by mending and fixing, by making do and going without. It was good preparation for the life she would lead as the wife of the cofounder of Alcoholics Anonymous.

It is true that, whatever the financial strains, Lois's family was accepted in social circles a family like Bill's could only dream about. But as the nineteenth century turned into the twentieth, the old order was collapsing. Bill's mother, former wife of a quarry foreman, became an osteopath, married an M.D., and made a new life for herself. Bill's sister, Dorothy, who wanted to be an actor, instead trained as a nurse. She married an osteopath and moved to New York City, where her husband's patients, many of whom were also their social friends, included trustees of the Rockefeller Foundation and the rector of Riverside Church, whose parishioners included the Rockefeller family itself.

Unlike Bill, Dorothy seems to have made the transition to a better life without difficulty. But Dorothy saw more of their mother than Bill did. Their father, whom Bill needed more than she, was the colder and more distant of their parents even before he disappeared from their lives.

Bill's memories of his father were of a happy man who was a good storyteller and immensely well liked. Before the divorce, Gilman spent time with his son and encouraged Bill's interest in science. Bill recalled that when he developed a passion for baseball during the family's time in Rutland, his father would play catch with him in the evenings after work. Apparently, however, none of this pierced his father's essential remoteness. When Gilman died in 1954, Bill would say that he had hardly known him.

Bill remembered his mother as a disciplinarian. Emily was a strong-willed woman with little capacity for warmth and understanding, particularly when it came to her son. Bill never criticized his mother, but his childhood letters to her are characterized by a plaintive longing for her attention and approval. In recollections of his childhood recorded in 1954, Bill recalled his mother giving him his first "good" spanking, administered with the back of a hairbrush, and he recalled the "agony of hostility and fear" with which he received it. Bill also said that he could never forget the experience.

The Burnhams were more like "real" Vermonters than many of the summer people the Wilsons and the Griffiths knew. They had left the social life of Manchester behind for the more rugged existence of the camp on Emerald Lake. Photographs of Lois's mother reveal her to be robust, strong, and vital, a woman who bore no resemblance to a cosseted Victorian matron. Lois's father prided himself on his physical daring-do, and he could easily have lain claim to being as rugged as any native-born man in the Green Mountain State.

Bill might have felt inferior to Lois, but he was a good and genuine young man of intelligence, physical stature, and looks. He had a winning personality, and he showed promise. Lois's family had known him most of his life, and they had known his family even longer. Given the kind of people Lois's parents were and their knowledge of Bill, it is not surprising that they would welcome their daughter's choice into the family and treat him as one of their own.

2

POWERING UP

Even as a child Bill Wilson was tall, well built, good-looking, intelligent, and friendly. However, none of this seemed to have elicited much of a response from his mother. Beginning long before his parents divorced, Emily was frequently absent from the family. She was thought to suffer from nervous disorders that required extended rest cures. Not infrequently, Emily took his sister with her and left Bill behind.

Bill often seemed to feel that he did not measure up. In spite of the largesse of a prosperous and generous grandfather, he believed that he had not had the advantages others did, and he was sure people saw him as their inferior. In order to get anywhere, the first thing he had to do was prove how wrong they were to look down on him.

Bill would later characterize this "I'll show them" attitude as "power driving," attributing it to an outsized ego that made it very difficult for him to form a true partnership with another human being. In Bill Wilson's case, though, the power driving seems to have had its roots in an underdeveloped, not an overblown, sense of entitlement. This feeling of inferiority manifested itself as shyness, awkwardness, and an inability to make friends. While Bill always knew many people, according to Lois, he only had two real friends in his life: Mark Whalon and AA cofounder Robert Smith. That neither of these men was his contemporary seems significant. Children who never experience the full attention and support of either parent often continue to regard contemporaries as competitors well into adulthood.

In 1903, when Bill was eight, the family moved to Rutland, Vermont, a place much as it is today, a small, predominantly working-class city. The public school Bill attended represented a big change from East Dorset's two-room schoolhouse. Bill's classmates were the children of factory workers and of the men who worked for his father in the marble quarry, yet he imagined that they felt him to be vastly beneath them. Instead of trying to make friends, he set out to prove them wrong, deciding that one of the ways he would do that would be to work himself impossibly hard to become the school's best baseball player. The team needed a pitcher, and Bill practiced long and hard; he became a pitcher and captain of the team.

Bill's insecurity probably had less to do with social status than family neglect. His mother had spent much of the prior year in Florida and she had taken his sister, Dorothy, with her. They left East Dorset in the winter of 1902, and they did not return until after school started in the fall. Bill's letters to his mother during this period are plaintive and pathetic. In virtually every one of them, he asks her when she is coming home.

By 1906, the Wilsons were back in East Dorset. His parents divorced in 1907. On the night they separated, Emily and Gilman had a bitter argument. Gilman walked out of the house. At bedtime, Bill's mother told him that she felt one of her headaches coming on and asked him to put his sister to bed. Bill was unable to sleep. Then, at about 10:30 in the evening, Gilman Wilson came home. Bill had learned to judge how much his father had had to drink by the lightness of his step. That night Gilman's tread on the stairs seemed very light, indeed.

In a scene more appropriate to a motion picture than real life, Gilman went into Bill's room and, with a jerk of his head, indicated that Bill should follow him. He walked back down the stairs and out the front door. A rented horse and buggy was standing in front of the house. His father got in, patted the seat beside him, and Bill climbed up and they started off. It was a long ride in the summer night, up a mountain road and through a quarry gate. Gilman drank periodically from a jug of whiskey, but he never said a word. When they were in the quarry, he stopped the buggy and climbed down. Then, taking the whiskey with him, Gilman entered a nearby shed. From the way he closed the door behind him, Bill knew that he was not expected to follow.

Gilman was in the shed for a long time. When finally he came out, he was still holding the whiskey, still silent, just standing there, looking out across the valley by the moonlight. Then he moved a couple of steps away and leaned back against a tree. In his first words of the evening, Gilman asked Bill, age eleven, to take care of his mother and his sister and be good to them. He cut off any possible reply by saying that he knew Bill would do it. Then, indicating that the "discussion" was over, he took a long pull on the jug of whiskey.

Perhaps when he was in the shed drinking, Gilman said to himself some of the things he planned to say to his son. Bill's father did not tell him that he was moving to Canada or raise the topic of divorce. And he seemed to have no regrets.

After another period of silence, Gilman simply started talking about the mountains and the moon and the stars and how they all had existed long before there was anyone to look at them. He walked over to a slab of marble and sat down. Bill joined him, and his father explained how they were all a part of something much vaster than anyone could possibly understand. After a while, they stood up. Gilman put his hand on his son's shoulder and led him back to the buggy.

Bill fell asleep leaning against his father's sleeve on the ride back home. In the morning, his sister woke him to say that his father was gone, and Bill did not see him again for nine years; it was an even longer time for Dorothy. Emily stayed with the children for a while, arranging for the divorce, then she, too, was gone, off to Boston and medical school. Like his father, Bill kept his silence about what his parents' divorce meant to him, but it plunged him into a depression that lasted a full year.

Imagining that people found him wanting, then setting out to prove them wrong, was a pattern Bill would repeat throughout his life. There was just one brief interlude when he seemed to have done this to his own satisfaction. The teenage Bill Wilson spent most of his high school years at Burr and Burton, a prestigious school in Manchester, Vermont. He had thought of himself as homely, awkward, and vastly inferior to his classmates. In fact, photographs of him at this time show him to be tall, broad-shouldered, and handsome, and he became president of his senior class, a star football player, and the star pitcher and captain of the baseball team. Bill also acted in the school's stage productions, and he was first violin in the student orchestra. The violin was an instrument he had actually taught himself to play.

At Burr and Burton, Bill encountered children from families better off than his own. Yet his family was hardly poor, and his grandfather saw to it that he was well dressed and well supplied with spending money. Bill did, in time, feel that he had proved himself the equal of his peers. For him this hinged, more than anything, on his having a girlfriend. Her name was Bertha Bamford, and she was the most beautiful and popular girl in the school. She was also the daughter of the rector of Manchester's Zion Episcopal Church, and her family welcomed Bill into their home.

There were times during the summer and into the fall of 1912 when Bill actually felt emotionally secure. He was deeply in love with Bertha, and she with him. Then, just when he seemed to be seeing himself the way others did, his newfound self-confidence was shattered. In November, Bertha went to New York City with her parents, where she underwent surgery in Flower Hospital and died from postsurgical hemorrhaging. Bill first learned what had happened when he was summoned to the school's chapel along with the other students to hear the tragic news of their classmate. The school held a memorial service, and Bertha was given a large public funeral. Her parents gave a brass pulpit to the church in memory of their daughter.

Bill reacted to the loss of Bertha in the same way he had to his parent's divorce and their subsequent departure from his life. This time, though, his devastation was even more severe. The depression he plunged into after Bertha's death lasted three years. Bill was forced to drop out of Burr and Burton. He suffered terribly, first with depression and then with panic attacks. As Bill saw it, in death he had come up against something that he could not overcome by willpower. As far as Bill was concerned, his ability to "show them" had earned him Bertha's affection. Then she was dead. The striving had not worked.

With the help of either of his parents, Bill almost certainly would have recovered more quickly from this tragedy. But Gilman was in western Canada, and Emily simply urged him to "snap out of it." After an absence of several months, Bill returned to Burr and Burton and completed his studies, but he failed German and was told that he would not receive his diploma. His mother was furious when she heard the news. She made a trip from Boston to argue with the principal about it. The principal would not budge, though, and Bill did not graduate with his class.

That summer, Bill went to live with his mother in Arlington, Massachusetts, a suburb of Boston, where he made up the German. Near the end of the summer, Bill, now age twenty, saw his father again for the first time in nine years. Although the family knew where Gilman was, he did not contribute toward his children's support, nor did he send them Christmas or birthday presents. Yet the spell he cast in his leave-taking must have held: astonishingly, Bill never blamed his father for his absence or expressed any anger toward him.

To re-unite with his father, Bill took a train from Boston to Montreal, where he boarded another train for the long trip across Canada to British Columbia. Gilman Wilson was now manager of the Marblehead quarries of the Canadian Marble Works. While there, Bill wrote several letters to his grandmother Wilson. He described in detail the Canadian Rockies, the oil and gas fields of Alberta, and the city of Medicine Hat, where the street lights ran on natural gas and were never turned off. But the letters don't mention anything about what it was like to see his father again.

WORSE

Upon his return to Arlington, Bill seems to have had no strong feelings as to a choice of career, but his mother did. Emily not only decided that Bill should become an engineer, she also picked the school: the Massachusetts Institute of Technology. Because of his poor performance in his last year at Burr and Burton, Emily decided that he should delay applying to MIT, so instead of going to college in the fall of 1913, Wilson attended Arlington High School. Although he was essentially repeating his senior year in an environment where the competition was certainly less keen, Bill did nearly as poorly at Arlington as he had at Burr and Burton.

The trip to see his father seems only to have deepened his sense of devastation and hopelessness. All of Emily's urgings to "buck up" were of no avail. Inevitably, Bill performed badly on the MIT entrance examination. Although he did go to college in the fall of 1914, instead of MIT, he enrolled at Norwich University, a military college in Northfield, Vermont.

Bill was miserable at Norwich. Had it not been for his inability to cope with the loss of Bertha, he almost certainly would have been accepted into MIT. Given his intelligence and aptitude, there is every reason to think he could have done well there. In 1914, the total enrollment at Norwich College was a mere 145 students. Yet Bill was sure he could not succeed in any of the arenas in which he had excelled at Burr and Burton.

At Norwich, Bill did not win a starting position on either the football or the baseball team, nor was his violin playing good enough to get him into the orchestra. The boy who had been president of his senior class in prep school did not get a single bid to join a fraternity. Fearful of letting his mother know the true state of things, Bill papered over this last failure in his letters. He even went so far as to say that he received bids from three of the school's four fraternities. The following semester, he wrote to her claiming to have had bids from all four. Bizarrely, he claimed that he hadn't joined a fraternity because he did not want to have the unfair advantages membership in a fraternity would provide when it came to military advancement at the college.

Bill also tried to put the best face on his poor academic performance. His grades ranged from a 94 in chemistry to a 53 in algebra. The true quality of the students he felt himself unable to compete against can be inferred from the fact that, in spite of his 53 in Algebra, Bill still ranked fifth in his class. He attributed his worst grades to having been sick the week before his exams, but they seem more clearly related to the amount of interest and natural aptitude he had for a subject.

Bill Wilson's lackluster performance seems to have caused his self-esteem to plunge even further. Then, as he was beginning his second semester at Norwich, he fell on a slippery sidewalk and hurt his elbow. The injury was not serious, but he insisted that his mother should attend to it, and he was given permission to leave school and travel to Boston. As a young adult, Emily had had her own problems in coping with ordinary life. Even so, such an obvious attempt to elicit some sympathy from her was not well received. She immediately sent Bill back to Northfield. As he boarded the train, he had a panic attack. His symptoms included heart palpitations, extreme shortness of breath, and the feeling that he was about to die. He somehow managed to keep himself together until it passed, but the incident left him convinced that he had a fatal heart condition and would soon be dead.

In Bill's first semester, military duty was his best subject. Despite a poor showing in most of his academic subjects, he had received a ninety-eight in military duty and one hundred in deportment. After returning from Boston, however, every attempt to perform physical exercise caused Bill to collapse. He would be taken to the college infirmary, but the doctors never found anything wrong with him. After several weeks of this, Bill was sent home. This time, he didn't go to his mother's but to his grandparents' in East Dorset.

Bill's grandparents were more welcoming, but the attacks continued. Each time, he would cry out for the doctor to be summoned, though the doctor could do little more than try to convince Bill that there wasn't anything physically wrong. Bill would later say that he felt as though he "wanted to die . . . and there wasn't any use in going on." His condition actually worsened in East Dorset, and he spent much of the early spring of 1915 in bed, complaining of "sinking spells," dizziness, a sour stomach, and heartburn. He would go for days either without eating or subsisting on a diet of "soft toast." In an April 1915 letter to his mother, Bill indicates his awareness of the hyponchondriacal nature of his complaints. He mentions that during one of the doctor's frequent visits the doctor told Bill's grandparents he thought Bill's complaints were the result of his not eating. When the Griffiths insisted it must be something more serious, he tried to steer a middle course by allowing that Bill was certainly in no condition to eat much. When Bill relates this incident in the letter, he indicates his appreciation of the fact that the doctor was practicing diplomacy rather than medicine.

In time, an event occurred that got Bill going again. When his grandfather told his wife, Ella Griffith, what he had learned about automobiles from a catalogue Bill had received, Ella said that it must be hard to learn how to "run a machine," because a neighbor of theirs had refused to learn how to drive his. It was an offhand remark, but it was enough to arouse Fayette's competitiveness. He replied that he was sure he could quickly learn how to do it. Then he began investigating the possibility of not only buying a car but also obtaining an agency to sell them.

Fayette was fired up, and Bill seems to have caught his enthusiasm. Soon the same young man who seemed hardly able to get out of bed was in Manchester, trying to interest people in buying automobiles. The depression had lifted at last. Except for the lingering palpitations, Bill's fear of death and the physical symptoms that accompanied it vanished. He had accepted a new challenge: like his grandfather, he would not only learn to drive an automobile, he would also sell them. In fact, they would become the first people in Dorset Township to do so.

In a subsequent letter to his mother, he told her that he had nearly sold a car to the Bamfords, the parents of his lost love. He also said that there was nothing he could talk about better than automobiles. The sinking spells and dizziness were gone, he could eat anything he wanted, and his weight and strength had returned to normal. Bill still described himself as nervous, and strenuous exercise was still causing heart palpitations. He now believed that these would leave the moment he succeeded in fully convincing himself that there was nothing wrong.

In the end, Fayette never got the automobile dealership, and Bill was to spend the summer selling kerosene burners. But his grandfather's enthusiasm for a new undertaking and the part Bill saw himself playing in it had done the trick. In addition to selling the burners, the violin playing that he had judged not good enough to get him into the school orchestra at Norwich was now providing him with a steady income from performing at dances, weddings, and other affairs. What's more, his opinion of his playing had so changed for the better that he was thinking that he could put himself through college by playing the fiddle. The summer of 1915 is also the summer a romance blossomed between Bill Wilson and Lois Burnham.

3

TRYING HARDER

It is hard to see how Bill Wilson could have gotten anywhere without Lois, and he acknowledged that she provided him with much-needed mothering. Before their courtship, Bill and Lois had already known each other for years, and he was friendly with Lois's brothers, Rogers and Lyman. Bill was particularly close to Rogers. (The two would later share many a drunken escapade.) When Bill and Lois were married, Rogers was Bill's best man. But Lois was more than three years older than Bill, and all the years she knew him only as her brother's friend she had never taken him seriously.

William Wilson and Lois Burnham had a quiet and countrified, courtship. Their dates mostly involved talks, walks, and swims, during which they discovered their mutual love of the outdoors. Bill confided to Lois his dreams of glory as well as his many doubts and fears. Lois thrilled to and believed completely in the former, sympathized and promised to help with the latter. By the end of the summer, they were secretly engaged.

Bill returned to Norwich that fall in a different frame of mind. The same young man no one liked the year before was now very popular. Bill discovered a talent for leading his fellow cadets in their drills, his size and bearing lending themselves to the task. When it came to barking commands, the voice that had an almost comical twang in ordinary conversation was deep and resonant. The depression Bill had fallen into in reaction to Bertha's death and the physical symptoms that accompanied it were gone, but his poor academic performance continued. The way he chose to cope with it was both nasty and self-destructive.

Bill's difficulties with algebra the year before had become a nightmare with calculus. Instead of simply studying harder, or seeking extra help, he chose instead to attack his professor's competence. In listening to his teacher answer other student's questions, Bill realized that while the man could teach calculus, he did not have a fundamental understanding of it. Bill buried himself in the college library, reading all he could find on the history of mathematics and the concepts underlying the subject he was failing. He then provoked a classroom discussion with his teacher about the theoretical basis of calculus. By Bill's own report, he made a fool out of the man in front of the class.

The incident reveals astoundingly poor judgment. Wilson could now justly claim to have a better understanding of the roots of calculus than did his teacher, but he still didn't know how to do the assigned work. The teacher he might have received help from gave him a zero for the course. In its arrogance and pointlessness, the episode was a harbinger of things to come.

That humiliating his teacher would not lead to a higher grade seems predictable, but Bill's motives seem self-destructive at best. If the humiliation had caused his teacher to throw himself in the Connecticut River, grade book in hand, Bill still wouldn't know the calculus he would need if he was going to be an engineer. Bill's teacher may not have had the power to expel him, but giving him a failing grade conveyed in the strongest terms possible that he didn't think Wilson belonged at the military academy.

Other aspects of Wilson's conduct at Norwich would soon cause the college's commander to reach the same conclusion. It seems that Bill was much better at giving orders than obeying them, and no amount of urging or discipline on the part of his superior officers could make him conform to the spit-and-polish appearance military schools value so highly. As would be true of his business clothes later in his life, at Norwich Bill's uniform most often looked like he had slept in it. The problem continued until the same commandant who had recognized Bill's prowess on the drilling field became determined to put him out of the school.

Bill's violin playing saved him from immediate expulsion when the school's music director managed to convince the commandant that the orchestra could not get along without Bill's violin. Even so, one has to wonder what would have become of Bill if World War I hadn't intervened. Because he was a military cadet, the boy who could not keep his uniform in order was nevertheless able to enter the army on a favorable basis. Bill started drinking in the army.

Military service was a tradition on both sides of his family; both the Wilsons and the Griffiths believed that serving one's country was patriotic and not serving was "slacking," a disgrace. Yet Bill had mixed feelings about going to war. At the turn of the nineteenth century, memories of America's Civil War, in which Barrows and Griffiths had fought, were still fresh. Bill's surges of patriotism alternated with a fear of death. Although he would later characterize this as neurotic, it seems to have had little in common with the earlier, unreasoning fear he had experienced in reaction to Bertha's death.

Many young men facing military service in wartime come to the realization that they are afraid to die. Often, this is the first time it occurs to them that they might not have the long and full life they had considered their rightful expectation. The difference in Bill Wilson's case is the extent to which he turned to alcohol in an attempt to numb his fear.

After basic training, Bill applied for officer candidate school and was accepted. His first experience with alcohol was at a reception given by the society ladies of New Bedford, Massachusetts, where he was stationed. As with so many others, alcohol produced in him instant feelings of completeness, invulnerability, and an ecstasy that approached the religious, and as is true for many alcoholics, Bill could recall his first drink in detail all his life. We have learned to see such a response to alcohol as a warning sign of alcoholism. With Bill, though, warning signs were hardly necessary. The first time he drank, he got so drunk that he threw up and was miserably sick the next day. This did not discourage him in the slightest. Alcohol may not have been what was missing from his life, but alcohol could certainly take its place. Bill kept drinking.

Bill Wilson never had a "social" drink in his life. Whenever he drank, he got drunk. There were times when, after taking a drink, he could delay getting drunk for a few days by marshaling his will. Once triggered, though, the compulsion was apparently undeniable. The only question was how drunk he would get, and how much damage he would do to himself and others before he was again sober.

Given the Wilson family's history with alcohol, Bill's reaction to his first drink isn't surprising, but what made alcohol so potent for him may also have to do with something he didn't get from his father or anyone else—an understanding of his parents' behavior. When a marriage ends, it is common for the children to feel responsible. When Bill's parents separated, they went off in different directions to pursue their own interests. Bill's mother had established a pattern of taking his sister with her and leaving him behind. This made it especially hard for Bill not to feel that he was the problem. Alcohol, though, made him feel whole and complete, and no matter how sick he became or how destructively he might behave while under its influence, he was willing, even eager, to go back to it again and again.

Bill's drinking steadily progressed while he was in the army, but outwardly it didn't seem to have any negative consequences. Because he had come from a military college, in basic training others looked to him to show them what to do. Here he was free from the self-doubt and insecurity new situations often brought out in him. Bill was only twenty-one when he completed his officer training. The years of failure or near failure he had experienced since Bertha's death were behind him: Bill Wilson was now a second lieutenant and a leader of men, and he relished the role.

When Lois visited him while he was stationed at an army base in Plattsburgh, New York, Bill's grandmother and his sister, Dorothy, accompanied her, and they never left them alone for longer than a minute. Lois's own parents were far less strict. When Bill was transferred to Fort Monroe in Virginia for artillery training, they allowed their daughter to visit him unchaperoned. Spurred by a rumor that he would soon be going overseas, Bill and Lois were married in Brooklyn Heights on January 24, 1918.

Before shipping out, Bill had a lot of time on his hands. He filled it with drinking and thoughts about both the dangers and the opportunities to distinguish himself that lay ahead. Bill's last stateside posting was at Fort Adams near Newport, Rhode Island. Although wives were required to live off post and the couple could be together only on weekends, Lois moved to Newport in April. During one of those weekends, they sat watching a sunset from a cliff looking out over the ocean and talking about their future together. Bill would later recall this as his first sense of what he would come to think of as a spiritual experience.

When Bill went overseas, he had a chance to do some sightseeing in London before crossing the channel to France. On a visit to Winchester Cathedral, he read doggerel on a tombstone about a soldier who had died, not in combat but from drinking. The army may not have been concerned about Bill's drinking, but the rhyme made enough of an impression on Bill for him to be able to quote it almost verbatim years later, when writing *Alcoholics Anonymous*, AA's *Big Book*:

> *Here lies a Hampshire Grenadier*
> *Who caught his death*
> *Drinking could small beer.*
> *A good soldier is ne'er forgot*
> *Whether he dieth by musket*
> *Or by pot.*

Wilson may have been touched by the fate of this soldier, but it does not seem to have had any immediate effect on the course of his drinking. Yet, sitting in the cathedral thinking about what might lay ahead of him in France, he felt aware of a powerful spiritual presence. Later, he said that he had been willing to have God with him in that moment, and He was there. Nearly sixteen years later, Ebby Thacher, a boyhood friend and drinking companion, would talk to Bill about a spiritual source of relief from his alcoholism. Fogged by alcohol and desperate to understand what his friend was saying, Bill would think about his experience in Winchester Cathedral.

The war was nearly over before Wilson made it to France, and drinking with his fellow soldiers was mostly the way he passed his time during the months he spent there. Except for an occasion or two that was chalked up to "boys will be boys" behavior, it never got him into trouble.

Bill had trained for war, but he had been fearful of what he would do when confronted with the "real thing." When an explosion rocked the British ship carrying him and his men to England, he discovered that his leadership ability extended beyond the parade grounds. Instinctively, he took charge and said the right things. His calm but firm orders quelled the panic and stopped his men from stampeding dangerously toward the stairways leading up to the deck. They had thought they were under attack by German U-boats, but it was only a depth charge dropped by a passing destroyer that had exploded near their ship. This event, and an artillery exercise that sent a shell nearly on top of his position, was the closest Bill came to combat.

4

IT'S OVER

When he mustered out in 1919, Bill found that the way he had spent his time in the army had not prepared him for what was supposed to come next. In civilian life, drinking was to be confined to evenings and week-ends, and even then, moderation was the norm. Moreover, he was expected to work at a job that required him to be in the same place at the same time every day and to do essentially the same thing he had done the day before. None of this was to Bill's liking.

Wilson got a job decoding cablegrams for an export company. He then worked for a time for Lois's sister Barbara's fiancé, who was the head clerk in the insurance department of the New York Central Railroad. At an-other point, he again worked for the New York Central, this time driving spikes in planks on one of its piers. No matter what the job, he either quit or was fired. His reasons why things didn't work out were vague, arbitrary, and sometimes even contradictory: he left his first stint with the New York Central because he believed the railroads should be nationalized, while his second go-around ended because he didn't believe in unions.

When Bill quit jobs or conducted himself in such a way that an em-ployer had little choice but to fire him, he seemed to act without regard for the consequences. Many of these jobs were acquired through the good graces of his wife's family or friends, but Bill evidently never displayed any concern about this.

When he was in the army, Bill drank primarily to calm his nerves and to fantasize about the glory he might achieve. He also drank to dream of the wonderful life he and Lois would have once the war was over and he had made his mark in the world. When he returned to civilian life, Bill again drank to calm his nerves and to dream of glory. He also drank to nurse his resentment about the unfair treatment that he, a war veteran and a leader of men, was receiving. Bill drank to feel sorry for himself because he hadn't had the advantages given to Lois and her brothers and sisters who, along with their spouses, all seemed to be doing much better than the Wilsons.

Many nights, all of these "reasons" to drink kept him at it until closing time, even when he had to work the next day. He also drank when his in-laws entertained or when he and his wife were invited somewhere. Even this drinking sometimes ended with him sprawled across the bed, vomiting into a pail. That he would still be expected to show up for work in the morning was, of course, another reason to drink.

It was in these first years of civilian life that Bill began to experience blackouts, periods when he would later have no recall of what he had done or said. Wilson was only twenty-four years old, but if he had had a different wife or no wife at all, his drinking might have taken him to the streets and an unmarked grave.

Bill's drinking played no small part in his inability to accept the limitations of a situation while working toward something better. Part of the problem was also the nature of the jobs he was taking. They may have been a true reflection of his self-esteem, but they were far beneath his intelligence and talents. For a time, Bill considered enrolling in an engineering school in New York, but then he dropped the idea.

This thrashing around was punctuated by extensive sojourns in the country, some of which lasted for months. These jaunts were usually Lois's idea; they were her way of getting Bill away from his habitual patterns. On one of their earliest getaways, the Wilsons walked from Portland, Maine, to Rutland, Vermont, a distance of several hundred miles. Getting her husband out of New York and into nature was a technique Lois would employ for many years, with some success.

The trips certainly had a positive effect. When Lois first began to employ this tactic, Bill would often be alcohol free for the entire period. Even when his alcoholism was far advanced, he would drink much less when they were in the country. At the end of one of these trips, Bill would return to New York ready to charge into the fray. He was, of course, essentially unchanged, and it was only a matter of time before his drinking was again interfering with his ability to cope with life. At first, he showed enough improvement for Lois, and perhaps even Bill himself, to believe that he had established some measure of control over when he drank and how much. False hope can be better than no hope, and believing that "this time it would be different" was all they had.

By 1921, Bill was drinking virtually full-time. Again, he and Lois removed to Vermont, where they embarked on a walking trip that ended at her family's camp on Emerald Lake. Bill dried out, and the exercise and fresh air were restorative, but he returned to the city with no better idea of what his next move should be.

Since Bill also drank to help himself think, he now resumed in earnest. Lois began to feel that his devotion to the bottle was tantamount to his establishing a life without her. With growing alarm, she quickly scheduled another, more extensive time out of the city. They walked the newly created Long Trail along the tops of the Green Mountains in Vermont. Lois's father, her brother Rogers, and an old beau of hers had helped to clear a section of it, and it ran for three hundred miles. At the end of their hike, they visited Bill's grandparents in East Dorset. Conversations with his grandfather led Bill to recall the desire to be a lawyer that the older man had instilled in him as a boy. This time, he returned to New York with a plan. Instead of becoming the engineer his mother had wanted him to be, he would study to be the lawyer that would make his grandfather proud.

Again with the help of his wife's family, Bill got a job investigating fraud and embezzlement for the United States Fidelity and Guaranty Company, a surety firm located in downtown Manhattan. He also enrolled in Brooklyn Law School. Lois was greatly relieved that her husband at last had both a job and a chosen profession. Working full-time and going to school at night would not be easy. But he would have less free time, and the drinking Bill did in his free time had made it hard for him to hold a job. It seemed like a good plan and it might have been, for someone else, but it wasn't for Bill.

Night school students are often more mature, dedicated, and disciplined than their day school counterparts, but Bill's life was so different from the way he wanted it to be that he found his new regimen intolerable. He didn't like his job in Manhattan and he hated commuting by subway. He also found much to object to in law school. Bill's grandfather had expounded eloquently on lofty legal principles, but schools like the one Bill was attending function primarily to ground lawyers in the legal details they needed to practice.

It is hard to find justification for Bill's dissatisfaction. His job was in the financial district in downtown Manhattan, where he had the opportunity to make contacts that might serve him well in the future. Law school certainly has its mundane aspects, but every profession requires knowledge of certain less-than-scintillating fundamentals. As for his complaints about the subway, Bill was living in Brooklyn Heights, just across the East River from Manhattan, then perhaps an even more desirable neighborhood than it is today. It is close enough to downtown Manhattan for many Heights residents to *walk* to their jobs in the financial district across the Brooklyn Bridge. Brooklyn Law School, located in downtown Brooklyn, was also within walking distance.

Bill didn't walk. He stuck to the subway, and, from his later recollection, he seems to have spent most of his ride feeling sorry for himself. After class, he would spend many nights in a barroom doing the same thing. Bill's "drinking work" was again keeping him in the bars until closing time.

It is doubtful that he could have survived law school without Lois. As often as she could, she arranged for weekend excursions out of the city to nearby New Jersey, the beaches of Staten Island, or the eastern end of Long Island. All of these locations offered the couple the opportunity to fish or clam for their supper and sleep under the stars.

With the aid of these respites, Bill managed to hang onto his job and stick with law school long enough to see his course work through to completion, but he showed up for his final exams so drunk that he couldn't read the questions. Bill was able to reschedule his exams and he passed them, but he never got his diploma. Although he had completed all of his course work and passed all his exams, to get his degree there was one requirement left to fulfill: he had to attend a commencement ceremony.

It was something Bill Wilson was unwilling to do. We may wonder why Brooklyn Law School was so strict about requiring students to attend commencement before granting the degree, but it is hard to imagine anyone not complying with that proviso. Bill Wilson didn't. Because he wouldn't attend his own graduation, he didn't get his degree. Without the degree, he could not sit for the bar exam. Even though Bill had dreamed of it since childhood and had successfully completed his course work and passed his exams, he never became a lawyer.

One has to wonder if there has ever been anyone else in the history of Brooklyn Law School, or of any law school, who failed to graduate only because he did not show up for a graduation exercise. Yet Bill didn't seem to feel that there was anything about his behavior that required explanation. Even after he got sober, all he ever said about it was that someday he ought to go back to the school and get his degree. Lois would only say that by the time he finished law school, Bill had already decided he wanted to work on Wall Street.

If so, why did he bother to take his finals? Are there no lawyers on Wall Street? Even if Wilson could already see himself as the successful stock analyst he would become, surely a law degree was not something to walk away from. Bill did say that much of what he did during his drinking years was probably motivated by a desire to prove he wasn't the stumblebum he was sure other people believed him to be. Implicit in this, of course, is the hope that gaining his detractors' approval would change how he felt about himself. It may be that the nearer he got to his goal, the harder it was for him to stay on course. With the finish line in sight and Bill still not feeling any better about himself, perhaps he just couldn't summon the will to take that last step. The idea that a law degree could have value independent of its effect on his self-esteem seems to have had little meaning for him.

By the time of Bill's law school fiasco in 1924, Lois had already experienced many disappointments over his drinking and false starts. At Christmastime the year before, Bill had written the first of his "temperance pledges" in the family Bible. He was only twenty-eight. Two months later, having failed to keep the first pledge, he entered another.

Yet Lois's faith in her husband and her conviction that he was capable of great things was unwavering. No matter what Bill did, she gave him all the support and encouragement she could muster. After the war, Lois worked as an occupational therapist with returning soldiers, including those whose nerves had been shattered by their battle experiences. It sometimes seems as though she greeted Bill's accomplishments with an enthusiasm that would have been more appropriate for one of her patients.

When Lois was well into her nineties, she was still talking proudly about the radios Bill built during his "flopping around" years after the army. Radio was at a relatively early stage, and radio stations were still amateur affairs. Like other people all over the country, Bill put his radios together from a kit, but Lois's pride in telling of her husband's achievement could hardly have been greater if he had invented the radio itself. That such an activity was vastly below the level of Bill's talents we have from no less an authority than Thomas Edison.

As a boy, Bill was always making things. He also had a chemistry set an uncle had given him, and on one occasion he was discovered by his father to be on the verge of making something dangerously close to nitroglycerin. Bill also learned while still a child what part of invention was inspiration and what part sheer hard work. When he was twelve, his grandfather said something one day about how curious it was that only the Australian aborigine could make a boomerang. Bill had never seen a boomerang and had no way of acquiring one, but he spent virtually all his free time over the next six months researching and experimenting, until he had succeeded in making a boomerang that returned perfectly.

Bill came to know Thomas Edison at the time he was deciding about going to law school. The great inventor had run an ad in the *New York Times* seeking recruits, and when Wilson responded, he was invited to go to Edison's New Jersey laboratory to take a test. Edison was a childhood hero, and at this time, Bill was still capable of showing up sober for a test. He was still at the test long after everyone had left, not because he was having a hard time of it but because he was able to answer questions the others had left blank. Edison was impressed, and he told Bill so on the spot.

A few weeks later, he received a letter from Thomas Edison offering him a job in his famous laboratory. In an article the *Times* ran on the lucky few selected, Bill was quoted as saying that he found the questions easy. The young man who had failed the entrance exam for MIT and turned in a lackluster performance at an obscure engineering school had received one of the highest grades on Edison's test.

There is no reason to think Edison was wrong about Bill. In spite of the years he had just spent, in his own words, "flunking and slumping," Bill's drinking had not yet impaired his remarkable ability to absorb and recall scientific principles and information. But Bill never worked for Thomas Edison. There can hardly be more than a handful of people in a generation who are given the opportunity to learn a profession by working with someone who is both the greatest living practitioner of that profession and their childhood hero. Yet Bill Wilson turned Edison down. He chose instead the existence he would so quickly come to despise: a full-time job and law school at night.

One of the more famous incidents from Groucho Marx's remarkable life concerns his long campaign to be admitted to an exclusive Los Angeles country club that barred Jews. When, after years of importuning, the club finally issued him an invitation, he wrote back saying that he refused to belong to any club that would have him as a member. Many an AA member understands perfectly well why the club's acceptance produced such a precipitous drop in Groucho's regard for it. Given Bill's low self-esteem, Edison's approval and acceptance may have been enough for him to lose his enthusiasm for the life of an inventor. All Lois would ever say about it was that Bill had already made up his mind to go to law school.

5

LOYALTY BEYOND MEASURE

Lois not only put up with Bill's behavior, she managed to make a life with him, come what may. She even saved some money. By the time Bill was limping away from law school in 1924, she had accumulated $1,000 (more than $11,000 in year 2000 dollars). When Bill announced his plans for it, she promptly handed it over.

As Bill's interest in law school faded, he was taken up by the investment frenzy his job with U.S. Fidelity was exposing him to. Bill wanted to use the money Lois had saved to validate what at the time was a novel approach to investing. Instead of merely picking stocks based on the buzz on the Street, he was trying to learn all he could about the firms that interested him. When the investments Bill made based on his research did well, Lois was also ready for the next step.

Bill was convinced that by visiting a company's production facilities, he could learn firsthand how the company was doing and what its plans were for the future. He could then write reports detailing his findings, enabling investors to benefit from this "inside" information. The big question was whether anyone would be willing to pay for these reports.

Bill had met some Wall Street people through his job with U.S. Fidelity, and through his wife's family and friends he made the acquaintance of some of the Street's movers and shakers, but he couldn't get any backing. About the only person who would listen to him was Frank Shaw, the husband of Lois's best friend. Shaw was a Wall Street investor and a principal in the firm of J. K. Rice & Company. Although he was hardly older than Bill, he had made himself a millionaire by shrewdly investing his wife's capital.

Shaw would not back Bill, but if Bill found a way to carry out his plan on his own, he agreed to read and evaluate Bill's reports. It was faint encouragement indeed, but Bill was so sure he was onto something that as far as he was concerned, the willingness of someone like Frank Shaw to take his research seriously virtually guaranteed his success.

Bill made a list of firms that interested him, and he and Lois laid out an itinerary. With the exception of General Electric, which was poised to enter the consumer field, the companies were utilities like Adirondack Light and Power and the Southern Power Company, or producers of raw materials like the Giant Portland Cement Company, the Aluminum Company of America, and American Cyanamid.

The year before, Bill and Lois had borrowed money from Lois's mother to buy a motorcycle with a sidecar and a tent to use on their weekend getaways. Lois now set to work modifying their kit for extended travel. She added a window to the tent, made a multilayered sleeping bag out of army blankets, and sewed waterproof bags for all their gear.

The Wilsons gave up their jobs and their apartment, put their furniture in storage, and set off for what even today would be an extraordinary adventure. Lois would later describe them as "motorcycle hoboes." They had spent nearly every cent they had to equip themselves. Except for the stocks Bill had purchased, which he was counting on to gain entrée to various concerns as a stockholder, they had about fifty dollars left.

Bill had an itinerary, but what he did not have was a timetable. Their first stop on this make-or-break venture was East Dorset. This detour was to have taken a week, but Bill and Lois stayed nearly a month. Bill's grandfather, Fayette Griffith, had died during Bill's last year of law school. His maternal grandmother, Ella Griffith, had died several years earlier, and with his mother remarried and living in Florida, it fell to Bill to settle his grandfather's estate, but he spent as much time drinking and reminiscing with his old friend Mark Whalon as he did on estate business.

The Wilsons had sunk everything they had into this venture, and already Bill's drinking had derailed them. But Lois was desperate to find some context in which Bill could function at the level of his capabilities. She had hoped law school would be a turning point for Bill, and in a way they had not anticipated, it was. It seems to have been the last time either of them thought the answer to Bill's difficulties lay in trying to get him to behave like other people. There is an old joke about where an 800-pound gorilla sits. The answer is, wherever he wants to. In respect to his alcoholism, Bill was like an 800-pound gorilla that would drink whenever he wanted to. Bill actually drank more when he was in law school than he had previously, and near the end, his drinking degenerated into a nearly relentless binge.

It would have been the last straw for many women when Bill walked away from his law school degree, and Lois was still in her early thirties, with no children. By this time, their relationship had become a one-way street; Lois did everything in her power to help Bill, and Bill apologized for not being able to return the favor. The history of Lois's pregnancies is a case in point.

In the previous two years, Lois had suffered three ectopic pregnancies. She recovered easily from the first. When the second proved more difficult, her husband was loyal and supportive. Then a third and equally difficult ectopic pregnancy occurred in May 1923, and Bill was so drunk that for days at a time he didn't even come to the hospital to see her.

Lois's motto seemed to be, "When the going gets tough, try harder." Admitting defeat wasn't in her nature. She had no idea whether Bill's on-site investigations would yield anything worthwhile, but what she did know was that he drank less when he wasn't in New York. Perhaps most important from Lois's point of view, the trip meant they would be together almost constantly, and she seems always to have wanted more time with her husband.

The best thing that can be said about the adventure is that it worked. Unlike anything they had tried before, it accommodated Bill's drinking. Because Bill had no one backing him, he had no one to answer to and no schedule to keep. His deeply felt need to renew his drinking bonds with his friend Mark Whalon resulted in their one-week Vermont stay becoming four. It also exhausted their meager capital, but this just meant that they would have to find jobs along the way sooner than they had anticipated. Nothing was lost.

The trip also showed that Lois was right about him: under the proper conditions, he could accomplish extraordinary things. Between drinking bouts, he functioned at a high level. He learned what he needed to know about the companies he was interested in and he incorporated this information into clear and comprehensive reports. When Frank Shaw read Bill's reports, he was impressed enough by them to act on the information they provided. Aided by the bull market of the 1920s, the results were nearly always positive.

The target of Bill's first investigation was a General Electric facility near Schenectady, in upstate New York. Bill put on the one good suit he had brought with him for the purpose and went to the company's main office. On the strength of his ownership of two shares in GE, he presented himself as a stockholder interested in learning more about his holdings. He also asked for a job at the plant. Bill did not get the job, but the GE employees he encountered did disclose useful information about the future direction of the company's products.

By the time they reached Schenectady, the fifty dollars was nearly gone. When Bill wasn't hired at the plant, both the Wilsons took jobs on a local farm. Bill did chores, something that he was familiar with from his grandfather's farm. Lois, who knew almost nothing about cooking, worked in the kitchen of the farmhouse, preparing meals to feed the farmhands. She may have been the only graduate of Packer Collegiate, an exclusive girls finishing school, to hold such a position.

The farm jobs actually turned out to be a lucky break. The farm's property extended all the way to the perimeter of General Electric's radio research laboratories, and when the farmwork was done for the day, Bill went over to the labs. As lab workers stepped outside to enjoy a moment in the summer night air, he would engage them in conversation. As soon as he could, he would work the conversation around to where he could express an interest in what they were doing. After several nights of this, the men invited him inside. It didn't take long for the fellow who scored so highly on Thomas Edison's test to realize that he was getting a preview of where the radio industry would be in five or ten years.

Continuing to meet their expenses by taking whatever jobs they could fine en route, the Wilsons worked their way down the eastern seaboard. Lois did most of the driving, while Bill studied his Moody's Manuals in the sidecar. The years of hiking and camping had seasoned both Wilsons to sleeping out of doors and bathing and washing clothes as the opportunity presented itself. They would live like this for an entire year before they would return to Brooklyn Heights.

Bill was having the time of his life. The work itself was, in essence, inductive reasoning put to the test. Bill would gather information, draw conclusions from it, and recommend a course of action. In one of his letters to Frank Shaw, he said that nothing gave him greater pleasure than seeing conclusions thus arrived at proven sound. Alcoholics Anonymous was in many ways also the perfect environment for Bill. Gathering information, drawing conclusions, and then recommending a course of action is the methodology he employed for more than thirty-five years in creating AA.

If trying to find a way to live with alcoholism is akin to trying to live with an 800-pound gorilla, in the year the Wilsons spent as motorcycle hoboes, they found a way to keep the gorilla happy. Although neither of them seemed aware of it, the trip also established that his alcoholism had progressed to the point where Bill was drinking for no apparent reason. He was drinking, in AA's terminology, simply because he drank. He had a liberal supply of the opportunities for individual expression and creativity he found wanting in ordinary life. He was also free from its boredom and restrictions. But Bill still drank, and when he drank, he got drunk. On one occasion, he even disappeared with all of his and Lois's money. She found him in a bar, drunk and incoherent. He had spent every penny they had getting that way.

According to AA lore, Bill Wilson pioneered the notion of stock analyst as a Wall Street specialty. Although other people had analyzed a company's finances, and others had also visited a company's facilities to obtain firsthand information, Bill seems to have been the first to make this work a full-time occupation and he gathered information in ways that no one else did: he posed as a working man and took a job at a plant in order to get inside it. He entered company grounds by climbing fences clearly designed to keep people out. He used field glasses to surreptitiously observe equipment and plant activity, and he plied company foremen and supervisors with alcohol to extract confidential information.

When the stocks moved as Bill predicted, he was on his way. Frank Shaw set up an account that Bill could draw on to meet further expenses. Shaw also bought and sold securities for Bill on credit, making it possible for Wilson to benefit directly from the information he produced. But an incident that occurred in Sanibel, Florida, illustrated that Bill's success did nothing for his self-esteem.

The Wilsons's trip down the East Coast was grueling, and their old and overburdened motorcycle had broken down frequently. Bill's mother and her second husband, Dr. Charles Strobel, had a houseboat in Sanibel, and the Wilsons were staying with them, resting and recuperating. While walking along the beach picking up shells, Bill and Lois encountered Henry Ford, along with his wife and other members of Ford's family. Lois was soon engaged in an animated discussion with the "Daddy of all flivvers." Bill hung back, ignoring Lois's entreaties to join them. When the Fords had gone on their way, Lois asked Bill why he had behaved as he did. All Bill would say is that he hadn't wanted to bother the great man.

Henry Ford was another of Bill's heroes. As someone who had made himself into a "master of the universe," Ford was exactly the sort of man in whose company he longed to be. What better way to cement his recent successes than by taking this opportunity to chat up Henry Ford. He might even be able to learn something about what this authentic genius might be up to next. Thomas Edison had a home near Ford's in Fort Myers, and Bill knew it. If Bill felt at a loss for something to say, why not let Ford know that he had made the acquaintance of his neighbor? Perhaps Bill was hung over that day, or perhaps, despite his recent triumphs, staying with his mother had let the air out of him. For whatever reason, when fate gave him the opportunity to make the acquaintance of one of the greatest men of his time, Bill did not think himself worthy of it.

The hobo lifestyle, once sampled, seems to have been irresistible to the Wilsons. Days on end were devoted to keeping their motorcycle in repair during their trip to Florida. Even with Frank Shaw paying, they stayed with it for the return leg. After an accident near the end of their journey, which left Bill with a broken collarbone and Lois badly banged up, they took a train, but only because waiting for the motorcycle to be repaired would have meant missing a family wedding.

The wedding bells had hardly stopped ringing before they were off again for another six months of "investigating." Bill now had a job, an expense account, and a $20,000 line of credit ($250,000 in year 2000 dollars) that he could use to buy stocks for himself. This time the Wilsons could have traveled by train and stayed in first-class hotels. Instead, they drove a secondhand Desoto that Lois had outfitted with curtains so that they could sleep in it alongside the road. Lois's concern about Bill's drinking made her reluctant to stray from a formula that had at least kept him sober enough to be able to accomplish something.

Bill Wilson's Wall Street career was all too brief. It ended badly, due in part to the stock market crash in 1929 and the Great Depression that followed. However, the fundamental reason Bill crashed along with the market, never to recover, had to do with the relentless progression of his alcoholism.

6

ON THE STREET

Wall Street in the Roaring Twenties was very much the sort of place it is today. What you had to offer counted for far more than who you were or where you came from. The Street's stars included people like Frank Shaw, who had started with a family fortune. There were also people like Joe Hirschhorn, the rough-hewn, self-made man Bill would later work for. Starting from nothing, Hirschhorn went on to establish a large fortune and a premier collection of modern art.

The Wilsons' motorcycle accident may have left them bruised and battered, but as their train pulled into New York, the successes Frank Shaw was having with the information Bill provided meant that Bill's place on Wall Street and the couple's future seemed assured. The best part of it was that Bill still didn't have a "regular" job. There was nowhere he had to be at the same time every day. Bill was making money now, big money, and increasingly, he was becoming someone smart investors listened to.

One might wonder why he had had to go to such lengths to prove himself. It was more than the newness of his investment approach that people resisted. Based on his appearance and the way he conducted himself, few people were likely to conclude that Bill was capable of great things.

Photographs usually show him looking quite dapper, but they were taken on occasions when Lois made sure that he looked his best. Most of the time, Bill's suits looked like he had slept in them. Bill also was a heavy and a sloppy smoker, and his clothes were usually covered with ashes and often had holes where live ashes had burned right through the material.

Then there was Bill's choice of headgear. He always wore what seemed to be the same misshapen, slouchy, brown homburg, and he wore it sitting square on his head. Sometimes he didn't take it off even when he was indoors. When he did, he must have kept it in range of the by-products of his smoking, because there were holes in the hat, too. The hat and the way he wore it were enough to make him quite an oddity in the formal world of the Street. Even many years later, it was what many people remembered most clearly about Bill Wilson.

Bill also set himself apart in other ways. He characteristically walked so slowly that he seemed to be leaning backward. There was also his manner of speaking. Although Bill could have insightful and important things to say, the way he stated his case was invariably expansive and long-winded. His speech pattern was also slow and deliberate. It had much in common with the actor Jimmy Stewart. Unfortunately, with Bill, an element made him much less attractive than Stewart. He would loosen up a lot after he stopped drinking, but during his Wall Street years, there was a stiffness in him that put people in mind of a Baptist preacher.

As if all this were not enough, there was also Bill's demeanor. He never stood when he could lean, and he never sat so much as slouched. He seemed to lie down whenever he found himself near an unoccupied couch, or even an open space on the floor that seemed particularly inviting.

Given the nature of Wall Street's high-pressure, high-stakes, high-risk world, we have to wonder if Bill was intentionally trying to make a bad impression or whether his eccentric appearance and behavior were calculated to make people take notice of him. Even after he stopped drinking, though, Bill seemed never to have any conscious awareness of how he was presenting himself.

Ironically, his behavior advertised him as a rube, the very quality he felt sure he could never overcome. It was as though he were saying, "I know you'll never accept me, but I'm not going to let you forget just who it is that is making you all this money." It is hardly surprising that the only person who would listen to him was the husband of his wife's best friend, and that even this man wouldn't back him until he had proved himself.

Bill was soon making money faster than he could spend it. He wrote his reports at home and in his own time. He didn't even have to keep his appointments. If a hangover made it inconvenient to have to be somewhere he could beg off on the grounds that something new, with the potential to be truly big, had just come up. If keeping the drinking under control seemed to require some time away from the city, he could pass it off as "research." It was the road trip raised to the level of a profession.

Unfortunately, Bill seemed to think less of himself now than when he was driving spikes on a pier for the New York Central. There were still times when alcohol helped him to feel as good as it had when he'd first discovered it. The next day, just because he had drunk so much, he would feel even worse. In his years of floundering, Bill's drinking had grown more severe with each failure. Now he drank more with each success.

Even as everything he touched turned to gold, he was now inclined to regard the help Lois's family and friends extended to him as having been motivated by pity for Lois. Convinced that they thought she had made a bad marriage, he was given to drunken scenes in which he taunted members of Lois's circle with the fact that he was now making more money than they could possibly imagine.

The less Bill thought of himself, the more he surrounded himself with the trappings of wealth. At his insistence, the Wilsons rented two adjoining apartments a few blocks from Lois's family home. Walls were removed to combine the apartments into one sumptuous suite of rooms. It was just the two of them, and Bill was rarely there except to sleep, but nothing could be grand enough.

Lois had misgivings about the negative effect of the good life on Bill's drinking, but as far as Bill was concerned, she had little reason to object. What counted was that he was making money, and more money, and then still more money.

By 1928, Bill Wilson was drunk virtually every day. Even on the good days, he started drinking with the clang of the stock exchange's closing bell. After downing the first few at a nearby speakeasy, he would work his way uptown, spending money with abandon. According to Wilson's own recollections, it wasn't uncommon for him to go through hundreds of dollars in a single evening. Many a spree ended with him broke and having to sneak onto the subway in order to get home. He was nasty now when he drank; no one was likely to lend him carfare, even if he had been sober enough to realize his need for it before parting from his "friends."

When the newly affluent Wilsons went to Vermont in these years, it was in grand style. The man who thought of himself as a rube from East Dorset took up golf and became a member of the exclusive Manchester country club his father-in-law had helped form. It thrilled him to think how impressed the people at the local bank must be by the size of the checks he was cashing.

There were still times, though, when the drinking caught up with him. Upon returning to the United States from a trip to Canada, where he had been on his best behavior, he left Lois at the border crossing with the excuse that he needed to buy some cigarettes. Hours later, she found him in a saloon, dead drunk. Liquor was legal and cheap in Canada, but that did not keep him from drinking up nearly all their cash.

Cheap liquor was also involved in another fiasco. On a trip to Cuba to investigate the sugar industry, Bill was so drunk he accomplished little. Word about his behavior filtered back to New York, and Frank Shaw wrote him, expressing concern.

Given what was to follow, Bill's letter in reply contains an astonishing admission. He said that drinking had always been a problem for him. He also said that he was through with alcohol forever, and told Frank that he was greatly relieved to have put it behind him. Then, as though the matter were settled, he went on to discuss other things.

In truth, nothing had changed. The drinking continued without pause. In time, it affected Bill's work in other ways.

When everything went sour in 1929, Wilson was deeply involved in a stock manipulation. Bill had made Pennick and Ford, a small company that made corn products, his pet project. Although Wilson had made his mark by investigating companies firsthand to determine their true worth, with Pennick and Ford, Bill "created" value by talking up the company. The stock went up based on nothing more than this talk.

Because it was a small company, Wilson could "peg" the stock's price by getting his friends to buy it. Whenever the price began to dip, he would bring someone in to shore it up. He told himself he was doing his friends a favor by not selling them the stock when it was at its highest. Later, Bill would characterize what he had done with the company's stock as little more than a Ponzi scheme, but this was almost certainly an exaggeration. While he truly felt bad about his manipulations, since Bill also noted that the company did recover from the '29 collapse, there does seem to have been some real value in Pennick and Ford.

NO RETURN

The stock market crash of 1929 (Black Thursday) caught Bill Wilson pushing the limits of the criminally lax margin requirements that had helped to fuel the Roaring Twenties. When the dust settled, the Wilsons were in debt to the tune of fifty thousand dollars, equivalent to more than half a million dollars today.

Many people in 1929 shared Bill's fate, but people whose perspicacity was no match for his own nonetheless made even greater fortunes buying and selling stocks at depression prices. The difference in Bill's case was his drinking. The binge he went on to drown his sorrow in the days immediately after he went bust seems to have loosened the floodgates forever. Everything he did to recover his financial losses and reestablish his professional standing was ultimately undercut by alcohol.

His drinking went far, far past the point of reason. Utter strangers would tell him that he must be crazy to drink like he did. Earlier, he was capable of responding with great hostility when someone criticized his drinking. Now, he could only nod helplessly in agreement.

The Wilsons had to give up their lavish apartment, which they sublet at a loss, and move in with Lois's parents on Clinton Street. Their welcome was not warm: members of Lois's family who had followed Bill's investment advice had also suffered heavy losses. Many of them were the same people with whom Bill had flaunted his success.

There seemed to be no one to turn to now. At the height of his "great man" frenzy, Bill had been determined to go it alone so that no one would be able to say that he owed anything he achieved to someone else. He had even broken with Frank Shaw.

He was drinking more than ever, but there were still days when he was able to pull himself together and head for the Street. Spurred by his old determination to "show them," he soon had something going. Dick Johnson, an old friend who headed up the firm of Greenshields and Company in Montreal, offered him a job. The market crashed in October. By Christmas, the Wilsons were in Canada.

The effects of the Great Depression on the national economy, and of Bill's drinking on his professional reputation, were less severe in Canada. Bill knew he had to be on his best behavior. Although there were lapses, for a while things seemed to go amazingly well, and Bill seemed to be on his way to repeating his Wall Street success.

The Wilsons weren't in Montreal very long before they were again living grandly, with a luxurious, furnished apartment on Mount Royal overlooking the city, a brand new Packard automobile, and a membership in the country club. The stock market closed at three, and by springtime Bill was spending the rest of the afternoon on the golf course, with dinner at the club to follow.

After the years of hellish binges, Lois allowed herself to believe that this time it would be different. For Bill, though, the entire Montreal experience was miserable. As desperately as he was trying to control his drinking, the lapses were nightmarish for him.

They were also indications of things to come. Soon enough, Bill was drinking and behaving as badly as he had in New York. Less than ten months after his arrival in Montreal, he was fired.

The Wilsons' leave-taking could hardly have been more inglorious. Bill's brief reversal of fortune actually deepened their financial plight. The Mount Royal apartment was also sublet at a loss for the remainder of the lease. The Packard was left with the dealership in hope that it could be sold for the payments still owed. The Wilsons had been living so close to the edge, they did not even have train fare out of town. When Bill tried to prevail upon his former employer, he was told that the fare would be advanced only if he could secure it with collateral. The only thing they had left that might serve the purpose was the life insurance Bill had obtained in the army. To his further humiliation, the policies were accepted and the money advanced.

During the years of his success on Wall Street, there did not seem to be anything Lois could do or say to slow the relentless progress of Bill's alcoholism. After the Crash, Lois endured the humiliation of their having to move in with her parents, then she packed up again and went to Montreal with him. But when Bill's drinking again destroyed all he had accomplished, she returned to New York and left him to attend to the details of their moving back to the States.

Bill proved woefully inadequate to the task. He got drunk and became belligerent in a hotel bar. When a house detective tried to quiet him, Bill started swinging and he was arrested and jailed. Fortunately, the next morning the judge was more impressed by Bill's status as an upper-middle-class businessman than with the hotel detective's complaint. Bill was released, but he started drinking again immediately and was soon in the midst of a blackout. He came to at Lois's parents' camp on Emerald Lake in East Dorset. With him was a disreputable Montreal character he had fallen in with during his spree. Sending the man back to Montreal took nearly all of the money Bill had left.

Reluctantly, Lois went to Vermont to collect him. Her mother was ill, and the diagnosis was bone cancer. When word came that her mother's condition had worsened, Lois returned immediately to New York. Left on his own again, Bill went back to drinking.

Lois's mother was being cared for in an apartment her father and brother had created for her in the house on Clinton Street. When Bill finally pulled himself together enough to make the trip, he and Lois moved into the large front room on another floor. Bill surely must have wanted to be a support to Lois during her mother's final illness. Her mother had treated him like a son, and Bill was very fond of her. Yet when she died on Christmas Day, Bill had been drunk for days, and on the day of her funeral, he was too drunk to attend. He stayed drunk for many days thereafter.

With her mother gone, Lois again devoted herself full-time to her husband. Bill eventually sobered, and he even got a job conducting investigations of companies whose fundamentals were still sound enough to make them good investments. It was a salaried position, and it paid a hundred dollars a week. Nothing compared with what he had been used to, but their living expenses were meager, and with the unemployment rate at 25 percent, there was reason to be grateful.

Through a superhuman act of will, Bill kept this job for nearly a year.

Then he got into a fight in a barroom with a taxi driver. Word got back to his employer, and he was out. Although he would never find full-time employment again, Bill did manage to work more or less steadily through the rest of 1931. On the day of his fourteenth wedding anniversary in January 1932, he came to collect Lois at Macy's, where she was again working. He presented her with a watch and a check for two thousand dollars.

The check was for work he had done for Joe Hirschhorn. Since they were still fifty thousand dollars in debt, it was a welcome sight. Lois's relief was tempered by the fact that Bill had already been celebrating his good fortune. Although he took her to an elegant restaurant, by the time the food arrived, he was too drunk to eat. Lois gave up and took him home. The next day, Bill asked for the check back. As was often true by then, there was something he hadn't told her. The money was earmarked for a new investment company founded by two men Bill had met through Lois's brother-in-law. Bill was to be manager of the company, but it was understood that if he got drunk, he would be fired, and the investment was nonrefundable.

By now, Bill knew that if he was to have a chance of staying sober, he couldn't drink anything at all, and aware that he was running out of chances, he actually became good at saying no. Then he was asked to go to New Jersey with a group of engineers from the Pathé Company to look at a new photographic process.

In the evenings, the men he was with played cards and drank "Jersey Lightning," a type of applejack Bill had never tried. Although they urged Bill to join in, once he made it clear that he wasn't drinking and didn't like cards, they left him alone. Bill was soon bored and restless. Eventually, the thought that he might die without ever having tasted Jersey Lightning proved too much for him. Bill tasted. Then he had a second taste, and a third.

Bill got drunk, and he stayed that way for three days. Word got back to the investors, and he was fired. This would prove to be his absolute last chance.

About the only two people in the world who had not yet given up on him were his wife and Joe Hirschhorn. Hirschhorn, already a multimillionaire and an expert "bottom fisher," was getting richer by the day cherry picking the stock of companies undervalued at depression-era prices. He always explained his affection for Bill by saying, "The son-of-a-bitch makes me money!" He also said that he liked having very smart people around him, and in his opinion, Bill was the best stock analyst he had ever met.

But this smart man was frequently so drunk now that he fell down in the lobby of the building where Joe had his office or collapsed on the street out in front. It became almost routine for Joe to drop everything and, accompanied by another analyst in his employ, charge downstairs to rescue the son-of-a-bitch who made him money. Together they would carry Bill to the elevator, and from the elevator to Joe's office. Bill would sleep the afternoon away on Joe's couch while Hirschhorn wheeled and dealed.

A good-hearted man of tremendous enthusiasms, Hirschhorn did not see the capacity for baseness Wilson was fast developing. Invited to a party at Hirschhorn's estate, Bill discovered his employer's cache of vintage champagne. Already drunk, he and a friend broke the necks off the bottles and poured the outrageously expensive liquid down their throats and over themselves and each other. Fortunately, their wives discovered them first and got them out of there. When Hirschhorn found out what had happened, he was apoplectic, but Bill had been relatively sober when Hirschhorn had last seen him, and Hirschhorn did not suspect him.

Eventually, though, even Joe Hirschhorn got tired of Bill. The last straw involved Canada again. It was 1933, and Hirschhorn was just beginning the uranium-mining venture that was to make him one of the wealthiest men in the United States.

Hirschhorn wanted Bill to help him evaluate a Canadian mining company he was interested in. Bill set off for Toronto by train from New York, but he was so drunk by the time the train reached the Canadian border that he was refused entry. To make matters worse, his protests turned so belligerent that he was arrested and jailed. Unable to bring himself to contact Lois, Bill instead telegraphed Hirschhorn, Hirschhorn was furious, but he sent his secretary to bail him out.

When Bill finally arrived in Toronto, in an attempt to keep him in line, Hirschhorn installed Bill in his own suite in the city's leading hotel. Bill still drank, though, and soon he was so drunk as to be virtually useless. Hirschhorn gave up and sent Bill back to New York.

7

DIFFERENT

By the fall of 1934, Bill Wilson was living to drink. He had also taken to writing raging, gin-fueled letters, many of them unfinished, to President Franklin Roosevelt, denouncing the New Deal. The letters themselves represented an exercise in self-destruction. Assuming the ones he managed to finish and mail could somehow have an effect, it would have deepened the Wilsons' crisis. It was only by the grace of Roosevelt's mortgage moratorium that they had a roof over their heads.

The Wilsons were still living in her father's house. Her father had defaulted on the mortgage, remarried, and moved out of New York. Because the moratorium forbade foreclosures, they were able to stay on by paying the mortgage company a small monthly fee.

By this time, Lois was working as an interior decorator in the furniture department of Macy's. Out of fear that Bill would go into withdrawal, she would leave him enough money when she left for work in the morning to keep him in gin until her return.

Their despair can hardly be imagined. In the preceding twelve months, they had tried the "trip to the country" cure for extended periods. They spent the summer of 1933 in Vermont, on the farm of Bill's sister, Dorothy, and her husband, Leonard Strong. The Strongs and their children were spending the summer in Europe, so the Wilsons had the place to themselves.

There were occasions that summer when Bill drank, and when he did, he drank horribly. He also chopped wood, did chores, and undertook a number of needed repairs. Bill even built a swimming pond, complete with waterfall. Lois always described that summer as a wonderfully happy time. New York, with its horrible memories and their enormous unpaid debts, never seemed farther away.

They both did a lot of reading. According to Lois, Bill was trying to find something that could help him with his drinking, and he focused on the self-help books of the period. At that time the most prominent representative of this genre was *Science and Health*, by Mary Baker Eddy, the founder of Christian Science. Bill read it several times, but he finally concluded that her approach could not help him. Christian Science required faith, and faith was something that, at this point in his life, he could not imagine himself possessing.

When they returned to the city, Bill was drunk in a matter of days, and he stayed drunk, too, drinking day and night. Literally fearful for his life now, Lois knew that her husband needed help she could not give him.

Lois Wilson may have come from a family of doctors, but it was a family that, following her father's lead, regarded illness and infirmity as a manifestation of a weak character. The Burnham men were themselves two-fisted drinkers, especially Rogers. As a young man, Rogers had no trouble keeping up with Bill on the occasions when the two of them would down most of the contents of Clark Burnham's liquor cabinet. However, the Burnhams prided themselves on knowing when to stop. Rogers's drinking never caused him to alienate anyone, let alone drink himself out of a career.

Lois did not turn to her father or her brothers for help but to her brother-in-law, Leonard Strong. Bill's brother-in-law had a thriving osteopathic practice among well-to-do New Yorkers. By nature a very compassionate man, he and Dorothy seemed to share Lois's high regard for Bill.

Leonard got Bill into Charles B. Towns Hospital on Central Park West in Manhattan. Although the word *hospital* was part of its name, Towns was devoted to drying out well-to-do tipplers. A stay there was not something Bill could possibly afford, but Leonard paid the bill himself. Unexpectedly, the Wilsons learned something during Bill's stay in Towns that, perhaps for the first time in their marriage, gave them reason to believe that a life free from the torment of Bill's need to drink might be possible.

Bill's treatment took place under the supervision of the hospital's medical director, Dr. William D. Silkworth, who would become a legendary figure in AA circles. Silkworth had little more to offer of a medical nature than the "belladonna cure." This involved a "purging and a puking" aided by, among other things, castor oil. Belladonna, a hallucinogen, was also administered to ease the symptoms of alcohol withdrawal.

But what Silkworth gave Bill that seemed invaluable was a theoretical explanation of *why* he drank as he did. Silkworth was the first person Bill had ever encountered who regarded alcoholism as an illness rather than a moral weakness or a failure of willpower. As E. M. Jellinek relates in his landmark work, *The Disease Concept of Alcoholism*, the view of alcoholism as a disease was put forth in the United States as early as the late 1700s by no less than the U.S. surgeon general, Dr. Benjamin Rush. The work of Rush and another early proponent of the disease concept, Dr. Thomas Trotter in England, initially did little more than provide fodder for the temperance movement, which seized on their descriptions of alcoholism's physical effects.

In the 1830s, Dr. Samuel Woodward, the first superintendent of the

Worcester State Hospital, Dr. Eli Todd of Hartford, and the Connecticut State Medical Society were among those suggesting the establishment of institutions for "inebriates." In 1872, a medical society dedicated to the study of "inebriety" was founded. The group published a medical journal that continued for nearly forty years, but it was the creature of people who owned and operated hospitals and homes for alcoholics, and neither the society nor its journal ever had much legitimacy.

As far as the temperance movement was concerned, alcoholism was a moral failing, and it vigorously opposed the disease concept of alcoholism. By the time temperance forces had succeeded in establishing Prohibition, the notion had been completely eclipsed in the United States. The view of alcoholism as a disease remained current in Europe, and its acceptance continued to grow. By the early 1930s, disillusionment with Prohibition and the temperance movement's belief that excessive drinking was a sin was widespread. For the first time in the United States, prominent men of medicine and science were writing about alcoholism as a disease.

Silkworth thought that people like Bill Wilson were suffering from a mental obsession with alcohol accompanied by a physical allergy that made compulsive drinking inevitable. Once Bill had even one drink, he would continue drinking. The only way to avoid drunkenness was to abstain from alcohol entirely. This view of alcoholism would form one of the basic principles of the AA approach. The AA slogan "It's the first drink that gets you drunk" may seem incomprehensible to nonalcoholics, but every alcoholic (in a sober state) understands it intuitively.

Bill and Lois were ecstatic. Dr. Silkworth seemed to be saying that Bill was like someone with an allergy to bee stings who kept getting stung by bees and was therefore constantly ill. For such an individual to stay healthy, he had to avoid bees. For Bill to stay healthy, he had to avoid alcohol. Wilson walked out of Towns Hospital alcohol free, and he returned home to a hero's reception.

Lois had filled the house with flowers and all of Bill's favorite things to eat. She had even bought him a portable golf green that he could use in the living room to practice his putting. They were massively in debt, and it was only by dint of the mortgage moratorium that they even had a living room, but for Lois the putting green was a symbol of the life the man she had married should have. Now that they had the solution to his alcohol problem, she thought he would have it.

That very evening, the Wilsons began to imagine wonderful weekend excursions. They would do all the things they had enjoyed in the early days of their marriage. They would camp on the Palisades in nearby New

Jersey and sail down the Hudson in a rented rowboat with a sail rigged from a bath towel. As a couple, they were starting over, and they would again have everything drinking had caused them to lose.

Within a month, Bill was drunk again. He would later insist that it must have been two months, or even four, that he had gone without a drink after learning from Silkworth about his "allergy." This may be an indication of how hard he had tried to stay sober and how difficult it had been for him.

FALSE HOPE

Given Bill's track record, it seems amazing that either of the Wilsons had believed this time would be different. Silkworth may have offered a new reason for Bill to abstain from alcohol completely, but swearing off was hardly a new approach. By 1934, the temperance movement had been in full swing for more than a hundred years. Prohibition had been repealed in 1933, but the sale of alcohol was still prohibited in some states and in numerous counties of other states.

As a youth, Bill Wilson had himself attended temperance meetings. Later in life, he had tried swearing off repeatedly. His attempts to renounce alcohol had reached the intensity of written pledges in the family Bible some ten years earlier, while he was still in law school. Even when failing to stay sober would mean the end of what seemed to be his last chance to revive his Wall Street career, Bill drank. Why, then, had the Wilsons been so excited about Silkworth's theory?

Bill and Lois may not have been religious people, but like so many who came of age as the nineteenth century turned into the twentieth, their faith in science was unyielding. Silkworth's theory provided a scientific, physical explanation rather than a religious one, for the common-sense observation that some people, once they taste alcohol, will continue to drink beyond any reasonable stopping point. When, less than a month after it seemed they were to have a normal life at last, Bill was drinking again, their disillusionment was bottomless. Silkworth may have been right about alcoholism not being subject to moral suasion, but it wasn't subject to the power of the intellect, either.

Bill spent the winter of 1933–34 doing little more than drinking. In March, Lois attempted yet another Vermont resuscitation. They went to the Strongs' farm again. The summer before, Lois had taken a leave of absence from her job. This time, determined to stay in Vermont for however long it might take to restore her husband's health, she simply resigned.

It was apparent from the start that this trip would be different from their last. Their first day on the farm, Bill went fishing, came across a fellow fisherman with a bottle, and got drunk. He had hardly recovered from that debacle when, in Brattleboro to have some dental work done, he used the money that was to have paid the dentist to buy a bottle.

Since they had no car, Wilson rode the mail coach to Brattleboro and back. Getting drunk with the coach's driver became a regular feature of these excursions. What is hard to convey is how hard Bill was trying *not* to behave this way. In between bouts, his remorse was boundless. Paradoxically, when he was drunk, his ravings frequently revolved around the deep guilt he felt about what he had put Lois through with his drinking.

Even at this late stage, Bill occasionally displayed evidence of his sincere desire to do the right thing. He had been of no use to Lois during her last two ectopic pregnancies, and he had only been an additional burden when his wife suffered the loss of her mother. When Lois injured a ligament in her knee during their stay on the Strongs' farm, he seemed determined to make up for these past failings.

For the three weeks Lois was laid up, Bill attended to her every need. Unfortunately, he was also drunk the entire time. As he staggered around the farmhouse with kerosene lamps slanted precariously, Lois could do little more than shout warnings to him and pray that she would be back on her feet before he burned the place down.

Eventually, Bill's dental work was completed, and he stopped going to Brattleboro. Since there was no alcohol on the farm, and nowhere to buy it in Greenfield, he stayed sober. With her husband returned to her, Lois would look back on this time as one of the fondest of her marriage.

Their days were filled with walks through woods and fields, their evenings with talking and reading aloud to one another. Possessed of a remarkably resilient constitution, Bill felt so restored after a few weeks of this kind of living that he was actually able to write articles on financial and economic topics. His always-fragile self-esteem had not recovered, though; he never submitted the pieces for publication.

Lois, too, had great resilience. On the strength of a few weeks' peace of mind, she wrote an article on the merits of veneered furniture. Although Bill, as was usual for him when it came to Lois's writing efforts, was very ungracious about the results, Lois stuck with her self-imposed assignment. She also submitted the final product to *House Beautiful*, which refused it, and then to *House and Garden*, where it was accepted and published.

In June, the Strongs arrived in Greenfield to take up residence for the summer, and Bill and Lois moved into a tent. Bill built a stone fireplace for them to cook on. It was of a type he had learned to construct as a boy, during the maple syrup season on his grandfather's farm, and he and Lois spent many cheerful evenings sitting in front of it to ward off the night chill. Bill's innate resourcefulness meant that, when he was sober, no matter how broke they were he could always find ways to help Lois feel cared for.

In July, the Wilsons returned to New York, intent on looking for work. Lois found a job in downtown Brooklyn in the furniture department of Loesers Department Store. Faced again with the responsibilities of real life, Bill simply started drinking. He was quickly in such desperate shape that Lois prevailed upon her brother-in-law to readmit him to Towns Hospital. This time, though, Silkworth seemed to be just as discouraged as the Wilsons were, and Bill left Towns with none of the confidence of his earlier stay. Convinced that nothing could keep him sober, he drank again almost immediately.

Bill's sufferings were making him almost nostalgic for the hell he had known on previous binges. He was sleeping on the basement level of the house on Clinton Street now. Lois had dragged a mattress down there to keep him from jumping out of a window in a fit of despair.

To Lois, Bill seemed to be enduring the impossibly cruel fate of a fatally injured animal whose survival instinct repeatedly drags it back from the brink. Just when it seemed as though the amount of alcohol he was consuming would at last claim him, something within Bill would rise up to fight his fate. Time and again, he stopped drinking and worked through the horrors of withdrawal, filled with fear, paranoid thoughts, and terrifying hallucinations.

Often, he would be sober hardly more than a day when he would start drinking agan, only to repeat the cycle in a few days' or weeks' time. Finally, Lois intervened in a way she never thought she would. Refusing to let her husband try to sober up another time, she kept him dosed on sedatives until Leonard Strong could again get him into Towns Hospital.

This time, purging and puking was truly all Silkworth could offer. The doctor confessed to Lois that his earlier hopefulness about her husband was based almost entirely on the evident strength of Bill's desire to stay sober. Now, Silkworth had before him a broken and defeated man. What was worse, even after Bill had been detoxed, the delusions and nameless fears continued. Silkworth thought this was a very bad sign. The vast quantities of alcohol Bill had consumed since his previous hospitalization seemed to have had a permanent effect on his brain.

The doctor was no longer offering theoretical explanations for why Bill drank. He told Lois that her focus now must be on keeping her husband alive, and that her only chance for doing so lay in committing him to a sanitarium. As Lois would say later, the fact that she did not commit Bill did not mean she thought Dr. Silkworth might be wrong. To admit Bill to a sanitarium would have required a change of course, and she simply didn't have the energy for it.

After Wilson's third trip to Towns, he left the hospital a deeply frightened man. Neither his doctor nor his wife had shared their pessimism with him. They didn't have to.

Sheer terror kept him sober for some months. He even found a little work on Wall Street. In real terms, it did not amount to much, but it did start to restore his shattered confidence. The fear was enough to keep him sober well into November. Unfortunately, as his confidence returned, his fear of alcohol began to recede.

On November 11, 1934, Armistice Day, the day set aside to commemorate the end of the Great War, the stock market was closed, but Lois had to work, and Bill decided to occupy himself with a round of golf at a public course on Staten Island.

To get there, he first had to take a subway into lower Manhattan, then walk to the ferry terminal. Once on the Staten Island side, a bus would take him halfway across the island to the golf course. The amount and variety of travel involved may itself have been a proximate cause of the debacle that followed. Almost certainly, the fact that, by awful coincidence, Bill's seatmate on the bus was carrying a rifle also played a role. Bill would say later that the rifle reminded him of one he had had as a boy. Traveling with a stranger with a rifle on Armistice Day must have put him in mind of other rifles as well.

When Bill struck up a conversation with the man, he learned that his new friend would be celebrating Armistice Day with some target practice. His destination was a rifle range even farther down the island than the golf course. As they talked, the bus was struck from behind by another bus. No one was hurt, but the bus they were on was damaged badly enough that they had to wait for a substitute bus. While they waited, Bill's new friend suggested they visit a nearby bar.

The man ordered scotch. When Bill ordered ginger ale, the man asked him why he wasn't drinking. In reply, Bill launched into a long-winded presentation of Silkworth's theory about alcoholism as a mental obsession accompanied by a physical alergy. He also recounted in some detail the difficulties he'd had before coming to the conclusion that he simply couldn't drink any amount of alcohol, ever.

The substitute bus arrived, and the men continued their journey uneventfully, arriving at the stop near the golf course around lunchtime. The man with the rifle disembarked to take another bus to the rifle range. At his suggestion, they decided to have lunch together at an inn near the bus stop.

Bill had another ginger ale with his sandwiches, and his friend had another scotch. As they were about to leave, Bill fell into a reverie about the wonderful time he had had on the first Armistice Day, which he had celebrated in a small French town. The bartender chose this moment to come over with two scotches and invite them to have an Armistice Day drink on the house.

Bill downed the scotch without a moment's thought. The man with him could not believe it. "You must be crazy!" he said. Bill, aware too late of what he had done, replied in the affirmative. The man went on to his target practice, but Bill continued to drink.

Somehow, he eventually made his way to the golf course. He purchased a bucket of balls at the course's driving range, but his shots were so erratic and he raised so many divots that he was ejected. Bill kept drinking. He finally arrived home at five o'clock in the morning, so drunk that he fell in the entryway under the stairs and gashed his head.

Lois, who had not slept all night worrying about him, raced downstairs as soon as she heard the commotion. She found her husband on the floor, unconscious and bleeding badly. His golf clubs were still over his shoulder, a sad reminder of her hope for a new life when she had bought him the putting green.

Their defeat was total now. Bill drank with a desolate abandon. There was no talk of either a return to Towns Hospital or a trip to the country. When Lois wasn't working or cleaning up after him, she was investigating sanitariums and gathering her strength.

8

CHANGED

They went on like this for weeks until, one day while Lois was at work, the phone rang. By then, Bill could not be counted on to take notice of such things, but he heard it and got himself to the telephone in time. The caller was an old friend, Ebby Thacher. He was in New York and wanted to pay Bill a visit. When Bill opened the door a couple of days later, he could hardly believe his eyes: Ebby was sober.

Ebby was the wayward son of a prominent family that made its mark in manufacturing and politics. Bill had known Ebby since high school. More recently, his friend was rumored to have fallen lower than Bill himself. The last Bill had heard, Ebby was to be committed to a state asylum. Yet there he was, standing on Bill's front stoop, sober.

Bill invited him in, sat him down at the kitchen table, and offered him a drink. When Ebby refused, Bill wanted to know why.

"I've got religion," was Ebby's reply. Bill's heart sank. Apparently, Ebby wasn't so well after all. Ignoring Bill's disappointment, Ebby went on to recount his downhill slide. Just when all had seemed lost, he had been rescued by a couple of fellows Bill knew to be hard drinkers themselves. One of them, Rowland H., alcoholic scion of a well-to-do New England family, had journeyed as far as Switzerland to seek the aid of Carl Jung. After trying unsuccessfully for some months to help Rowland stop drinking, Jung told him that he thought his best hope lay in religion. It seems Jung had known several alcoholics who, after having a religious conversion experience, found they could stay sober.

In the 1930s, religious conversion experiences were attaining legitimacy not previously known in modern times. Most of them occurred among people who already believed in God. They were believers who had either lost touch with, or never had a sense of connection to, something larger than they were. Spiritual conversions have in common a sudden revelatory experience followed by a 180-degree shift in the way the individual feels about himself (or herself) and the world. Connectedness, benevolence, and optimism replace feelings of isolation, alienation, and hopelessness. Jung believed that what could not be accomplished with alcoholics by psychoanalysis could sometimes be achieved through a spiritual experience.

Rowland left Jung and went forth in search of enlightenment. He found it in the Oxford Group, and he stopped drinking. Rowland introduced Ebby to the Oxford Group, and Ebby was able to stop drinking as well.

The Oxford Group, originally known as a First Century Christian Fellowship and later as Moral Rearmament, was an evangelical sect that was founded by Frank Buchman, a Lutheran minister. Its leader in New York was Sam Shoemaker, an Episcopal minister who was the rector of Calvary Church in Manhattan. Both men were highly intelligent and educated individuals who had had their own transformational experiences, and both said that before their conversions they had had no personal knowledge of God.

The Oxford Group was composed almost exclusively of intelligent, educated people. Most members were upper-middle-class businessmen and professionals. A few were wealthy or prominent or both. The Group also counted among its membership many ministers still active in mainstream churches.

The movement wasn't English, and it had no connection with Oxford University. The Oxford Group specialized in the production of spiritual conversion experiences. It had a set of principles for bringing about a spiritual transformation. Standardized, one-size-fits-all, it was an approach to spirituality that could hardly be more American. Bill Wilson, an admirer of Thomas Edison and Henry Ford, always said that, shorn of their Christian rhetoric and with the holes plugged that an alcoholic might escape through, the Oxford Group principles became the Twelve Steps of Alcoholics Anonymous.

Frank Buchman was intent on changing the world by "converting" the most prominent people in the country to an awareness of a present and active higher consciousness. Although Buchman was not an alcoholic, when he found that alcoholics could benefit from the Oxford process, he stopped drinking. Buchman's interest in alcoholics was fueled in part by his desire to help people. He also knew that having alcoholics in the Oxford Group would speak volumes about the Group's power and effectiveness.

Ebby was still telling Bill why he couldn't have the drink Bill had offered him when Lois came home from work. As Ebby related his experience with the Oxford Group, Bill was trying to listen, but he wasn't exactly sold. He had seen people "witnessing" to such conversions at the tent revivals he attended as a boy, and he had his doubts about how genuine they were. Some of the people testifying only seemed to have religious impulses when the revivalists' tents were up. Now, after all the years of alcoholic hell he had endured, he didn't think he could ever again believe in anything, let alone in a God who would strike him sober.

As Ebby talked, it became evident that not all his troubles were behind him. He was living at Calvary Mission on Twenty-third Street near Second Avenue in New York. The mission was run by Sam Shoemaker's Calvary Church, located a few blocks away on Fourth Avenue (now Park Avenue South). It was a mainstay of the down and out during the depression, when over the years it served some two hundred thousand people.

Bill wanted to scoff at many of the things Ebby was saying. His friend had apparently been "saved" at a mission, where "giving witness" was a routine event. Still, there was no denying one thing: Ebby was sober. What was even more amazing to Bill was that he seemed relaxed and happy about it.

After his friend left, Bill kept drinking. But he was also thinking.

Ebby came to see Bill again a few days later, and this time he had Shep C. with him. On his earlier visit with Bill, Ebby's tone had been conversational, but Shep was very aggressive in putting forth the Oxford case.

After Ebby and Shep left, Bill drank with a vengeance. Shep had made him angry, but after seeing Ebby a second time, it was even harder to deny that something had changed him (and maybe Shep, too) for the better.

The next morning, Wilson decided to pay a visit to the mission. Although he cleaned himself up and put on a suit, he had no intention of going there sober. He was drunk before he even got on the subway. Just to be on the safe side, he got off the train in Manhattan a good distance from the mission and worked his way toward it from bar to bar.

It was in one of these saloons that he struck up a conversation with a Finnish angler and sail maker named Alec. After a few drinks, Bill talked Alec into coming along with him. As it turned out, Alec would be in Bill's life for months to come.

It was late afternoon by the time they finally arrived at the mission. Wilson was very drunk, but by the mission's standards, he was dressed well enough for one of its inhabitants to describe him and Alec as "an elegant man and a down and out." Bill must have also felt himself to be a cut above, for he immediately let everyone know he had something important to say. He was so rowdy that one of the men in charge threw them both out.

Bill and Alec went back, but again Bill's loud insistence that he was someone to be listened to led to their ejection. This happened several more times, until finally the two men were given a seat on a bench in the chapel downstairs. Bill was still sure that he had something important to say, and he kept interrupting the service. He was on the verge of being put out for what would probably have been the last time when Ebby arrived and took them both upstairs for some food and coffee. This seemed to settle Bill down, but no sooner were they back in the chapel than he started interrupting the service again.

He was told that he would be given a chance to speak later, but this was not good enough. It is tempting to think that his insisting he had something important to say was inspired by some dim memory of the story of his grandfather Wilson storming East Dorset's Congregational Church after returning from Mount Aeolus.

Finally, the person leading the service let Bill come up front. Although Bill had no recollection of it later, he told everyone that Ebby had explained what was expected of him. If what they were selling had helped Ebby, he was sure it could help him, and he was willing to try it. Bill then returned to his seat and, to Ebby's great relief, sat quietly.

Near the end of the service, people were invited to come forward to give testimony. Both Bill and Alec went up front and knelt down. Later, Bill's companion was invited to take a bed upstairs for the night. After talking it over with Ebby, Bill decided to go to Towns Hospital.

SOMETHING HAPPENS

Bill did not go to Towns. Instead, he went home, and the next morning, he started drinking as soon as Lois left for work, and for the next three days, he did little else except drink and contemplate his fate. As Bill saw it, he was on the horns of a dilemma. To keep drinking meant a certain alcoholic death or institutionalization, but stopping drinking by embracing religion seemed to be trading one odious dependency for another. He could not see how he could give up his intellect to embrace the tenets of any faith and still call himself a man.

No matter how Bill struggled, though, he also could not escape the image of Ebby Thacher, sober. That he was a changed man seemed incontrovertible, and Ebby did not seem to think he had given up anything worth having.

On the third day, Bill knew what he had to do. He had to stop drinking, and he had to talk to Dr. Silkworth about all of this. After leaving Lois a note, he headed for a grocery where he had a charge account and bought four bottles of beer. When he arrived at Towns, he had one bottle left. He had bought the beer merely to ensure that he did not go into withdrawal along the way. The date was December 11, 1934. Although he did not know it yet, Bill Wilson had taken his last drink.

During Bill's fourth stay in Towns, on the second, or possibly the third, evening, Ebby came to see him. Bill asked his friend to describe again how this Oxford Group business worked. Ebby repeated the formula that had worked for him: realizing he was defeated, he admitted it, and turned his life over to the care of God. It seemed so simple to Ebby, but after he left, Bill didn't feel himself to be any further along. He was also filled with guilt and remorse over his bad behavior, particularly toward Lois.

He knew he was defeated. He did not have any trouble admitting it. In a few days, he would have to leave Towns. Absent some kind of miracle, he felt sure that when he hit the street, he would drink again. The prospect terrified him as nothing had before, but he wrestled with what Ebby had said about having to surrender his intellect to the unknown and the un-knowable. To someone who prided himself on his rational, scientific ap-proach to life, this seemed an insurmountable barrier. In the depths of his torment, Wilson issued the unknowable a challenge: "If there be a God, let Him show Himself now!" he shouted.

As if in response to his demand, the room suddenly filled with light. It was bright and white, a benign, enveloping presence that seemed more than a match for the terror he had been feeling just moments before. Then he saw himself on a mountaintop, with a wind blowing toward him. The wind moved closer and closer, then through him. Then the man who had been bound up in a seemingly irresolvable internal struggle felt profoundly free.

When the wind and the light were gone, Bill could again see the walls of his room. Everything returned to normal, except for one thing: Bill Wilson would never be the same again. Bill lived another thirty-six years after that night, and he spoke about his "hot flash" experience frequently. Yet he was never able to expand significantly on the above description of what had caused him to lose all desire to drink.

Wilson spoke to Silkworth about it almost immediately. What had hap-pened was so extraordinary Bill was afraid that his doctor was going to tell him that his descent into alcoholic insanity was a fait accompli.

Dr. Silkworth listened carefully, and he asked Bill a number of ques-tions. It went against his medical training and all his experience with al-coholics, but Silkworth could not deny that his patient seemed different. Happy. Relaxed. Energized. Even years younger.

Silkworth could not explain what had happened, but neither did he think Bill was crazy. Clearly, his patient was better off than he had been.

The doctor's advice was to stop trying to understand. Bill should focus instead on hanging onto what the experience had given him.

A few days later, Ebby brought Bill something that would help him to hang on: a copy of the psychologist William James's book *The Varieties of Religious Experience.* In it, Bill was to encounter a number of stories similar to his. Desperate people who had surrendered, given up on their own power, and asked for help.

Here in a book written by the country's most eminent psychologist was confirmation of the efficacy of what he had experienced. Rowland, Shep, and Ebby had also engaged in a process of spiritual change. None of them had a sudden transformational experience like Bill or the people James was describing, but they had changed. That they were all sober was the proof.

The change in Bill was so dramatic that Lois could see it instantly. She had made her way to Towns in a very foul mood. She was angry that Bill had gone back to the hospital without consulting her. If he had, she would have been against it. There was no reason to think it would do him any good, they had no means of paying for it, and there was no one left she felt they could turn to. Lois walked into Bill's room ready for a fight.

"He was different," she would say later. "I knew it right away. And I knew that he would never drink again." Over the next fifty-three years, Lois would be asked perhaps thousands of times to describe her reaction to seeing Bill for the first time after what Bill would later characterize as his "hot flash." She would never waver on either point.

"How could you tell?" I asked her myself, in 1988.

"I just could," she replied, looking at me as if I had just asked how she knew the sky was blue.

Bill Wilson *was* different. So different that others who had known him as a drinking man would also be able to accept completely that he had stopped drinking for good. After his experience in Towns Hospital, people meeting Bill for the first time often instantly accepted him as the extraordinary figure Lois had always felt him to be.

His personal problems were certainly not all behind him. The bubble of Bill's optimism would eventually burst. In time, personality deficits that had been manifest before he started drinking would seem to dominate his life much as his alcoholism once had. Initially, though, being free from his losing battle with alcohol produced in Bill an unassailable buoyancy and dynamism. In the months and years to follow, he would overcome all the obstacles to achieving what was soon to become his life's work: the creation of Alcoholics Anonymous.

9

WHAT WAS IT?

In trying to explain Bill's experience at Towns, we might point to his having just listened to Ebby's and Shep's stories. He had also read Mary Baker Eddy's book and heard about what Carl Jung had said to Rowland about the power of a spiritual conversion experience.

Bill had been to the mission, where he had heard people "witnessing" to the power of God to relieve them of the need to drink. Also, belladonna was administered at Towns, and a number of other drugs with hallucinogenic potential were used there, as well.

There is the similarity between Bill's description of his spiritual experience and the terms his grandfather used to describe a moment of truth atop Mount Aeolus. It seems impossible that Bill did not know this story about his grandfather Wilson. Even as his sister, Dorothy, approached her ninetieth year, she was able to recall it with great clarity.

Whatever happened to Bill Wilson that evening in Towns Hospital, the fact remains that, before that event, he seems to have been a hopeless drunk. After it, he never drank again.

Bill was not a religious man before or after that night in Towns Hospital, and he frequently had grave doubts about himself as "a going concern" all the rest of his life. Yet there were certain things he never again doubted. He believed unquestioningly that there was a divine force in the universe, that he had been touched by it, and that he owed to this experience his freedom from the need to drink.

Wilson's transformation was of a different order entirely from what his friend Ebby had experienced. In discovering the Oxford Group, Ebby found people who would take him in and take care of him. Time would reveal that Ebby was always able to stay sober when he had someone to look after him and was never able to when he did not. Ebby had been sober two years and seven months when, in 1937, after moving back to Albany, he started drinking again. Many more relapses were to follow. Bill, ever faithful and loyal, would always do whatever he could to help his friend. When Ebby was in his cups or just particularly down on his luck, he often came by the AA office for a handout. Bill always came through for him, even during the years when he would have to borrow money from someone else in order to help Ebby. Whenever a grateful AA member asked Bill if there was anything he could do for him, Bill invariably replied, "Well, I just wish there was something we could do to help Ebby." On more than one occasion, people would try, and it was because of their efforts that Ebby enjoyed his longest periods of sobriety. (Rowland, too, eventually returned to drink.)

In Bill's case, his experience at Towns, the information from Silkworth about the nature of alcoholism, and his deeply felt need to redeem a failed life combined to provide him with something that had been missing at the height of his Wall Street success: Bill Wilson now had a calling.

He began to think about helping other alcoholics while he was still a patient at Towns. As he lay in his hospital bed, he could see the help spreading from one drunk to another, until alcoholics all over the world had what he had.

Bill shared his thoughts with Lois when she came to visit him again. He was very aware that he had put his wife through hell. What had happened in his hospital room in the middle of the night may have saved his life, but he was under no illusions as to who had made it possible for him to survive long enough to have that moment.

In December 1934, Lois was nearly forty-four years old. She was profoundly grateful that her husband was a well man, but this did not mean the nightmare that had been their life together was entirely over. They were still broke, they still had no assurance of a roof over their heads, and there were still all those debts. Moreover, he was unemployed, and seemingly unemployable, in the only profession he knew.

Yet Bill was never much for small talk, and when he was excited about a new idea, small talk was out of the question. With little more than a "hello," he plunged in. He told Lois what he wanted to do, and how much difference he thought it would make. His enthusiasm and his vision knew no bounds.

Bill could not tell his wife what contribution his desire to help drunks would make to solving their problems, or when, but it did not matter. Lois was entranced. She was a schoolgirl again, listening to her boyfriend talk about the great things he would do in the world. If she had so much as a moment when she thought, "Wait a minute, what about me?" she was never known to have admitted it.

"I thought it was a splendid idea," she would say later. "I was all for it, right from the start."

When Bill left Towns, he "graduated" from the mission to Oxford Group meetings at Calvary House, adjacent to the church. It was here that he learned more about the Group's methods for living life on a higher spiritual plane. This was also where he came to know Sam Shoemaker, who would become a lifelong friend.

Perhaps most important, Bill quickly discovered the gang of Oxford Group members who met at a nearby cafeteria for "the meeting after the meeting." These people had something in common with each other that they didn't share with other members of the Group: they were sober alcoholics. Bill liked and admired Sam Shoemaker and others among the nonalcoholic members of the Oxford Group, but it was with the Oxford Group members who were also ex-drunks that he felt truly at home.

The Bill Wilson who had shown up drunk at Calvary's Twenty-third Street mission was hoping to find something that would save his life. The Bill Wilson who attended Oxford Group meetings at Calvary House was doing research. Bill did not go to Oxford Group meetings for himself. He went to learn how the Oxford Group was able to help alcoholics stay sober.

Although the profound nature of Bill's spiritual conversion resulted in an enthusiastic welcome, it was clear almost from the beginning that Bill Wilson was not well suited to be an Oxford Group member. Frank Buchman's, and even Sam Shoemaker's, interest in alcoholics was of an entirely different order than Wilson's. Conversely, Wilson's interest in the Oxford Group was very limited. He never shared in, or had much sympathy for, the Oxford Group's goals.

Buchman was out to "Christianize" people by introducing them to the "real" Christian experience. At its founding, Buchman called his movement A First Century Christian Fellowship, but he coupled his back-to-the-future theology to some very twentieth-century marketing methods.

He promoted the Oxford Group not as another religion but as something more like a "religion enhancement." Joining the Oxford Group did not mean giving up or converting from one's present faith. It was instead a means for making that faith more personally meaningful.

Bill Wilson always said that the essence of the AA program came from the Oxford Group. He did indeed learn much from Frank Buchman that would be of benefit to AA. Like the Oxford Group, AA believes in "spiritual equality," opposing on principle any hierarchy based on class, racial, sexual, or religious differences. Like the Oxford Group, AA employs religious symbolism and expressions of religious faith as part of a program designed to bring about spiritual conversion. Also like the Oxford Group, it did these things in a way that did not threaten the hegemony of established religions.

Yet there is also much about the Oxford Group that is not carried over into AA. Alcoholics Anonymous is not a Christian fellowship. There are no specifically Christian references in any of its literature. Alcoholics Anonymous is open to all people, regardless of age, class, race, gender, nationality, or sexual orientation. The Oxford Group professed spiritual equality, but its membership was almost exclusively upper-middle-class white professionals. Its teams actively pursued prominent cultural, political, and business figures.

Buchman saw the Oxford Group as eventually encompassing people from all walks of life, but he felt that the best way to promote its growth was to focus on prominent people. In all his years at the helm of the movement, the prominent were always his targets. Bill Wilson, on the other hand, was interested in helping drunks.

In Buchman's view, it was important for the Oxford Group to be able to say that it had the power to save souls. He was always on the lookout for opportunities to attract attention to his movement through the achievement of a dramatic conversion. Members of the clergy were particularly encouraged to join. The movement included leading clergymen who felt they had discovered in the Oxford Group what it truly meant to have God in their lives.

BEING USEFUL

Jews were also encouraged to join. Buchman might have been delighted to have prominent Jewish cultural, political, or business figures in the Oxford Group. However, with all the references to Jesus as the source of spiritual healing, one has to wonder how any Jew could possibly have felt welcome. The Oxford Group was clearly a specifically Christian fellowship, and saying that Jews were welcome would seem nearly the equivalent of saying that Jews are welcome to join the Roman Catholic Church, which they are, if they are willing to give up their faith.

Perhaps the most important point of difference between Bill Wilson and the Oxford Group had to do with alcoholism. Bill thought William Silkworth was right about alcoholism being a disease. Frank Buchman thought alcoholics were sinners. OGers believed that a personal experience of God hinged on the acceptance of four absolutes: honesty, purity, unselfishness, and love. They were also actively against sin, and excessive drinking was a sin.

Smoking and sexual adventuring were also regarded as sins. The Oxford Group was opposed to medical or psychological explanations for any human failing. It also opposed psychotherapeutic remedies for the same. Buchman drew people out by talking about his own failings. He also possessed unusual insight into other people's problems. Both characteristics must have been useful in his work with alcoholics. However, unlike Bill Wilson, Buchman was not interested in alcoholics per se; he tried to help them because doing so was a way to do good and promote the Oxford Group.

Bill emerged from Towns armed with enthusiasm, energy, and determination to succeed. Unfortunately, he had no experience in trying to convince another alcoholic that he should, or could, quit drinking. For Bill, the Oxford Group was the place to learn.

As far as the Oxford Groupers were concerned, Bill was a "star pupil" before he attended his first class. Thanks to Ebby, the Oxford Group already knew about Bill's visionary spiritual conversion experience, so when Bill went to his first meeting, he received a hero's welcome. To the Oxford Group, a sober alcoholic was a saved sinner. The more dramatic the saving, the more value the alcoholic had to the Group. Bill's "saving" could hardly have been more dramatic, and the Oxford Group was ready to take credit for it.

Bill certainly owed his relief from his need to drink to a conversion experience, but he had had almost no exposure to OG doctrine and practice. He hadn't read any of the Group's literature or attended a single Oxford Group meeting, and when he went to the Calvary mission he was so drunk he later could barely recall being there. Bill had talked to Ebby, and then Ebby and Shep, about the Oxford Group, but each time, he was drunk. When Ebby visited him in Towns, he had to ask Ebby to repeat again his version of the Oxford formula.

Bill Wilson was so far from being a saved sinner the Oxford Group could legitimately take credit for that he didn't even believe that drinking was a sin, but his story was certainly dramatic. Although he had a loyal wife to keep a roof over his head, his drinking could hardly have taken him further down. Yet so profound was the effect of his experience in Towns, the man who had been at the door of a lifetime commitment to a sanitarium now beamed with energy and confidence. Bill was still only thirty-nine years old, and he was tall, slim, and handsome. His health—this time without the benefit of the "Vermont cure"—had never been better.

In the beginning, Wilson was frequently called on to give witness at New York area meetings and "house parties," the primary means through which newcomers were introduced to the Oxford Group. He was also asked to travel to other cities along the eastern seaboard to speak at OG events.

James Houck, a surviving member of the Oxford Group who met Bill

Wilson in Baltimore in 1935, described Bill as a big, good-looking, and pleasant fellow with a ready wit. He also saw Bill as someone who "carried a powerful message of personal redemption," but Houck's assessment of Bill as an Oxford Grouper is far less positive.

"He was an atheist before he stopped drinking, and I don't think he ever really stopped being an atheist." Houck said. "He was never interested in the things we were interested in. All he ever wanted to talk about was alcoholism." Moreover, according to Houck, the only people Bill ever wanted to talk to were the other alcoholic members.

Before his spiritual conversion experience, Wilson described himself as an agnostic. Afterward, while Bill never subscribed to a specific religion, he saw the universe as being essentially spiritual in nature, and he always professed a deep and abiding faith in a higher power, which he referred to as God.

The Oxford Group itself used the terms *higher power* and *God* interchangeably. That Houck would see Bill as an atheist reflects a tension between Wilson and the Oxford Group that extended well beyond their cross-purposes.

Bill did not think drinking was a sin and he did not share the OG's view of other human failings, either. Still aglow from his spiritual experience and a life free from alcohol, he had no interest in giving up smoking, and Bill seems always to have been ladies' man. Men who knew him during his Wall Street days attest to it, and his time in the army doesn't seem to have been any different. Even when his womanizing seemed certain to threaten his status as AA's exalted founder, he was not known to have made any attempt to curb his behavior.

Bill does seem to have controlled his sexual impulses in Oxford Group circles, if for no other reason than the fact that his wife was usually with him. Yet he also seems to have been unconcerned about the Group's views on the subject. Houck recalls that he often regaled its male members with tales of his exploits.

Fortunately for Bill, the Oxford Group was tolerant of sin and sinners. Neither smoking nor drinking was banned from Oxford Group circles, but Frank Buchman didn't smoke or drink and neither did Sam Shoemaker. Oxford Group members were encouraged to stop even if they did not have a drinking problem.

Giving up alcohol and tobacco was virtually de rigueur for anyone who wanted to be regarded as "maximum," a term reserved for members who were truly "on the program." It was an outward manifestation of the power of the Oxford Group to change lives, and it made the Oxford

Group more welcoming to those seeking a safe haven from both big and little vices.

Oxford Group members made a practice of seeking guidance during meditations, not only for themselves but for other members as well. The process through which they shared the guidance they got for another member was known as "checking." Bill was frequently checked for his smoking and womanizing, but he simply ignored these admonitions. Whenever Bill offered checking to another member, it was to a fellow alcoholic, and the guidance was always about drinking.

In the end, Bill's stubborn single-minded focus on helping alcoholics was too much for the maximum Oxford Group members. His continuing refusal to even regard being "maximum" as a worthy goal also diminished his value in attracting people to the Oxford Group.

Alcoholic OG members began meeting at the Wilsons' home on Clinton Street in 1935. These meetings were devoted to just one topic: staying sober. By January 1938, they were no longer attending Oxford Group functions.

According to Lois, she and Bill were more or less "kicked out" of the Oxford Group. Near the end of 1935, the alcoholics at the Calvary Mission were told that they could not attend the meetings the Wilsons were holding in their home. As Bill and Lois saw it, this was tantamount to their being told they were no longer welcome in the group. However, the prohibition issued at the Calvary Mission was done while Sam Shoemaker was away on vacation, and the members were far from unanimous in the condemnation of Bill's focus on drunks. Buoyed by the Oxford Group members who supported their work with alcoholics and feeling that there was still much to be gained from participating in Oxford Group activities, the Wilsons persisted.

As far as the maximum members were concerned, though, the Wilsons quit. Some of them even saw their withdrawal as a betrayal. According to Lois, both Shoemaker and Buchman were furious. Buchman never got over it, and Shoemaker did not speak to Bill for years.

THE CRUSADERS

Bill may not have been well suited to Buchman's purposes, but the Oxford Group could hardly have been better for Bill. Some 10 percent of its membership were made up of alcoholics, and other alcoholics were always investigating the group to see if it might be able to help them. There was also the Twenty-third Street Mission. It might seem surprising that Sam Shoemaker, a principal of the Oxford Group, which had catered to the high and mighty, would be associated with such a project. But while Shoemaker liked and admired Frank Buchman, his own conversion experience gave him an interest in helping people life had dealt with more severely than most. This interest would always claim as much of Shoemaker's energy as his desire to change the world through promoting the Oxford Group.

Although the mission did not exist to serve alcoholics per se, many of the men who ended up there were desperate drunks. Towns Hospital was also a source of prospects for Bill. Charlie Towns and William Silkworth were so impressed with his recovery that they let him work with any Towns's patient who was willing to listen.

In the first few months after he joined the Oxford Group, not one of the men Bill tried to help stayed sober. Not even Alec, who was one of the dozens of drunks he brought home to live with him.

Why Lois put up with Bill's turning what had been her family home into an unstaffed residential treatment facility may be something that she herself never fully understood. Since all their "patients" were nonpaying, the entire operation was dependent on Lois's department store earnings. What is more, when it came to housework, none of the men under her roof were interested in breaking new ground. Lois did the shopping, cooking, and cleaning.

Besides Lois's multiple contributions to the material well-being of the men Bill brought home, she also spent countless hours trying to help them. Bill made the initial contacts, but once an alcoholic was in residence, he unburdened himself to whoever was available to listen. Since Bill was spending a lot of time working at the mission or Towns Hospital, Lois was often the person these men turned to for counsel.

Annie Smith, wife of AA cofounder Robert Smith, was also directly involved in trying to help other alcoholics. So were the wives of many of the other early members. In fact, Lois considered herself a member of AA as well as Al-Anon. According to her, all the wives who joined their husbands in working with alcoholics during AA's formative years saw themselves as AA members.

Some of the men the Wilsons took in were undoubtedly grateful for Lois's efforts, but there was also the fellow who chased her around the house brandishing a kitchen knife. The episode was provoked by her rejection of his amorous advances. Another man killed himself on the premises. Later, they realized that he had been stealing and selling all their best clothes. In addition to such major events, it was almost routine for at least one of these men to come home drunk and make a mess or create a ruckus, or both.

Lois had to be grateful that Bill was not among this lot, as he might have been just a short time earlier. However, Bill was not home much. When he was not at the mission or Towns working with drunks, he was at Towns with Dr. Silkworth or at Calvary House talking with Sam Shoemaker, sometimes into the wee hours of the morning. Lois must have resented this and found it unfair. Yet she seemed never to have wanted anything more than to have her husband succeed, and though she certainly had more than enough cause, she was never known to have complained, though most people would feel that Bill certainly gave her cause to do so.

Lois did admit to resenting Silkworth and the Oxford Group because they had been able to help Bill where she had failed. In the first weeks after his transformation, she felt useless and even depressed. While no one could have been happier than she that Bill was at last sober, her primary purpose in life—helping her husband in his battle with alcoholism—had been taken from her.

Lois's negative feelings toward the Oxford Group came to a head one Sunday as she and Bill were preparing to leave for an Oxford Group meeting. Bill, fearful of being late, urged her to hurry. Her response was to take the shoe she was about to put on and throw it at him.

"Damn your old meetings!" she shouted.

(Lois throwing her shoe is memorialized in Al-Anon circles as the first awareness that alcoholism can also seriously affect those who are close to an alcoholic. When I knew her fifty years later, Al-Anon members were still sending her miniature shoes as an expression of solidarity and gratitude.)

She was as surprised by her behavior as Bill. Later, she would say it was her first realization that the feeling of moral superiority she had enjoyed for so many years was perhaps not entirely justified. Her response to this insight is a tribute to the remarkable person she was. Lois began to attend Oxford Group meetings, not merely to accompany her husband, but for the help they might provide her in overcoming the shortcomings in her own character. The knowledge she gained about herself in this period provides insight into her dedication to her husband's mission. Bill's being successful served as the ultimate vindication of her choice of mate, and his creating an organization to help people to overcome alcoholism also represented a special kind of triumph for her.

Lois may have been as ego-driven as Bill. Bill wanted to conquer the world, but Lois wanted to be someone who had the power to change people. As a child, Lois managed to convince herself that she could do this by merely exposing them to the magnificent goodness of her personality. In her memoirs, *Lois Remembers,* she recounts a childhood daydream in which she surprises a burglar stealing the family silver. Inspired by her sweet example to want to be good, he puts the silver back.

She seemed to regard both her parents as paragons of nineteenth-century virtue. According to Lois, her mother was a woman who "could change bad people into good ones" by exposing them to her strength of character. Lois attributed her need to believe in her power over people to a desire to be like her mother. This is why she took such tremendous pride in her husband's accomplishments. Becoming an officer in the army, building radios out of kits, passing Thomas Edison's test, completing law school, inventing a way for himself to become a Wall Street success—it all represented a vindication of Lois Burnham's power to change Bill Wilson for the better.

This is also the root of her enthusiasm for Bill's wanting to make helping drunks his life's work. When Lois heard about Bill's latest plan, it must have seemed to her that his conversion experience had converted him to *her* way of life. She could not take credit for Bill's getting sober, but now that he was sober, she had someone with whom to march through life changing bad people into good ones.

Lois also felt a genuine compassion for the alcoholics Bill brought home. To her, they weren't bad men but childlike and immature ones. She even felt this way about the fellow who chased her around with a knife, and she never doubted the sincerity of a drunk's professed desire to stay sober.

After four or five months of unrelieved failure in their efforts to help alcoholics, both the Wilsons were quite discouraged. As a result of attending Oxford Group meetings, conversations with Silkworth about alcoholism, and with Sam Shoemaker about spiritual conversion, Bill's understanding of his drinking and how it had been arrested had grown exponentially. Unfortunately, he had yet to find an effective way of conveying this information to the men he was working with. On the plus side, the transformation he had experienced showed no sign of fading: he still wasn't having any trouble staying away from alcohol.

Neither of the Wilsons thought about giving up, but they did feel that it might be time for Bill to go back to work. He had already done some exploring among his old contacts on Wall Street. Many had been burned too badly by the Bill Wilson of old to be willing to consider the possibility that he had changed. For others, though, the change was self-evident. Bill looked different, and he sounded different. They were also impressed by his heartfelt willingness to acknowledge the error of his previous ways.

In addition to looking for work, Bill sought out Silkworth's opinion as to why he was not getting anywhere with his efforts to "fix" drunks. Silkworth thought Bill was doing two things wrong. One of them was proselytizing.

When Bill talked to a drunk, he came on very strong. Ironically, the manner and tone he employed seem not to have been very different from what he had objected to in Shep C.'s behavior. Bill Wilson had changed in many ways, but the difficulty he sometimes had in making an effective case for something he strongly believed in was still with him. Later, this same difficulty would turn some of his efforts to effect positive change in AA into a battle royal.

Dr. Silkworth also thought Bill was making a mistake by insisting that an alcoholic's only hope lay in the kind of "hot flash" spiritual conversion experience Bill himself had. Most of the alcoholics who had gotten sober through the Oxford Group had come by their new perspective slowly, through trying to live in accordance with Oxford Group principles. Not surprisingly, Silkworth was of the opinion that Wilson should be telling drunks that alcoholism was a mental obsession combined with a physical allergy; unless something was done to unhinge this combination, an alcoholic would drink until death or insanity intervened.

As he was in most things, when it came to communicating, Bill was a man of extremes. When he was not in "monologue mode," he was actually a very good listener. Bill listened to what Silkworth was trying to tell him. His willingness to heed the doctor's advice may actually have saved his life. At the least, it was crucial to his being able to help Dr. Robert Smith, AA's cofounder.

A NEW MAN

It is hard to appreciate how different Bill seemed to be after his spiritual experience in Towns Hospital. One is tempted to think the good opinions of his wife and his doctor, who had seen him at his worst, would not necessarily be shared by anyone not judging him against this standard. In the spring of 1935, Wilson renewed his old contacts on Wall Street. Cliff E., the Wall Street acquaintance who had introduced him to Joe Hirschhorn and years later joined AA, introduced him to Howard Tompkins, a principal of the Wall Street firm Baer and Company. Tompkins was involved in an attempt to take over the National Rubber Machinery Company (NRMC). Based on Akron, Ohio, the company made equipment used in tire production. Bill's services were quickly enlisted in the attempt to collect proxies from NRMC shareholders. What's more, if Tompkins's group succeeded in gaining control of the company, Bill was to be the company's new president.

That he would be considered for this venture at all, let alone as the president of a multimillion-dollar company employing hundreds of people, is a measure of the new man he seemed to be. Bill had never run a company. In fact, except for his time as an officer in the army, he had no management experience at all. If this was still the Roaring Twenties, and his new business partners were drinking men, their proposal might not seem so remarkable. Yet it wasn't, and they weren't.

The Depression had left many people feeling old, used up. Bill, on the other hand, felt reborn, brand-new. There was a spring to his step and an eagerness to take on new challenges. Many of his Wall Street friends found this irresistible.

In the past, Bill had often done poorly in new situations. Not knowing what was expected of him seemed to aggravate his self-doubt. He had never gotten along very well with regular employment, either. The previous time he'd tried it, more than ten years earlier, had culminated in his drinking so much and feeling so poorly about himself that he never got his law school degree.

Yet, neither Bill nor Lois, who certainly knew more about Bill Wilson than his new partners, seemed to have any doubts about his being an asset to the enterprise. That they shared his partners' confidence is a measure of how much he had changed, and how solid they regarded his so-briety to be.

In April, Bill and his partners went to Akron to continue their proxy fight. After several weeks of trying to persuade National Rubber Machinery Company stockholders to give them their proxies, Bill's side seemed to be winning. The shareholders meeting had been delayed until May, but it looked as though they would be able to vote more shares than either the faction they were struggling against or the company's management. The company presidency included a salary of $14,000, which would be about $165,000 today. Bill made a quick trip back to New York, filled with hope for a better life.

Then, shortly after he returned to Akron, a number of shareholders switched sides, and the other faction joined forces with the company's management. This new, combined group controlled 60 percent of the company's voting stock. What had seemed a sure thing now appeared all but lost. Leaving Bill behind to see what he could learn about why those shareholders had switched, his partners returned to New York. In their haste, they didn't ask Bill how he was fixed for cash. By then, Wilson had been chronically broke for years, and he was too embarrassed to bring up the subject.

Still stinging from their defeat, Bill found himself alone in the lobby of Akron's Mayflower Hotel with only a few dollars in his pocket. He could hear the sound of laughter and conversation coming from the bar at one end of the lobby. To his surprise, it actually seemed tempting.

Since Bill had left Towns Hospital for the last time, he had stayed away from situations in which alcohol was served unless he'd had a good reason for being there. When he had been around booze, he had remained confident of his ability to stay sober. Now, though, this confidence was gone. As Bill surveyed the lobby, he realized that he did not know when he would again be able to talk with another alcoholic about the nature of his affliction. Akron had an Oxford Group chapter, but he had no idea whether its membership included alcoholics. Oxford Groups were not listed in the phone book, and Bill did not know the names of any of the local members.

It wasn't Oxford Group meetings that he missed. It was the alcoholics he had met through the New York group, and the alcoholics he was working with at Calvary Mission and in Towns Hospital. None of them were staying sober, but as the sounds from the bar beckoned, Bill saw that the energy he had devoted to talking with other alcoholics had in fact accomplished something: it had helped *him* stay sober.

This notion is a cornerstone of AA. It is captured in the AA slogan "You have to give it away in order to keep it," and it did not come from the Oxford Group. Oxford Group members worked with others because it served the Group's goal of changing the world. That this activity could enhance the spiritual health of the person carrying the Oxford Group message had never been explicitly identified.

After realizing that working with other alcoholics had helped him stay sober, Bill walked to the other end of the lobby, where he had noticed a church directory. After trying to decide which minister was the most likely to know about the Oxford Group, he settled on the Reverend Walter Tunks. Like Sam Shoemaker, Tunks was the rector of an Episcopalian church.

When he called, he learned that the Reverend Mr. Tunks was himself an Oxford Group member. Tunks didn't know any alcoholics, but he gave Bill the names of some people who might. Bill called nine of the names without getting anywhere. The tenth call was to a man who said he knew a woman who had been trying to help an alcoholic. The man gave Bill the telephone number of a Henrietta Seiberling.

This was enough to send Bill back to pacing the lobby. He had been able to call a minister he had picked at random, and then call ten strangers the minister thought might be working with an alcoholic. However, calling a woman named Seiberling in Akron, Ohio, was not something Bill felt prepared to do. In more prosperous days, he had actually met Frank Seiberling, the founder of Goodyear Tire and Rubber and, later, of Seiberling Tire. Now, feeling broke, isolated, and increasingly desperate about his prospects for getting through the evening sober, he was supposed to call up a woman he assumed was this great man's wife and tell her that he wanted to talk to someone who was looking for help with a drinking problem.

The sounds from the bar still beckoned. Bill knew too much to be able to kid himself about what could happen if he succumbed to his desire for some easy camaraderie. He made the call.

That he did so stands in sharp contrast to the incident on the beach of Sanibel Island. Even buoyed by the presence of a wife who was both socially connected and socially graceful, Wilson had not been able to bring himself to speak to Henry Ford. That he called Henrietta Seiberling is a measure of how much he had changed.

To Bill's surprise, Henrietta Seiberling, who was actually the estranged wife of Frank Seiberling's son, could hardly have sounded more delighted to hear from him. She did indeed know of man who was seeking help with his drinking. To Bill's greater surprise, Henrietta Seiberling immediately invited him to her home.

When he arrived, Mrs. Seiberling told him about Dr. Robert Smith, an Akron proctologist she had been trying to help for the last two years. Henrietta described him as an Oxford Group member, although at the time, Bob might not have agreed. What is certain is that Bob's wife, Anne, was an Oxford Group member, and she and Henrietta were good friends. Anne had been dragging her husband to Oxford Group meetings and "house parties," and Henrietta had nearly made getting Bob sober her life's work.

WHAT BILL KNEW

There is some reason to wonder about Bill's account of how he came to meet the man who would become AA's cofounder. Walter Tunks was one of the founding members of the Akron Oxford Group. As such, he was someone of whom Sam Shoemaker and other New York Oxford Group members were certainly aware. As for Henrietta Seiberling, given the Oxford Group's penchant for celebrity and Tunks's position in the Akron Oxford Group chapter, that Tunks himself did not know Henrietta Seiberling and her efforts to help Robert Smith seems hardly credible.

Bill Wilson was many things, not the least of them a showman. He was famous for exaggerating AA's membership figures and the attendance at AA events, but it was something he did almost openly. His longtime secretary and administrative assistant, Nell Wing, reports that whenever he would put forth an inflated figure in her presence, she would try to set the record straight. Invariably, Bill would complain good-naturedly that she was "trying to spoil his fun."

Wilson was also not above expanding and embellishing on a story to increase its dramatic impact. As he told it, having been abandoned virtually penniless by his partners compounded his anguish in the lobby of the Mayflower Hotel. However, the $10.00 he had was the equivalent of $120.00 in year 2000 dollars. While this was hardly enough to survive on for very long, there was never any thought that he would have to do so.

Before his partners returned to New York, they made contact with their local allies, and a strategy for the next phase of the battle was hastily sketched out. Bill was to stay in Akron as long as it took to see the fight to its conclusion, and money would be wired to defray his expenses.

The case for the essential truthfulness of Bill's version is, however, stronger than it may appear. The issue goes to the heart of his relationship to the Oxford Group. Walter Tunks may have been a household name to Sam Shoemaker and other maximum Oxford Group members in New

York, but the testiness of Bill's relationship with the OG and the single-mindedness of his focus on alcoholism make it plausible that he wouldn't know much about the Akron Oxford Group.

Certain defining characteristics of Akron's social fabric also help to make Bill's version of these events credible. Akron was the home of family dynasties, the Seiberlings, the Firestones, and others, who competed with each other in the rubber business. None of them thought much of losing. The competition spilled over into most anything the families or anyone connected with them did. Consequently, the rubber capital of the world was also one of the world's most faction-ridden cities.

By the time of Bill's arrival in Akron, Robert Smith's drinking had come to have implications well beyond its effects on his family and his medical practice. Henrietta Seiberling may have been estranged from her husband, but she was still Frank Seiberling's daughter-in-law, and she was living in the gatehouse of the Seiberling estate.

Although Henrietta had been trying to help Bob Smith for two years, Bob's drinking had only gotten worse under her tutelage. Smith knew that he was powerless over alcohol, but try as he might, he could not stay sober. Give the investment Henrietta had made in him, this would not have been an acceptable outcome under any circumstances. The history behind the formation of the Oxford Group's Akron chapter made the prospect of a Seiberling failure even less palatable.

In 1928, an OG member named James Newton moved to Akron to become personal assistant to Harvey Firestone, Sr., founder of the Firestone Tire and Rubber Company. Newton quickly became close to one of Firestone's sons, Russell Firestone, also known as "Bud." Bud was bright, good-looking, well educated. He had made a good marriage, and he seemed to have inherited his father's talent for business. He had everything going for him, except for one thing: he could not control his drinking.

Newton took him in hand, and together they tried to apply the Oxford Group approach. Although Firestone seemed totally sincere, he kept drinking. All this changed when he accompanied Newton to a church conference in Denver. Other Oxford Group members were there, Sam Shoemaker among them. After the conference, Shoemaker joined them on their train trip east. During the trip, Shoemaker and Firestone had a private talk, and Bud emerged from it a changed man. He stopped drinking, and this made his father a believer in the Oxford Group.

In January 1933, Harvey Firestone sponsored an Oxford Group conference in Akron. Frank Buchman was there, accompanied by a twenty-nine-member Oxford Group team. There were ads in the local papers and stories listing the names of the Akron notables who attended meetings held in churches, factories, and other locations, including the Mayflower Hotel.

Russell Firestone and his attractive wife represented proof of the power of the Oxford Group to change lives, and they were frequently called upon to give witness. The blitz proved extremely successful: almost overnight, Akron had a large and solid contingent of OG members. Henrietta Seiberling first learned about the Oxford Group at this conference. It is where T. Henry and Clarace Williams, who would later be mainstays of Akron OG activity with alcoholics, became members. It would also seem to be where Robert and Anne Smith learned about the Oxford Group. Bill Wilson was reluctant to contact an Akron Oxford Group member about working with an alcoholic, but it was because of the help Oxford Group members had extended to an alcoholic that there was an Oxford Group in Akron at all, and helping alcoholics would be the focus of many Akron Oxford Groupers for years to come.

All this was behind Henrietta's delighted response to a telephone call from an alcoholic Oxford Group member from New York. It was also, of course, behind the way Reverend Tunks had responded to Bill. The Oxford Group in Akron was inextricably a part of rubber family politics. Everyone in Akron who was not directly connected with the rubber families was at the least concerned not to do anything to offend them. Tunks was certainly aware of Henrietta Seiberling's Oxford Group membership. He may well have been aware of her friendship with Anne Smith and her efforts to help Robert Smith stop drinking. Telling Wilson about Seiberling or Smith may not have been viewed as sporting by the Firestones. At the same time, giving him the name of someone who *would* tell him about Seiberling may have come naturally to Tunks. Seiberling would later say that she had met Bill because "a man" had given Bill a name to call, and this person had referred him to her.

Henrietta Seiberling's personal investment in Bob Smith, and the unique social setting in which it took place, may help to explain why, long after Bob stopped drinking, she continued to have such a strong personal interest in Alcoholics Anonymous. That in helping Bob Smith, Bill Wilson succeeded where she had failed, may also help to explain something else. A decade later, Bill announced his plan for the establishment of a governing structure for AA based on democratic representation. Among other things, the plan was designed to guarantee that AA would never become an "Oxford Group for alcoholics."

Seiberling reacted by announcing publicly that "Bill Wilson had finally lost his mind completely." To defeat this proposal, she then mounted a personal campaign, which included traveling to AA groups around the country to urge its rejection. The campaign had the tone of a personal vendetta against Bill, and in a way, it was. There has never been another example of a nonmember taking such an extraordinary interest in the affairs of the fellowship, but Henrietta and many of the others who were so vehemently opposed to Bill's conference plan seemed to sense how much was at stake. If the ultimate control of AA were to devolve to the groups, a battle for the heart and soul of the organization would be lost. With the group conscience determining the direction of the fellowship, AA would be immune to the importuning of those both within and outside the fellowship who thought that alcoholics should undergo the sort of complete spiritual overhaul the Oxford Group advocated. With the group conscience in charge, the constant flooding of newcomers into AA would guarantee that the organization's sole focus would forever be exactly what Bill had envisioned for it: helping alcoholics stay sober.

1 2

THE ·MEETING

On the evening Henrietta Seiberling and Bill first met, she listened as he related something of his experience with the Oxford Group in New York and explained his need to work with another alcoholic. Then she promised to arrange for Bill to meet Bob Smith on Saturday afternoon.

When Bill arrived, he and Henrietta chatted briefly, then she called the Smiths, who lived nearby, and asked them to come over. After hanging up from her call, she told Bill that he would not be able to meet Robert Smith just then. Because Sunday was Mother's Day, Bob had gone out to get his wife a potted plant. Unfortunately, he had come back potted himself. The plant was on the kitchen table, and Bob was on the floor under the table.

This must have sounded very familiar to Bill. Dr. Bob Smith had tried to do the right thing, no doubt, to make up for past failures. Instead, he had just made things worse. Again.

Henrietta rescheduled the appointment for 5:00 P.M. on Sunday. This would give Bob time to recover from his plant-buying expedition, but Smith seems to have suffered no ordinary hangover.

Bob was never as bad off as Bill had been, but there was not much left of his medical practice, his finances, or his good name. He knew that he owed it to his wife, and to Henrietta, to grant their simple request to see this fellow from New York. However, he would say later that he could not remember ever having felt worse. He was certainly in no mood to be more than cursorily polite.

"I'll give him fifteen minutes. And that's it," he declared to his wife.

His son Bob, age seventeen, also accompanied him to the Seiberling estate. Henrietta gave them all dinner, but Smith was too sick to eat much. After dinner, Henrietta suggested that Bill and Bob retire to the library.

At first, the dour Vermonter sitting across from him, a type Bill knew well, tried not to let Bill see how much his hands were shaking. Bill must have put the fifteen minutes to good use. As sick as Bob was, the first conversation between the men who would be known as AA's cofounders continued until eleven o'clock that evening.

At first, Bill concentrated on letting Bob know that he understood firsthand the torments of active alcoholism. The ease with which Bill sat there talking about these things told Bob something else: this man who knew so well what he was going through no longer had to drink. Before they parted, they made a plan to talk again the next day.

Bob Smith was fifteen years older than Bill, and they were very different personalities. Yet they also had a number of things in common. They were both tall and lanky Vermonters—Bob was from St. Johnsbury in the heart of Vermont's "Northeast Kingdom." Both possessed the sense of independence and community that so characterized the small-town rural life of their childhoods.

As bright, talented sons of families of some local prominence, both had been expected to make something of themselves, but each had been severely affected by alcoholism quite early in their lives. Bill was too drunk to take his law school exams; although he did graduate, Bob had a similar problem with his exams in medical school. Both also had occasion to journey home to Vermont in search of a respite from the rigors of the drinking life.

Dr. Silkworth's advice to Bill about talking with, rather than at, his prospects was important to the success of his encounter with Robert Smith. Bill also brought to his first meeting with Smith the knowledge he had gained from his scare in the lobby of the Mayflower Hotel. It was the first time he had felt a desire to drink since his spiritual awakening in Towns. His wanting to drink made him think that he might not have been struck permanently sober, after all. More than anything else, it was this that made him feel closer to the prospect sitting across from him in Henrietta Seiberling's library than he had felt to the other men he'd tried to help.

From their first conversation, Bill thought he had made a connection of a different order. He was immediately able to relax and be himself with Robert Smith, or "Smithy," as he would soon come to call him. For all that Bob Smith had been prepared to cut and run, he quickly found that he felt the same way around Bill. That evening and over the next few days, the two men talked about what they had been through, and their instant liking began to grow into a friendship.

In those first hours of conversation, Bill told Bob everything he knew about alcoholism. One thing Bob heard from Bill was the notion that alcoholism was not a sin but an illness. This wasn't what he was hearing from the Oxford Group. After letting Bob know he knew what he was going through from personal experience, he concentrated on the hopelessness of Bob's plight, emphasizing that death or insanity lay at the end of the road. This was done in an attempt to bring about a surrender or, as Bill would later come to put it, an "ego deflation at depth." The idea of having "to give up, in order to win" is something Bob was familiar with from the Oxford Group.

As Bob would recall, though, it was not anything Bill said that made a difference. It was the fact that it was Bill who was saying it. For Bob, what was important about the evening was that Bill "spoke his language" from personal experience.

The National Rubber Machinery Company fight kept Bill in Akron through the spring and into the summer, but Bob Smith seems to have been the focus of his energies. Henrietta Seiberling arranged for Bill to move from the Mayflower Hotel to the Portage Country Club, Akron's poshest. The club was just down the road from the Seiberling estate, and it also put Bill closer to the Smiths.

Officially, he was the guest of club member John Gammeter, a self-made man with whom Bill felt himself to have a lot in common. Bill golfed at this club throughout his stay in Akron. His energy, positive outlook, and picture-of-health demeanor no doubt stood him in good stead with this crowd, and their acceptance of him must have done much to keep up his confidence. For Bill, the primary value of living at the country club seems to have been its proximity to the Smiths' home, where he spent most of his time.

It is not clear whether, at this point, Bill himself knew what he was doing in Akron. Lois certainly did not. "I couldn't understand why he didn't come home," she would say later. "There didn't seem to be very much happening in the proxy fight. Bill wrote me about this other alcoholic he was working with, but working with alcoholics was something he could just as well do at home. And I can't say I liked thinking about his playing golf at this fancy country club, while I was working at Loesers."

Lois's confusion only increased with the news contained in Bill's next letter. Bill had abandoned Akron's best country club for such hospitality as a down-at-the-heels proctologist and his desperate wife could offer. This, too, bothered Lois. "I tried not to be jealous," she told me, "but I couldn't help wondering what they had to offer that I didn't."

Bill had been living with the Smiths for several weeks, with Bob staying sober and the two of them trying to work with other alcoholics, when Bob decided he was well enough to attend the upcoming American Medical Association convention, to be held in Atlantic City. In years past, Bob's attendance at the AMA convention had always resulted in a drunken spree, and his wife was against his going. Bill sided with Bob. He even encouraged him to go.

Smith boarded the train for Atlantic City brimming with confidence. He was drunk before he arrived, and while there he drank so horribly he came home early. Bill could hardly have felt worse about this. He apologized profusely to Bob and especially to Anne, telling her that he was wrong not to have given more weight to her opinion. To Anne's credit, she seems to have borne Bill no ill will over this. Instead, they worked together to get Bob sober. He was scheduled to perform an operation in three days. Having to cancel was unlikely to affect the patient's outcome, but it would have a devastating effect on Bob's already battered professional reputation.

EMPATHY

The bond between Bill Wilson and Bob Smith seems to have been cemented by Bob's relapse. Bill shared a bedroom with Smithy, and he and Anne nursed him around the clock. On the morning the operation was scheduled, Bob pronounced himself ready. Just before he got out of the car to enter the hospital, Bill Wilson handed Bob Smith a bottle of beer to help steady his nerves. This was Dr. Bob's last drink. As the two of them would remember it later, the date was June 10, 1935. It would be some years before there would be anything like a formal organization, or even a name, for what Wilson and Smith were doing. Yet Alcoholics Anonymous, the organization based on the principle of one drunk helping another, is thought to have begun on that day.

It's more likely that the two of them first knew they had something going at four o'clock that morning, when Bob turned to Bill and announced, "I'm going through with it."

Bill at first thought he meant the surgery, but Bob said, "That, too, but what I meant is the things we've been talking about."

After the surgery, Bob called his wife and Bill to tell them of his success. On his way home from the hospital, he stopped by the offices of several colleagues, and the shops of several creditors, to whom he felt he owed amends. He wanted to convey to them his intention to live life in a new way. The Oxford Group recommended making amends, but it was not something Bob had done in the two years he had been going to Oxford Group meetings, or in the weeks he had gone without alcohol after meeting Bill Wilson.

Much of what followed in Akron would parallel Bill's experience in New York. Bill and Bob brought people home to live with the Smiths. Some of these men did recover, though most did not. One man who lived with the Smiths nearly a year eventually started the first AA group in Detroit. What was different about Akron was that, when Bob and Bill called on another drunk, there were two sober alcoholics trying to help one alcoholic stop drinking. Pitting two sober alcoholics against one still-active alcoholic is a practice AA members still employ when answering a request for help.

There was also something else. Thanks to Bill's insight in the lobby of the Mayflower, both he and Bob believed that, in trying to help other alcoholics, they were doing something they had to do in order to stay sober themselves. The importance of this discovery can hardly be overemphasized.

The sense of isolation alcoholism imposes on those who suffer from it has always been a major reason why efforts to help alcoholics fail so miserably. As Bill had discovered, it's very difficult even for sober alcoholics to bridge the chasm an active alcoholic experiences between himself and anyone not sharing his condition.

Bill himself had felt sure that he would never drink again. However, after he found himself in the lobby of the Mayflower, enticed by the convivial sounds coming from the bar, he realized that, while his conversion experience was real, it was not what had kept him sober. He had been able to stay away from alcohol because of his efforts to help other alcoholics. By witnessing the agony these others were enduring, he had kept alive within himself the awareness of what his drinking had done to him.

Suddenly Dr. Silkworth's advice, "Let them know that you know what they're going through," made sense to him. This was important to the different approach he took with Bob Smith. Although Bill was sober, Bob could feel certain that Bill knew exactly what he was suffering. The bond thus formed between the two men could make it possible for both of them to stay sober.

Bill's agreeing to become a part of the struggle for control of the National Rubber Machinery Company had seemed to mean at least a temporary end to his efforts to help other alcoholics. Instead, the proxy fight led to his meeting Bob Smith, and it also made it possible for Bill to stay in Akron long enough for them to develop an effective approach to helping alcoholics. Within weeks of Bob's stopping drinking, he and Bill were able to succeed with Bill D., an Akron attorney later to be immortalized in the fellowship's history as "AA no. 3."

Wilson stayed in Akron through the summer, and Lois was finally able to join him in July, traveling by bus to Akron to spend her two-week vacation with her husband and the Smiths. She would later say that as soon as she met the Smiths she understood immediately what Bill's letters had not been able to convey.

"It was clear that Bob and Annie were very special people. So warm, giving, and caring. I now understood why Bill didn't come home. Together he and Bob were making a beginning on accomplishing what we had been trying to do in New York. When the time came for me to go back, I didn't want to leave, either."

Lois's husband and his new friend were living her dream. The work was not easy, and there were many more failures than successes. Nevertheless, Bill Wilson and Bob Smith were changing people's lives by exposing them to their own changed personalities.

As Lois had in New York, Anne Smith in Akron tried to help both alcoholics and their spouses. Lois was introduced to Bill D. and his wife, whose name was also Henrietta. Like Bill Wilson, Bob Smith, and virtually all alcoholics, Bill D. had previously gone without drinking for countless periods. Many of them were equal to or greater than what he had known since meeting Bill and Bob. Bill D. did not have a transformation experience of the sort that had been visited upon Bill Wilson, and Henrietta D. was far from convinced that this period of sobriety would endure. But when she asked Lois whether she ever worried about her Bill drinking again, Lois answered immediately, "No. Never."

Anne Smith had given the same answer. In Annie's case, an unshakable belief in the permanence of her husband's sobriety had resulted from the changes she had seen in Bob following the convention debacle. Henrietta D. would later recall how important Anne's and Lois's convictions were to her coming to believe that *this* time her husband would stay sober.

THE MANAGER

In the end, the outcome of the proxy fight hinged on the decision of M. D. Kuhlke, head of what had been the Kuhlke Machine Company, one of the four firms merged in 1928 to form National Rubber Machinery. Kuhlke controlled enough shares to swing the tide either way. He waffled maddeningly for months, but finally went with the opposition. His decision was based in no small measure on the fact that Nils Florman, the other side's candidate for president, seemed much better qualified for the position than Bill.

Given Bill's history of self-sabotage, lack of management experience, and his knowing almost nothing about either the rubber business or the rubber machinery business, one has to wonder if he truly believed himself capable of running the company. Yet while he had his difficulties when it came to taking direction, he never exhibited any doubt about his ability to manage and lead. Overcoming his low self-esteem may have driven him to become captain of the baseball team and president of his class at Burr and Burton, but drive alone did not give him the skills he needed to be good at these assignments. Similarly, his experience in the army seems to have provided him with an opportunity to demonstrate rather than acquire leadership ability.

The proxy fight was a nasty, angry battle, as issues that had never been resolved in the merger of the four companies, all of them family owned and managed, flared anew, and accusations and insults were hurled back and forth. One may wonder at the contrast between the struggle Bill was engaged in for control of the National Rubber Machinery Company and the work he and Bob were doing in trying to help alcoholics. However, the way Bill approached his NRMC work led many Akron Oxford Group members to regard him as a savior of sorts. They believed that he had been "guided" to come to Akron to restore a sense of civility and community.

Years of wrangling had produced a tremendous amount of dissension within the company, and Bill seems to have felt that his main assignment was to dissipate this internal tension. In his letters to Lois, he sometimes reported that the other side was engaged in underhanded maneuvers. As Bill saw it, his best strategy was to focus on making peace, restoring confidence, and convincing people of his side's good intentions.

At one point, Bill wrote Lois about another man of ability who wanted to do the right thing by the company. His name was Paul Frank, and he was prepared to throw in with Bill's faction in return for being made president of the company. Although Bill had been counting on this position for himself, he wrote that he thought Frank would be excellent in the job. The battle was over before Frank could join them, but events proved Bill right: the faction Bill lost to was not able to run the company, and in 1941, a group headed by Frank forced them out. Frank was installed as president, and he managed the company successfully for the next twenty-five years.

Bill's attitude toward the Rubber Machinery Company battle reveals a man starkly different from the one who, at the height of his Wall Street success, was luring his family and friends into stock manipulation. When his stock scheme collapsed in 1929 along with the market, he was so full of anger and self-pity that he nearly drank himself to death. Yet in the spring of 1935, some six months after his spiritual awakening at Towns Hospital, Wilson was writing his wife that for him the most important thing in the National Rubber Machinery struggle was that he try to do his best by all concerned. He also told her that he would not have any regrets if he lost.

In time, Bill would demonstrate a remarkable ability to organize and manage. As AA's guiding light, he employed to great success both the visionary and the unifying skills he had seen as being necessary to affect a successful outcome for National Rubber Machinery. He did this in spite of the characteristic resistance even sober alcoholics have to being led, and he did it well enough for Aldous Huxley to characterize him as the twentieth century's greatest social architect.

It is tempting to think of the similarities between the management challenges Bill faced with AA and those his father had to deal with in keeping the hard-drinking, brawling individualists who were his quarrymen pulling in the same direction. Gilman Wilson was so well thought of by the men who worked for him that when he moved to British Columbia, Canada's westernmost province, many of them went with him. There was also the example of Bill's maternal grandfather. As a farmer, lumberman, and landlord, Fayette Griffith had many opportunities to exercise management and leadership skills, and Bill was often at his heel when he did so. Fayette may not have been well liked, but he was perceived as honest and fair, and he was respected and successful.

Repeatedly, Bill would make choices that reconfirmed his commitment to helping alcoholics ahead of making money. Yet he felt a need to make money, and given his enormous debts, big money. This struggle would endure the rest of his life. Bill's position as AA's guiding light would make it impossible for him to serve both masters. But that he was unable to do so contributed to his continuing doubts about himself as a "going concern."

Although Wilson and Smith experienced many failures, there were successes, too. By the time Bill left for New York at the end of August, there existed in Akron a core group of five or six alcoholics with genuine prospects of remaining sober.

Throughout Bill's stay, he and Bob spent countless hours talking about what to say to the men they were trying to help, and how to say it. This marked a critical departure from Oxford Group practice. It was the beginning of a process during which these two men, whose orientation would always be more practical than ideological, tested what they had learned from the Oxford Group in the crucible of experience.

Important changes took place in Bill's understanding of how to help other alcoholics. Initially, his drive to produce in others the experience he'd had in the middle of the night at Towns Hospital led him to try to duplicate the events that had let up to it. If he said the things Ebby had said to him, then they, too, would have a spiritual conversion, and their desire to drink would be lifted.

His experience with Robert Smith convinced him that alcoholics did not have to be "struck sober." Dr. Bob's awakening had been gradual, actually taking place over a period of weeks. There was, ultimately, a key event, but a flash of light did not accompany it—Bob simply realized that he was both willing and able to do what Bill Wilson, Henrietta Seiberling, and others had been telling him he had to do in order to stay sober. He was willing to do it because it was what Bill Wilson had done, and unlike the way Smith had felt in his previous attempts to stay away from alcohol, for Bill, staying sober was a very positive experience.

After that, Bob caught Bill's drive to make getting sober a process that could be reproduced according to a set of instructions. They were working out their own methods, not for recruiting new members to the Oxford Group but specifically for helping drunks. It was religion and medicine, Henry Ford, Thomas Edison, and tent-show revivalism, but it was working: people were staying sober!

One of the most critical discoveries made during Bill's first Akron stay was the usefulness of the "twenty-four-hour" concept. This is the AA notion that the alcoholic can deal with the desire to drink by postponing drinking for just one day—or, when the desire seemed particularly strong, just one hour, or even one minute, at a time.

The Oxford Group emphasis was on change: follow its principles and you will *be* changed. The difficulty with this for alcoholics has much in common with why the traditional psychotherapeutic approach to alcoholism had failed so miserably. Therapists had felt that, once the reasons behind the drinking were uncovered through the therapeutic process, the need to drink would be alleviated. Unfortunately, the alcoholic's drinking most often makes it impossible to follow either prescription.

The twenty-four-hour concept, which Bill and Bob seem to have stumbled on in their discussions, proved to be an indispensable tool. If the awakening is to take place in stages, the alcoholic needs to have some means of dealing with the desire to drink while waiting for it to be lifted. The twenty-four-hour concept enabled him or her to buy enough time away from alcohol to come to an understanding of what permanent relief required and how to effect it.

In addition to making a beginning at working out the program that would become AA, something else occurred during Bill's months in Akron. A deep bond, based on mutual affection, respect, and admiration, formed between Bill Wilson and Dr. Bob Smith. It became the basis of a friendship that would endure the challenges ahead. Bob would live only another fifteen years, but by the time of his death in 1950, AA would be an international organization, with a membership of more than one hundred thousand sober alcoholics, and the essentials of a governing structure designed to ensure that AA would outlive both its founders would be in place.

Ruth Hock, AA's first secretary, always said that while Bill and Bob often disagreed, they were able to work out their disagreements in ways that left them both satisfied. She also said that they seemed to trust each other completely. Bill would always claim that there had never been a harsh word between him and Smithy.

Lois and Annie also hit it off, and the Wilsons visited the Smiths in Akron at least once a year. The Smiths also frequently traveled east to stay with the Wilsons. The couples were so close that at one point, Bill and Lois contemplated moving to Akron to be near the Smiths. At another, the Smiths thought about buying a home near the Wilsons' home in Bedford Hills, New York. After Annie, Bob, and Bill were dead, Lois and the Smiths' children, Sue and Bob, continued to stay in touch until the end of Lois's long life.

A NEW APPROACH

When Bill returned to New York, it was with a certain amount of disappointment that they had not accomplished more in three months of work. But he was leaving behind him two sober alcoholics, Dr. Bob and

Bill D., who seemed rock solid, and there were several others who weren't drinking and whose prospects seemed promising. This was more than he had to show for the six months that he had spent trying to help people before he went to Akron. He also was aware that much else had been gained.

His realization that even an alcoholic who had been "struck sober" needed to work with other alcoholics in order to stay sober amounted to a second awakening. It was largely because of this realization that he and Smithy were able to fashion a new, more successful approach, one that empathized with the alcoholic's plight yet made no bones about its hopelessness.

The idea was to produce a surrender; the alcoholic had to give up on the idea that by himself he would somehow, someday conquer his affliction. The empathy prospects could feel from these sober alcoholics, coupled with the experience they provided of someone like them who actually *enjoyed* not drinking, bought time. This made possible the spiritual conversion experience they believed would so change the alcoholic as to relieve him of the desire to drink.

Rapid and often simultaneous developments characterized the years following Bill's return. Robert Smith made some effort to revive his medical practice, but the major share of his energies was devoted to helping drunks. As a result, the Smith family never recovered financially from the losses Bob's drinking had imposed.

Bill would conduct some investigations of firms with possible investment potential for Frank Shaw and, later, Clayton Quaw, another Wall Street acquaintance. But it was never steady work, and Quaw paid him based on the profits he made from trading on the information Bill produced, which made what little income he derived from this activity uncertain and unpredictable.

Both the Wilsons and their alcoholic nonpaying boarders continued to be dependent on Lois's department store earnings. The Smiths managed to hang onto their heavily mortgaged home, but the Wilsons' impoverishment caused them to lose theirs, inaugurating a two-year period between April 1939 and April 1941, during which they had no permanent place to live. Dependent on the charity of friends, during this time they moved, by Lois's count, fifty-four times.

We have to wonder why both the Wilsons and the Smiths did not simply give up. Today the nation's best alcoholism treatment centers report success rates ranging from 25 percent to 50 percent. During Bill's stay in Akron, he and Bob calculated their success rate to be about 5 percent, and among the few who seemed to catch on, not all of them were able to maintain consistent sobriety. The first edition of AA's *Big Book,* published in 1939, contains the personal recovery stories of many of AA's earliest members. Some years later, Bill made notations in the first copy of the book to come off the press, indicating which of the individuals portrayed therein had stayed sober. A good 50 percent of them had not.

We can perhaps only begin to comprehend the ability of the Wilsons and the Smiths to sustain their commitment by trying to understand the high personal value they put on their efforts to help alcoholics. Bill and Bob were themselves desperate to stay sober. "Right living," which included morning prayers, readings from the Bible, and regular attendance at the weekly gathering of fellow sufferers, were considered necessary in order to stay sober. However, both believed that the most important element was their work with other alcoholics.

There was never a good time for them to cut back. The worse their money problems got, the greater the worry that they might resort to relieving their anxieties in the way they knew best—by getting drunk.

After he got back to New York, Bill's clearer understanding of what he was trying to accomplish produced two quick successes at Towns Hospital. Although Bill would become fast friends with both men, they could hardly have been more different. Hank P., an oil company executive from nearby New Jersey, was a tall, broad-shouldered former athlete with a salesman's drive and enthusiasm. Fitz M. was a blue blood from a suburb of Baltimore. The son of a minister, Fitz had been a salesman, a bookkeeper, a teacher, and a farmer. Lois described him as a dreamer and "the most impractical man" she had ever met.

As different as they were, both Hank and Fitz seemed to instantly grasp what Bill was talking about. Hank was the unofficial cofounder of the New York AA group, and he was instrumental in raising the money to publish AA's *Big Book*. Hank's story appeared in the book under the title "The Unbeliever." Although Hank was initially wildly enthusiastic for the sober life, he stayed that way for only four years.

Fitz would stay sober until his death in 1943. His story appears in the book as "Our Southern Friend." Fitz, his wife, Elizabeth, and Lois and Bill would also become close friends. Lois said that she and Bill had "practically commuted" to Fitz's home in Cumberland, Maryland, and Fitz visited them as often in New York.

Fitz's sister, Agnes, played a critical role in AA's early history. When in 1941, Works Publishing, the company Hank had formed to publish the *Big Book*, was unable to pay the printer, Agnes lent it $1,000 (nearly $12,000 in year 2000 dollars), in return for which the printer agreed to release the books he was holding—the first printing of *Alcoholics Anonymous*.

As different as these men were, and as different as they both were from

Dr. Bob, Bill was able to form and maintain a close relationship with all three. Even after Hank started drinking again in 1939 and broke with Bill, attacking him and trying periodically over a number of years to turn other AA members against him, Bill continued to be supportive toward Hank where he could.

The office furniture Bill used all the rest of his life, first in AA's head-quarters office in New York City, and later in his studio at Stepping Stones in Bedford Hills, New York, had originally belonged to Hank. When Hank, drunk, refused to turn in his shares in Works Publishing, Bill enticed him to do so by offering to buy the furniture from him for $200 (nearly $2,400.00 in year 2000 dollars). In future years, Hank would ap-proach Bill several more times about the furniture, claiming he had never been paid for it. Each time, Bill's response was to buy it from him again.

Initially, Hank and Fitz were convinced that every alcoholic could catch on as easily as they had. As soon as they were released from Towns, they plunged into the work with enthusiasm. For the next few years, Bill, Hank, and Fitz would be a triumvirate ever ready to go anywhere in the greater New York area to try to help another drunk.

The enthusiasm they brought to this work is evident in a scene Robert Thomsen describes in his book, *Bill W.* The three of them were riding down Park Avenue one night in Hank's convertible, when Hank suddenly stood straight up and shouted for all of New York to hear: "God almighty! Booze was never this good!"

While Hank and Fitz certainly bolstered Bill, their belief that any alco-holic could see the light as easily as they had seems to have knocked Bill off course. Always prone to excessive optimism concerning an idea he was hot on, after his success with Hank and Fitz, Bill seems to have forgotten what had worked with Robert Smith, Bill D., and the other men who had responded positively in Akron. Instead of spending hours engaged in a mutual conversation that established a bond of empathy, he was now more likely to spend an hour trying to argue a drunk sober. Some men did recover, though, through his efforts and those of Hank and Fitz.

This evident lack of patience was something that would return period-ically throughout Bill's years as AA's "head man." It seems to be the root of the complaint that he was "a lousy sponsor," or even, "the worst spon-sor a man could possibly have." Well into the 1980s, crusty, longtime New York AA members could be heard making such remarks. They were men who had known Bill and had loved him, but they had obviously taken de-light in exercising their AA egalitarian right to tweak him while he was alive, and after his death they seemed never to miss an opportunity to re-mind newcomers that Bill Wilson was human, too.

TWO PROGRAMS

During Bill's first stay in Akron, he and Bob together worked out an effective approach to alcoholics. In other ways, though, early developments in Akron and New York were on divergent courses. Part of this is due to the different environments in which each man worked. There is also the fact that in Akron, AA was being built around a physician.

When they were looking for a drunk to help, Bob was able to call Akron City Hospital, where he was an attending physician, and ask if there were any patients with a drinking problem. Invariably, there were, and many of those patients looked up one day to find two men at their bedside with information about a new way to stop drinking. That one of these men who seemed to know so much about alcoholism was a doctor was certainly a factor in the successes they had.

Before long, Bob was not only calling on drunks previously hospitalized, he was able to admit the men he and Bill were working with, albeit through the subterfuge of another diagnosis. Until Sister Ignatia, who was not an alcoholic, established an alcoholic ward at St. Thomas Hospital in Akron in 1939, virtually no general hospital admitted alcoholics for the treatment of their alcoholism.

There were also great differences in the attitude of the Akron and the New York Oxford Groups toward alcoholics. Henrietta Seiberling, a maximum Oxford Grouper, was an enthusiastic and influential supporter of Bob's desire to confine his Oxford Group activities to working with other alcoholics. Dr. Bob also had the unconditional support of two other Akron Oxford Group members, T. Henry and Clarace Williams.

T. Henry Williams was a descendant of Roger Williams, the founder of Rhode Island. Williams had been chief engineer at the Rubber Machinery Company and still had some involvement with the company. He and Bill had actually met near the beginning of Bill's stay in Akron, but neither knew the other was involved with the Oxford Group.

Although, like the New York contingent, many Akron alcoholics were uncomfortable with the Oxford Group's emphasis on sin, they never felt less than wholeheartedly welcome in the Oxford Group. With the exception of Russell Firestone, the Akron OG members never tried to use its alcoholic members to attract new membership. Nor did it urge Robert Smith, or any of its other alcoholic members, to quit smoking. This is in sharp contrast with the treatment accorded Bill and other alcoholics in New York.

There were OG members who supported Bill's desire to work only with alcoholics, but in New York alcoholic OGers sometimes felt used, manipulated, and barely tolerated. By contrast, in Akron, the alcoholics felt almost as though the Oxford Group existed just for them.

The weekly Oxford Group meetings attended by Bob and Anne and the others were held at the comfortable, upper-middle-class home of T. Henry and Clarace Williams, which the Williamses had virtually turned over to alcoholic Oxford Group members and their families. In recalling who attended, one of the alcoholics who was there described the group as the alcoholics he knew, plus a few Oxford Group members. Neither of the Williamses drank. Both were very religious people, but their main interest in the Oxford Group seems to have centered on its ability to help alcoholics. Long before the Oxford Group came to Akron, T. Henry was aware of, and deeply concerned about, the devastation alcoholism wrought on the victims and their families. There is no indication that other OG members in Akron objected to the Williamses' devotion to helping alcoholics.

Bill had a good relationship with the Oxford Group leader Sam Shoemaker, but even Sam wanted to exploit his dramatic recovery to attract people to the Oxford Group. Sam's tolerance of Bill's dissidence seems to have been based on the belief that in time Bill would conform. Perhaps the difference between the atmosphere in which AA began in Akron and New York can be best illustrated by the way the Akron Oxford Group felt about Bill Wilson. On his many visits to Akron, Bill seems to have been more warmly received by the Akron Oxford Group than he was in New York.

The Wilsons began hosting meetings for Oxford Group alcoholics and their spouses at the end of the summer in 1935, after Bill's return from Akron. They would maintain their ties to the Oxford Group for another two years—Alcoholics Anonymous's official history gives 1937 as the year the New York alcoholics broke with the Oxford Group. Akron alcoholics would eventually break as well, but they did not do so until the end of 1939. Even then, it was an action taken more to show solidarity with the New York and the (by then) Cleveland groups than from any felt need to be free of the Oxford Group.

Akron's "alcoholic squadron" never met separately from the Oxford Group until the break. In New York, OG alcoholics were already meeting by themselves when Bill joined the Oxford Group near the end of 1934. The New York break created a rift between Bill Wilson and Sam Shoemaker, whereas in Akron, the Williamses and Henrietta Seiberling maintained an interest in Alcoholics Anonymous all the rest of their lives.

Bill's not being a physician made the New York Oxford Group's attitude toward the work that he was doing with alcoholics particularly unfortunate. At the time, the Oxford Group probably presented the most likely pool of prospects available to him. He also worked with the alcoholics among the "down and outs" at Calvary Mission, but it's not known whether any of them recovered. What is known is that, like Bill D., the successes were professionals with intact families who still had at least some semblance of a career. Even today, it is alcoholics who fit this profile who are most able to effect recovery.

The patients at Towns Hospital generally did not make good prospects, either. The high cost of a stay at Towns meant that virtually all its patients were still well-to-do, but most of them were there only to find relief from the physical consequences of their alcoholism. They had no interest in stopping drinking on a permanent basis.

In 1936, the Oxford Group underwent a shift in emphasis that left the bands of alcoholics gathered around Bob Smith in Akron and Bill Wilson in New York feeling as though the Group was abandoning much of what the alcoholics liked best about it. The Oxford Group's focus on small, intimate meetings was replaced by the staging of large events accompanied by a massive public relations blitz. They included a rally held in the Berkshires, accompanied by lavish national publicity. Ten thousand people attended, and it lasted for ten days. The Oxford Group also underwent other changes that made it less attractive, and even inimical, to what Bill was trying to accomplish. Its dogmatism increased, making it less a "religious enhancement" and more a religion. The Group's new dogmatism was also the source of its objections to Bill and Lois holding meetings exclusively for alcoholics.

Then Frank Buchman was quoted in the national press as saying "I thank heaven for a man like Adolf Hitler." Buchman later said that he was not endorsing Hitler's Nazism but his anti-Communism. Buchman said he had made his statement, which went on to talk about what it would mean to the world if Hitler "surrendered to God," as part of his "prospecting" efforts. As incredible as it sounds, his hope was that saying something nice about Hitler would lead to an opportunity to co-opt him into the Oxford Group.

Buchman was not a Nazi, or even a Nazi sympathizer, but he had certainly become something of a megalomaniac. He was also someone who courted controversy, and he seemed to want to put the Oxford Group squarely onto the political stage. All this was far removed from the OG Bill Wilson had known.

Subsequent events would reveal that the Oxford Group, renamed

Moral Re-Armament, had clearly lost its way. In the meantime, a small, intimate, nonpolitical, nonsectarian, tolerant, open-minded group of OG members continued to meet on Clinton Street in Brooklyn. In seeking recovery from the ravages of alcoholism through right living, carrying the message to others, and deepening their spiritual awareness, they had more in common with the Oxford Group as it had been in the past.

Bill struggled to maintain his OG ties as long as possible. When we recall the way Bill had responded to criticism before his spiritual awakening, his behavior in regard to the Oxford Group is especially striking. The badgering he received about his smoking and womanizing could hardly have been more personal. Maximum OGers also challenged the legitimacy of the guidance he claimed to be receiving, as part of the Group's meditation practices, which told him to focus on alcoholics.

TAKING IT

None of this hostility produced a reaction in kind. When we consider how much of the criticism Wilson had reacted to in the past was imagined or, at best, grossly exaggerated, his refusing to act in a self-destructive way to the very real criticism he received from Oxford Group quarters seems even more significant. He had gone to the OG in the first place because he wanted to help other alcoholics find sobriety, and he maintained his association with them as long as to do so still served his purpose.

There were AA members, particularly in the Midwest, who criticized Bill for the public silence he maintained concerning AA's Oxford Group roots in the years immediately following his withdrawal. However, the controversy swirling around the Oxford Group was such that he was extremely reluctant to encourage any public perception of a link between it and AA.

In letters he wrote on the subject, Bill objected to the Oxford Group's aggressive evangelism, personal publicity seeking, use of coercion, and intolerant attitude toward nonbelievers. He felt the same way about the Group's growing dogmatism: it now insisted that members accept the "guidance" they received as coming directly from God and that they engage in evangelism for the Group. Such demands made it impossible for Catholics, among others, to be associated with it.

Although Sam Shoemaker was so upset about Bill's and Lois's withdrawal from the Oxford Group that he did not speak to Bill for years, Shoemaker himself would break with Frank Buchman in 1941. He later wrote a letter of apology to Bill, stating that he and other OG members were wrong to oppose Bill's desire to work solely with alcoholics and to focus only on helping these individuals to stop drinking. As Shoemaker looked back on Bill's association with his movement, he characterized the desire to control Bill and bring him into line as "stupid," and he apologized for it.

Bill's efforts with alcoholics may have been unappreciated by many who observed them in Oxford Group circles, but Charlie Towns was certainly impressed. Charlie had started Towns Hospital in 1901, but it was the rising tide of alcoholism in the Roaring Twenties that made it a success. Towns was a tall, handsome man who exercised two hours a day; his healthy energy and enthusiasm made him stand in sharp contrast to his patients.

Admissions to Towns Hospital dropped dramatically after the Crash in 1929. Since a big part of the hospital's revenue was from repeat business—drying out drunks who did not intend to stop drinking permanently—another man might have banned Bill Wilson from the premises, but Charlie Towns was a compassionate man. He decided on a different approach to turning around his hospital's sagging fortunes.

In 1937, Charlie offered Bill a job at Towns as a lay therapist. Bill's compensation was to be structured in a way that always appealed to Bill when he worked on Wall Street: a drawing account that provided a regular weekly income, to be offset against Bill's share of the profits. Bill greeted the proposal with great enthusiasm. He saw it as both a ringing endorsement of the work he had been doing and a permanent answer to his financial difficulties. There was a precedent for it, too.

Richard Peabody was an alcoholic and a lay therapist who worked with alcoholics. Author of *The Common Sense of Drinking,* published in Boston in 1931, Peabody had gotten sober in the Boston Emmanuel Movement, started in 1905 by Dr. Elwood Worcester and Dr. Samuel McComb in Boston's Emmanuel Church. Originally organized as an Episcopalian answer to Christian Science, the movement worked closely with medicine. The idea was to combine the best science had to offer with the best spiritual support religion could muster. The movement started a clinic that at first focused on holding educational and inspirational meetings for poor people who had tuberculosis. Later, it became an important force in helping alcoholics. When the clinic closed in 1939, Worcester continued his work under the auspices of the Craigie Foundation.

Courtenay Baylor, an alcoholic who was helped by the Emmanuel Movement in the 1920s, became an alcoholism therapist within the movement. Richard Peabody was one of his patients. Like Baylor, Peabody worked with other alcoholics and he trained other lay therapists as well. When Bill Wilson started going to Oxford Group meetings, Peabody was treating clients in his home on Gramercy Park, less than a block away from where the Oxford Group met at Calvary Church.

Bill Wilson owned a copy of *The Common Sense of Drinking* and he may well have been familiar with it before Charlie made his offer. It seems certain that he had read this work before he wrote the *Big Book* in 1938. Several of the earlier work's ideas are paralleled in the *Big Book,* including the notion that alcoholism is a disease of the body, mind, and spirit. Certain phrasings are also remarkably similar: Peabody: "Halfway measures are of no avail." Wilson: "Halfway measures shall avail us nothing." Peabody died in 1936, but the Emmanuel Movement coexisted with AA for a period in the 1930s and into the 1940s before being informally absorbed into AA. Like Peabody himself, the Emmanuel Movement was slanted toward a more distancing, clinical approach to alcoholism. According to alcoholics who started out in the Emmanuel Movement and subsequently joined AA, the movement never had AA's spirit and energy.

The sense of fellowship and joy that Bill identified very early among sober alcoholics can commonly be found in AA today. He thought its source lay in their being people who had found a common solution to an all-consuming, life-threatening problem. To Bill, this joy was the glue that held the fellowship together. He would always try to nourish it in everything he did and said. In time, Bill's interest in preserving this aspect of AA would be reflected in one of the most interesting features of the fellowship's decision-making process. Alcoholics Anonymous may be the only organization in the world that, in adherence to one of its governing principles, can fail to take a proposed action because of the opposition of a *minority* of its members. It was Bill's hope that this principle would help guard against AA ever straying from its primary purpose of helping alcoholics to stay sober.

Wilson's own sense of fellowship with other sober alcoholics, and the joy he took in their company, may have been the glue that kept him involved, as well. He first experienced it in Stewart's cafeteria after an Oxford Group meeting. It was what kept him hopeful of, and positive about, AA's eventual success when none of the people he tried to help were staying sober. It was also what kept Bill, Bob, and the other very early members going, when nineteen out of twenty of the alcoholics they tried to help failed to recover.

Bill was able to recognize and appreciate the importance of preserving this bond even when his fellow alcoholics were telling him he was dead wrong about something. Charlie Towns's job offer seems to have been the first occasion when this was put to the test. Bill's first indication that there might be something wrong with the career solution that had seemed heaven sent came when he told Lois about it. Given what she had had to put up with financially for most of their marriage and the intense struggle she had endured since his emergence from Towns, Bill had expected her to be ecstatic. Instead, her response was only lukewarm. Later, Lois would say that while she had instinctively felt it would be wrong for Bill to take a job at Towns, she hadn't been able to verbalize her misgivings in the face of his enthusiasm.

The regular Tuesday night meeting of the alcoholic squadron had no such problem. The ground rules for this emerging organization had yet to be worked out, but there was one thing he and Bob had been sure of from the first: there could be leaders, but no bosses. They had to stick together, all of them. No decision could be taken in opposition to what the majority wanted.

What is more, no decision was to be taken that created divisions, or classes, of members. Everyone had to be able to feel at home. No matter what their differences in money, position, or background might be, in regard to the reason that brought them together, they were all equal. No AA member has ever more fervently believed in, or more closely adhered to, this principle than Bill Wilson.

In what seemed a demonstration of the wisdom of this approach, one of the group's newest members, someone sober just a few months, spoke most clearly about why Bill shouldn't accept Charlie's offer. If Bill were to take money for doing what the rest of them were doing for nothing, he would no longer be one of them. What's more, others would soon follow his example, either by trying to get a paid position helping alcoholics themselves, or by not helping them at all, because they were not being paid for it. The bond would be broken, and the joy would be gone.

Because Bill's financial situation was so desperate, and his desire to devote himself full-time to what he most wanted to do was so strong, he argued on for a while. But it was clear to him that the newcomer was expressing how they all felt, and in his heart, he knew they were right.

Bill turned Charlie Towns down, as he would any similar proposal in the future. In doing so, he was confirming the course Robert Smith, already a health professional, had chosen, which was never to take money for helping someone to stay sober. It was what the groups wanted, and it was what felt right to them both, but it didn't solve the problem of how AA's founders were to be supported financially without setting them apart from the rest of the membership. This was something the fellowship would grapple with for years to come.

IMPOVERISHMENT

In 1937, the differences between the way the program was developing in New York and Akron put the bond between Bill Wilson and Robert Smith to a critical test. The economy, which had shown some faint signs of recovery, worsened dramatically that year, and the little work Bill had been receiving from Clayton Quaw dried up. The downturn also had a dramatic effect on Lois. She had given up her department store job and was trying to work independently as an interior decorator, and most of her clients canceled their projects.

In November, Bill went to Detroit and Cleveland as part of an attempt to get something going in the securities field. The trip was a failure, but he was able to spend some time in Akron. The Smiths' finances were also at an all-time low, and they were closer to losing their home than they had been when Bob was still drinking.

In December, it would be three years since Bill had stopped drinking and conceived his plan to help other alcoholics do the same. He and the Smiths decided to take an inventory. Among those they had tried to help, the failures were endless, and many of those who seemed sincerely willing to try their approach were struggling. When they were done counting, though, they realized that between Akron and New York there were now forty alcoholics staying sober, and half of them had not had a drink for more than a year.

Their program was working, and their gratitude at this realization was such that the three of them wept. Then, as they tried to grasp the full significance of their discovery, Bill's emotions began to drive his thinking. What happened next shows the clear influence of Bill's association with Hank P.

Hank was a marketing man. In 1936, Bill had joined Hank in Honor Dealers, an enterprise Hank had conceived, as much as anything, in order to get back at the oil company that had fired him. The venture was to provide selected gasoline stations with the opportunity to buy gasoline, oil, and automobile parts on a cooperative basis, but the company never got anywhere. This was partly due to the economic downturn in 1937, but while there was much conversation about how best to get their message out to the stations, Bill seems to have had little to do with the enterprise, and Hank's focus also seems to have been elsewhere.

Ruth Hock, AA's first secretary, had originally been hired by Hank to run the Honor Dealers office in Newark, New Jersey. As she remembered it, very little gasoline business was ever conducted. A lot of people did stop by to discuss their drinking problems, and on more than one occasion, Ruth observed Bill and Hank kneeling in prayer by the side of Hank's desk with one of these visitors (an Oxford Group practice when seeking God's guidance).

The influence of the daily activity in the Honor Dealers office, where the conversation seemed to move seamlessly between marketing and helping alcoholics, seems evident in the turn Bill's thoughts took when he and Bob and Annie discovered that forty alcoholics were staying sober. That the forty were the result of trying to help hundreds of desperate men might seem discouraging, but millions of alcoholics wanted to stop drinking. If reaching out to hundreds produced forty sober alcoholics, reaching thousands would produce hundreds, reaching tens of thousands would produce thousands, and if they could get to the tens of millions of alcoholics all over the world who wanted help, their forty sober alcoholics could become a million or even forty million.

The numbers were breathtaking, but they were very much in keeping with the exhilaration of the moment. It was the realization of Bill's original vision, while still a patient in Towns Hospital, of a chain reaction of one alcoholic helping another. It had taken them a couple of years to hone an approach, but the forty successes were proof that they were truly on to something. The rest was simply a matter of scale.

Had this been 1999, Bill's thoughts might have been on direct-mail campaigns, infomercials, Web sites, and treatment centers. But it was 1937, and they turned to books and pamphlets, paid representatives, and drying-out hospitals. If they had these things, the message of hope Bob and Bill had brought to the bedside of Bill D., the third man to stay sober, could be carried to alcoholics everywhere.

Bob's enthusiasm for all this was tepid, at best. He thought Bill could be right about the need for literature, but he was not sure hiring paid representatives and creating specialized hospitals were such good ideas. The one thing Bob and Bill always agreed on, though, was the need to present a united front. A special meeting of the Akron alcoholic squadron was called—eighteen sober alcoholics assembled at the home of T. Henry and Clarace Williams—and the results of Bill and Bob's review were presented. Then, riding the wave of good feeling this produced, they put forward Bill's vision for the future.

Bob went first. He spoke very briefly, but there was nothing in what he said to indicate that he was himself less than 100 percent behind Bill.

When it was Bill's turn, the group listened politely to what he had to say, but as soon as he had finished, the objections were vehement. Most of them were dead set against establishing a network of paid representatives and special hospitals. Most did not see the need for literature, either.

With Bob's help, Bill pressed on. In making his presentation to the New York alcoholics regarding his going to work for Charlie Towns, Bill had sensed he was wrong even before the others voiced their objection. This time, though, he wasn't asking anything for himself, and he had no such presentiments. That he made headway seems due to the truth in what he had to say about the objections the Akron alcoholics raised.

Bill pointed out the uniqueness of the Akron situation. Virtually all the very early members were late-stage alcoholics. For them to stop drinking without medical supervision would be foolhardy and could even be life threatening. The Akron group didn't feel the need for specialized hospitals because one of its members was a sober doctor. Bob was able to have the prospects that needed hospitalization admitted, and he had obtained permission for members of the alcoholic squadron to work with these newcomers without regard for visiting-hour restrictions. He also got permission for members of the Akron group to work with other prospects among the hospital's patient population.

Akron alcoholics didn't feel the need for their own literature because, thanks to the Williamses, Henrietta Seiberling, and the Akron Oxford Group's history with alcoholics, they were in an environment that could hardly have been more welcoming. But even in Akron, there were differences between the alcoholic squadron's and the Oxford Group's way of doing things, and the experience of the New York alcoholics showed only too clearly how Oxford Group practices and principles could be interpreted in ways that severely hindered their work with other alcoholics.

Akron didn't need paid representatives to introduce their approach to helping alcoholics. Well, New York didn't need them, either. Akron and New York were where this program was developed, but they certainly couldn't rely on the Oxford Group to carry the message to other cities. Given the Oxford Group's new emphasis on mass meetings, publicity campaigns, and political involvement, there was no reason to think the approach to alcoholics they had developed would find a warmer reception with other Oxford Group chapters than it had in New York.

These were sound arguments and, coupled with Bob's lobbying, they had their effect. By one vote, the Akron alcoholics pronounced themselves in favor of the project, but Akron would not be doing anything to raise the money it would require. This did not discourage Bill in the slightest; he seemed to think getting the money would be the easiest part.

Bill's plans found a much better reception with the New York contingent. Fitz M. was all for it and Hank P. was wildly enthusiastic. Millions would be required, and the Great Depression had just hit a new low, yet none of the New Yorkers seemed to think this would be a problem. Clearly, there was something no one was acknowledging. Bill was still massively in debt. He was also out of work, with no prospects. For the last nineteen years, he had been able to count on Lois for financial support whenever the going got tough, but she was now a freelance interior decorator, with no paying clients. Honor Dealers to the contrary not withstanding, Hank, too, was essentially out of work, as were Fitz and many of the other members of the New York contingent.

The decision about Bill accepting Charlie Towns's offer to become a paid lay therapist had settled the issue of whether any of them could make money from their approach to helping alcoholics that they all could claim some credit in developing. Yet the enterprise Bill envisioned would, of course, require centralized management and control. Given their financial situations, the enthusiasm of the New York contingent must have been at least partly motivated by the thought that some of the money would be used for the salaries of a director and his management team.

The millions never arrived, and AA never had either paid representatives or hospitals. But being paid for management-related contributions, rather than for helping alcoholics directly, is the principle upon which Bill and Bob would eventually be compensated.

MR. ROCKEFELLER

It might have been the Great Depression, but New York was still replete with wealthy individuals and charitable foundations. Hank and Bill put together a list of possible funding sources, but a month later, the list had been exhausted and not a dime had been raised. It seemed that moneyed New York wasn't much interested in giving large sums to a bunch of alcoholics.

Bill was horribly discouraged, even bitter. He didn't drink, nor does he seem to have been tempted. But instead of feeling, as he often did when he was down, not good enough for the world, he was sure that the world wasn't smart enough to be able to appreciate what he had accomplished. It was while Bill was registering this complaint with his brother-in-law Leonard Strong that the tide changed. Leonard remembered that a Willard Richardson, the father of a girl he had been close to in high school, worked for John D. Rockefeller, Jr. Leonard called Richardson, and when Richardson agreed to see Bill, he wrote a letter of introduction endorsing the effectiveness of Bill's work with alcoholics. The next day, Bill found himself seated in a chair that had just been vacated by Mr. Rockefeller himself.

Bill described for Richardson his own battle with alcoholism and how it had culminated with a spiritual epiphany that had left him free of the need to drink. He also talked about what had transpired since then, in his effort to help other alcoholics find a spiritual basis on which to remain alcohol free.

Willard Richardson was an ordained minister, and he was impressed by the idea of a "spiritual" cure for alcoholism. In the next few days, he related what Bill had told him to four other "Rockefeller men." All of them mirrored his enthusiasm. The Reverend Mr. Richardson then wrote Leonard Strong, reprising both his own reaction and that of the men he had spoken with. He suggested that Leonard and Bill join him for lunch so that they might discuss how Mr. Rockefeller might be of help. Bill could hardly have been more excited: it seemed as though he had struck the mother lode.

At the luncheon, which took place a few days later, Richardson proposed a larger gathering, and a dinner meeting was arranged. Bill, Leonard, and Dr. Silkworth attended along with several other New York alcoholics. Dr. Bob and another alcoholic from Akron joined them. The Rockefeller men present included the Reverend Mr. Richardson and Albert Scott, chairman of the board of trustees of Riverside Church.

The meeting lasted five hours. After listening to the alcoholics' stories of devastation and redemption, Scott thought that the movement they had begun, with its emphasis on carrying the message and one individual helping another without thought of personal recompense, sounded like First Century Christianity. Then he said, "What can we do to help?"

Bill had a ready answer: money was needed, and a lot of it, to carry forward his plan for expanding beyond New York and Akron to embrace the world. Millions of dollars were required, but millions of lives would be saved. Scott did not think much of Bill's equation: he thought large amounts of money, rather than guaranteeing the success of their venture, could be the end of it. The other Rockefeller men were not so sure. In the end, it was decided that one of them would go to Akron to explore the possibility of establishing a hospital for alcoholics.

Frank Amos, one of the Rockefeller associates, went to Akron in February 1938. In addition to spending time with Bob Smith, he met with Henrietta Seiberling and T. Henry Williams, and both of them verified the crucial role Dr. Bob was playing in the movement. He also met with G. A. Ferguson and Howard Seal, two of Ohio's most prominent physicians and with Judge Benner, a former probate judge who was the chairman of the board of Akron City Hospital. The three men were all full of praise for Robert Smith's skills as a surgeon and his work with alcoholics, and the doctors expressed concern about the financial difficulties Smith's devotion to helping alcoholics had created for him.

When Amos returned to New York, he wrote a report on his trip for Mr. Rockefeller. Bill's version of Amos's recommendations varies strikingly from what the report actually said. As Bill told the story, both in print and in numerous talks, Amos said that an initial sum of fifty thousand dollars was needed. The money was to be used in building either a hospital for alcoholics or a "recuperating home" and to compensate Smith for his efforts in directing the establishment of one of these facilities over the next two years.

Amos's report, which was submitted by Willard Richardson with a cover letter stating that its conclusions were endorsed by Richardson, Scott, and Chipman, suggested that Rockefeller provide a total of $10,000, $5,000 a year for two years, and it makes no mention of hospitals or recuperating homes. The money was to be used to buy Bob a decent car, pay down the mortgage on his house, and provide him with a bigger office and a secretary, all of which would make it possible for him to spend more time working with alcoholics.

While the report addressed the Akron situation alone, Frank Amos was hardly unappreciative of Bill's role. Amos had asked Bill for help with an alcoholic friend, and when Bill willingly complied and the man responded immediately, Amos was both impressed and deeply grateful. He and the other Rockefeller men appreciated that financial assistance would also be necessary in New York, if the work were to go forward there.

In the end, Mr. Rockefeller wrote a check for five thousand dollars that was to be used to help both Bill and Bob. The check was made out to Riverside Church, to be administered by Scott and the other Rockefeller associates. The mortgage on the Smiths' home was paid off, and the Smiths and the Wilsons were given an income of $30.00 a week (about $350.00 in year 2000 dollars). Bill realized the entertainment value in a story about the millions that got away. He always credited the richest man in the country's belief that too much money would ruin AA with helping to make the fellowship self-supporting. John D. Rockefeller, Jr., certainly did that, but he also did much more in helping to launch Alcoholics Anonymous.

That Rockefeller would agree to help, yet provide only half the amount his own representative told him was needed was completely consistent with the principles underlying his philanthropy. Rockefeller either made an open-ended commitment to provide all the support an organization needed for however long it might take to accomplish its goals, or he provided only half of what was required until the organization could develop the means to become self-supporting. In AA's case, he felt so strongly that the fellowship must become self-supporting that, in agreeing to provide half of the ten thousand dollars Amos was requesting, he told his associates not to ask him again for money on its behalf.

John D. Rockefeller, Jr.'s interest in what Bill and Dr. Bob and the others were doing had solid precedence. The Rockefellers were strict Baptists who didn't allow either smoking or drinking in their homes, and the family had long supported efforts to do something about alcoholism. This interest had found two means of expression: religious and secular.

The family had been among the early supporters of temperance movements, not as a means of proselytizing for their faith but in the hope that temperance would be an effective means of curbing a serious public health problem. The Rockefellers also created the Bureau of Social Hygiene, which was dedicated to alleviating societal ills such as alcoholism through pragmatic and nonsectarian means. As was true for much of the nation, by the mid-1930s the Rockefellers' disillusionment with temperance had grown quite profound, and their support of temperance movements had been scaled back dramatically.

Rockefeller's faith did have a direct bearing on his interest in AA. Like Albert Scott, he was taken by the similarities between AA and First Century Christianity. Mr. Rockefeller also believed that his own faith required him to devote a measure of his time and energy to helping people in need. It is clear that he helped Alcoholics Anonymous as an expression of his felt need to do this "Christian work" for many years.

By placing his five thousand dollar gift in the treasury of Riverside Church, Rockefeller guaranteed that the efforts of this small group of sober alcoholics to help other alcoholics would become known to Riverside's parishioners, many of whom were themselves prominent and successful people. Word of mouth soon carried the news about John D. Rockefeller, Jr.'s support of this Oxford Group offshoot beyond the confines of Riverside and into the worlds of New York society and business at the highest levels.

Mr. Rockefeller also put some of his most trusted advisers at Bill's disposal, including, in addition to Frank Amos and the Reverend Mr. Richardson, A. Leroy Chipman and various Rockefeller Foundation attorneys. Experienced business executives with an intimate knowledge of the world of New York philanthropy, AA's "Rockefeller men" helped create the Alcoholic Foundation, and they served on the foundation's first board of trustees. In time, the Alcoholic Foundation would be known as the General Service Board of Alcoholics Anonymous, which, along with the General Service Office and the General Service Conference, compose one leg of the triad of structures that now run AA on the national level. The very active association of these men with the fledging enterprise provided AA with legitimacy and a visibility it could never have aspired to otherwise.

Mr. Rockefeller received regular, detailed reports on AA's activities. Most frequently, they were authored by A. LeRoy Chipman, the Rockefeller man who became the first treasurer of the Alcoholic Foundation, but Willard Richardson, who became the first secretary of the foundation, also corresponded with Rockefeller on the subject of AA, as did Frank Amos. The Rockefeller archives contains hundreds of letters, many of them very moving, that John D. Rockefeller, Jr., wrote on the subject of AA. They reveal both the strength of his interest and the care and thought he put into determining what he could most effectively do on the organization's behalf.

The letters were directed not only to the Rockefeller men who were directly involved in helping AA but also to family members, friends, and business acquaintances. A number were written in response to appeals for help with a drinking problem. On these occasions, Mr. Rockefeller's replies always recommended AA, and a copy of A.A.'s *Big Book* usually accompanied the letters.

Although he had told his associates not to ask him again for money for AA, Rockefeller left his associates free to disagree with him on this issue. Richardson, Chipman, and Amos continued to believe in the need for AA hospitals, and they worked for many years toward raising the money to establish them. When they felt the need was urgent, they also asked Mr. Rockefeller for further financial assistance. Except for one occasion, when Rockefeller declined to buy a building for a foundering AA clubhouse for seamen, an organization he had been supporting for years, there is no indication that he ever turned them down. But John D. Rockefeller, Jr., never changed his mind about the need for AA hospitals, and no money was ever raised for this purpose.

In 1940, the early fellowship was undergoing what was perhaps its most severe financial crisis. The *Big Book* had been written and printed, but it was not yet selling, and AA was near bankruptcy. Rockefeller responded by hosting on AA's behalf a dinner to which he invited some four hundred individuals of great wealth and influence. A sober alcoholic was seated at each table.

On the night of the dinner, John D. Rockefeller, Jr., was ill with a severe cold and, on his doctor's orders, confined to bed. A number of letters testify to how disappointed he was not to be able to attend. His son Nelson stood in for him, and the man who would go on to become governor of New York and vice president of the United States told the assembly that his father knew of few things more deeply affecting or promising than Alcoholics Anonymous. He also expressed his father's continued hope that the fellowship would become self-supporting, and he said that until this happened, his father felt there was a need for financial assistance.

Bill made a presentation, and Dr. Bob offered some brief remarks. There were also testimonials from a prominent clergyman and an equally prominent neurologist. After the dinner, John D. Rockefeller, Jr., wrote to each of the men he had invited, endorsing AA and telling them that he was giving the fellowship $1,000 (nearly $12,000 in year 2000 dollars). Accompanying the letter was a copy of the *Big Book* and transcripts of the talks given at the dinner.

Bill and a number of other members still thought that this might be their opportunity at last to land millions for the cause, but they didn't reckon with the strength of Rockefeller's vision for their new organization or the personal energy he was willing to commit to seeing to it that it did not stray from the course he felt best. Perhaps only someone who had lived his entire life rich as a Rockefeller could have developed such a keen appreciation of the limitations of money, but by the time his agents approached him to help the fledgling organization, he had been devoting the major share of his energy to philanthropy for many years.

Mr. Rockefeller had become skilled at determining how he could best come to the aid of a particular cause, and his correspondence reveals a continual concern that he wield his great influence in the way that would be the most beneficial. To the alcoholics present, the remarks his son made in support of AA may have seemed designed to unloose the floodgates, but they were in fact calculated to have the opposite effect. Rockefeller was telling those assembled that from a philanthropic standpoint AA was his project and it was his desire that any support they might care to give it follow his lead.

The letters he received in response to his solicitation were full of praise for all AA had accomplished and expressions of confidence in the movement's bright future. A number indicated that they would follow Rockefeller's example in recommending AA to friends, relatives, and business associates. But many of Mr. Rockefeller's fellow millionaires declined to make any contribution, citing, by way of assuring him that he need not fear any future intervention, the severe economic conditions and other causes to which they were committed. Those who did enclose a check took their cue from Rockefeller's $1,000 donation and sent checks for as little as $10.00. The largest checks were for $250.00. Altogether, these wealthy men made contributions to AA totaling around $2,000.00.

The AA members may have been disappointed, but the result seems to have been exactly what Rockefeller had in mind. He personally acknowledged all the letters. He even wrote a millionaire who had sent a check for fifty dollars to tell him he had only anticipated ten dollars from him. Rockefeller then asked the man for permission to return the check, so that he could replace it by one for the smaller amount. When the man declined to do that, Rockefeller finally relented and accepted the fifty dollars, but not without again thanking the donor for his generosity in terms more than profuse enough to convey the message that, should his friend be thinking that this might be the first of many contributions, it was John D. Rockefeller, Jr.'s strong opinion that he had already done more than enough.

The dinner John D. Rockefeller, Jr., gave for AA was like other dinners he had sponsored to introduce to New York's charitable community causes that he felt worthy of support. In AA's case, it proved to be of greater value than the millions would have been, for it produced the fellowship's first surge of national publicity. Newspapers all over the country ran stories with headlines such as ROCKEFELLER DINES FORMER TOSSPOTS. The articles made thousands of people aware of AA for the first time, and on a most favorable basis.

Given Rockefeller's strong feelings about the kind of help that AA needed, the dinner seems a stroke of genius. It allowed him to reinforce publicly his support of the group. It guaranteed that the fellowship would receive the money it needed for its immediate survival; and it all but ruled out the possibility that AA would receive the kind of money he thought would do it more harm than good.

Alcoholics Anonymous solicited contributions from Rockefeller and his dinner guests each year for the next four years. It received donations averaging about $3,000 a year, which was used to pay the expenses of the AA office in New York and to continue to support Smith and Wilson. In 1942, A. LeRoy Chipman asked this group for a loan of $8,500 for use in buying back the remaining outstanding shares of stock in Works Publishing, the company formed to finance the writing and publishing of the *Big Book*. After much soul searching, John D. Rockefeller, Jr., lent $4,000, and Nelson Rockefeller $500. Other dinner guests lent the additional $4,000.

Mr. Rockefeller was concerned that he and his son were contributing too large a share of the loan. But he was even more worried about the crisis that had erupted within the fellowship over the unconventional way the publishing of the *Big Book* had been financed, and he wanted to see the matter put to rest as quickly as possible. As was his custom when he lent money to a cause, one dollar of the money he and Nelson had lent would be forgiven for every dollar repaid. Several of the other lenders provided the same terms. Still others forgave their share of the loan entirely.

A FOUNDATION

John D. Rockefeller, Jr.'s endorsement of and continuing interest in AA ushered in a period of tremendous growth and activity. By 1945, the last year in which support was received from Mr. Rockefeller and his dinner guests, AA was an internationally known organization with a membership numbering in the tens of thousands. It was also autonomous, fully self-sustaining, and well on the way toward establishing the formal structure that would make it possible, with one alcoholic helping another, for millions of alcoholics to find relief from the need to drink.

Given his history with the rich and famous, the way Bill conducted himself during this period is remarkable. The philanthropic activities of John D. Rockefeller, Jr., were already legendary. Moreover, just because the Depression was in its eighth year, the focus on his charity could hardly have been more intense. Willard Richardson had no doubt listened to countless petitioners, but Bill presented himself and his case in a way that was impressive and credible. He was also able, with his wife's assistance, to arrive at Rockefeller Center looking his beaming, picture-of-health best. His suit was clean, free of holes and freshly pressed, and he was apparently able to restrain his smoking enough not to set anything on fire.

The letter of introduction from Leonard, whom Bill seemed always able to accept as being genuinely well disposed toward him, may have helped. There is also the fact that Lois and John D. Rockefeller, Jr., were distantly related. For whatever reason, Bill's tendency toward belligerence and a defensive arrogance when presenting a new idea were not on display.

He was able to dazzle Richardson with his recently reinvigorated vision of the glorious future his plan for helping drunks could have. Richardson was so impressed that he immediately discussed Bill's proposal with other key Rockefeller associates, and together they began thinking about how best to help him. Anyone who has ever sought funds from a philanthropic institution knows this is not the pace at which things usually proceed.

Given that only five of every one hundred prospects ever caught on in those very early days, the success Bill had with Frank Amos's college friend involved more than a smattering of good fortune. It would not have happened at all, though, if Bill had gone at him the way he had others before connecting with Robert Smith, or if he had given him the one-hour-lecture approach he had taken to using with new prospects after his success with Hank P. and Fitz M.

Even though these men made it clear at the outset that Bill wasn't going to get from them the kind of money he was seeking, he was able to build on his initial favorable impression. Like Mr. Rockefeller himself, AA's Rockefeller men subsequently made the fellowship a major focus of their "Christian work," and Bill made lifelong friends of these men who were better born, educated, and connected than he was.

The Alcoholic Foundation gave the fellowship its first formal structure. It was also to serve as an indispensable tool in AA's future fund-raising activities. Willard Richardson, Frank Amos, and John Wood, the attorney Frank Amos brought in to handle the necessary legal work, were the new foundation's first nonalcoholic trustees. Robert Smith and a New York alcoholic were the first alcoholic trustees.

The Alcoholic Foundation received the proceeds from the Rockefeller dinner list solicitations and income from the sales of the *Big Book*. Richardson, Amos, A. LeRoy Chipman, and Leonard Harrison, another "Rockefeller man," would serve on the foundation's board in various capacities for many years.

That Bill did not serve as trustee points to an essential difference in the roles that he and Bob played during AA's formative years. Bill was the problem solver, the initiator, the conceiver and implementer of plans for AA's future. Bob served as a brake, a sounding board, a source of balance, and a leavening perspective. Establishing the Alcoholic Foundation helped to formalize this relationship. It also put in place a check on Bill that would survive the death of the older man.

The nonalcoholic members were given majority control as a way of instilling confidence in the stability of the organization. There was also a genuine fear on the part of the alcoholics about the damage that an alcoholic might do if he drank again. A provision of the foundation's charter called for the automatic dismissal of any alcoholic trustee who relapsed. This fear seemed justified when the New York alcoholic who was one of the first trustees relapsed. He was immediately replaced. Though the board would be expanded several times, its nonalcoholic members would remain a majority for nearly thirty years.

SPREADING THE NEWS

Alcoholics Anonymous is, without question, one of the greatest success stories in the history of publishing. It has been in print nearly sixty years, and it can be found in virtually every country in the world. In addition to the European languages, it is also available in Afrikaans, Arabic, Chinese, Japanese, Korean, Persian, Swahili, Thai, Turkish, and Vietnamese. To date, more than twenty million copies have been sold, and it continues to sell at the rate of more than a million copies a year.

Of the things Bill wanted to do to extend the reach of the fellowship, producing literature was the one most members deemed essential. When it was decided that the book describing their program of recovery would also contain personal recovery stories, several of the members who had initially opposed the project began clamoring to have their own included. Resistance was also muted by Hank P.'s projections regarding the money the sale of such a book would bring in. According to Hank, the *Big Book* would hit the million-copy mark in just a few short years.

It would actually take until 1973 to sell a million copies. By then, though, AA had become such a national treasure that the millionth copy was presented to President Richard Nixon in the White House. Hank's estimates seem to have been based on nothing more than his enthusiasm for the project. They also failed to take into account the resistance people would have to its $3.50 price tag, more than $40.00 in today's dollars. Still, there may never have been a *Big Book* without Hank; his optimism most certainly helped to reduce the resistance to going forward with the project.

Writing and publishing the *Big Book* tested all of Bill's professional and personal skills. He wrote the book's first eleven chapters, and he was involved in selecting and editing the recovery stories contributed by other members. That he would later describe his contribution as more refereeing than writing is an indication of the intensity of controversies and squabbles that marked the book's production. The project also tested his commitment to creating a movement capable of realizing his desire to help alcoholics the world over rather than, as many members wanted, an organization that would have been more like an Oxford Group for alcoholics.

Bill also wrote AA's famous Twelve Steps. In doing so, he was putting on paper the movement's program of recovery. Because the Twelve Steps have long been the treatment model embraced by nearly all substance-abuse treatment programs, it is hard to imagine that they could have been produced amid swirls of controversy. Yet, before the book-writing project, precisely how the by now one hundred alcoholics in Akron and New York had recovered had never been documented. When the project got under way, there seemed to be nearly as many programs of recovery as there were alcoholics who had recovered. That Bill was able to write the Steps and then, with a few modifications, obtain general agreement that they did indeed represent the recovery process all the members had undergone, in itself represents a miracle of diplomacy.

Getting agreement on the book itself was even harder. Yet, in spite of the number of voices contributing to its content, the text does not seem cobbled together out of disparate parts. Many people have criticized the language for being corny and cliché ridden, but the work is also an undeniably powerful piece of writing. The first eleven chapters present, in one seamless polemic, both the devastation of alcoholism and the effectiveness of the AA program. The tone is clear, direct, and down-to-earth. Its images are succinct and colorful, and the reader has the sense of a story being told by a favorite uncle. Bill had never written anything longer than an analysis of a company's investment potential or anything more personal than a letter. He had never written at all on the subjects of religion or medicine. Yet, if he had never done anything else, his authorship of AA's basic text alone would have qualified him for a listing among the one hundred most influential individuals of the twentieth century.

Bill even wrote the *Big Book* chapter entitled, "To the Wives." Quite naturally, Lois saw this as something she was much better qualified to do. Had she written this chapter, it is quite likely that the content would have been different. The chapter Bill wrote seems to assume the ideal spouse to be someone with no other interest but the welfare of her husband, whereas Lois always had other interests. The chapter also seems to hold the spouse substantially responsible for maintaining her alcoholic husband's emotional stability and a positive outlook once he stops drinking. The futility of such a life, and the depth of the anger produced by trying to live it, were among the lessons Lois had learned for herself as the result of her shoe-throwing "epiphany."

"I've never understood why he didn't want me to write it," Lois told me when I asked her about it. "I was so mad, and hurt. I don't think I have ever gotten over it. It still makes me mad just to think about it."

That Bill urges still more patience and endurance from the already long-suffering spouse may be an example of his determination to go to whatever lengths possible in helping alcoholics to recover. In all things, Bill Wilson was, first and foremost, an advocate for the still suffering alcoholic. It is hard to appreciate today the tentativeness of the early sobriety of the typically middle-aged, late-stage alcoholics he was familiar with. As heartless as it might seem from the wife's point of view to ask her to continue to treat her husband as a fragile child, if it could buy him precious time to achieve some degree of emotional stability before her long bottled up resentments boiled over, it was something that Bill would do.

While Bill seemed to be asking the impossible, it's likely that he was realistic enough to know that any indulgence he might succeed in obtaining would not long endure. It may be that in doing so he was employing a favorite tactical ploy: trained as a lawyer, he was not above asking for more than he could reasonably expect to get as a way of achieving his unstated goal.

The *Big Book* project also introduced the subject of money in a way that could no longer be dealt with by simply denying its necessity. Among other things, income from book sales was supposed to provide the wherewithal to compensate AA's cofounders for their full-time involvement with AA. When, as the result of book sales, the fellowship began to expand beyond Akron and New York, the demand on the founders' time precluded their doing anything else. But because book sales grew at the rate that was far below what had been anticipated, the Smiths' and the Wilsons' impoverishment endured long after Alcoholics Anonymous had been firmly established.

Bill wrote, edited, and rewrote the manuscript at home on legal pads. Then he brought his much-revised text to the Newark office of Honor Dealers and dictated it to Ruth Hock, who typed the manuscript. Ruth had been hired as a secretary for Honor Dealers, but by the spring of 1938, the office had also become the headquarters of the Alcoholic Foundation, and Ruth had become AA's first paid employee.

The typed copies were in turn regarded as a draft that was circulated both in New York and in Akron for comments and suggestions. Unfortunately, virtually all the evidence of the labor that went into writing the *Big Book* was lost when, as part of moving the Alcoholic Foundation's office from Newark to New York, an overzealous secretary "cleaned house." When I worked for Lois at Stepping Stones, though, we discovered what appeared to be a fragment of an early draft of the manuscript, and more recently I received from a German AA member a copy of what also appears to be a fragment from an early draft. In both cases, the manuscript is typed on oversized paper; each line is numbered, and in the wide left-hand margin there are handwritten comments made by Bill and others.

The fragments seem to be early attempts at putting on paper the kernel that would in time be expanded into the first eleven chapters. Both start with Bill's own story, except that in the fragments his story starts with his parents divorcing and his going to live with his grandparents, while in the version published in the *Big Book* as chapter one, "Bill's Story," it starts with Bill already in the army. The fragments go on as though the entire recovery program could be told out of Bill's own experience. There is even an itemized description of the AA process of recovery that seems to predate the articulation of AA's Twelve Steps of recovery.

Bill worked frantically at this project. He and many other people, who by this time included the Rockefeller men, were feeling a great sense of urgency about getting the program down on paper and spreading the word about its effectiveness. Yet one of the things Ruth Hock would later recall most vividly was Bill's willingness to interrupt the work whenever anyone stopped by. Bill seemed always to regard a conversation with another alcoholic as more important than anything else he might be doing. In 1938, the volume of people stopping by was low enough that his work on the *Big Book* still went forward.

By summer, general agreement among the membership had been reached on what would become the first two chapters of the book, "Bill's Story" and "There Is a Solution." Copies were printed for use in a new fund-raising project. The sample chapters did not raise any money, but they did lead to an important and solid endorsement of the project. Rockefeller associate Frank Amos got Bill an appointment with Eugene Exman, the editor for religious books at Harper Brothers publishers. Exman read the chapters and, after Bill had satisfied him as to his ability to finish the manuscript, agreed to publish it. He also offered Bill a fifteen hundred dollar advance, a generous sum in those years for a nonfiction book by an unknown author.

Exman's enthusiasm gave the project a big boost. Again, Bill and the others were dreaming big dreams. The Rockefeller people thought Bill should accept the Harper offer, but Hank P. saw Exman's confirmation of the commercial value of what they were doing as all the more reason why the fellowship should publish the book itself. To everyone's amazement, when Bill told Exman about the self-publishing idea, he was all for it. Exman's feeling was that, in spite of the perils associated with self-publishing, it was important for AA to control its own literature.

It is hard to appreciate the kind of courage it took to turn down

Harper Brothers. The thirty dollars a week the Wilsons and the Smiths were reach receiving from the treasury of Riverside Church kept the lights on and food on the table, but it didn't do much else, and even this financial support was scheduled to come to an end in about eighteen months. Although it was financially riskier, both couples thought that the fellowship should own and control its own literature, and they thought that self-publishing had the potential to produce a much greater income. Inquiries were made as to the actual cost of printing a book, and Bill and Hank learned that it was only about 10 percent of the retail price. At $3.50, they could pay as much as a dollar per book for distribution and still realize a profit of $2.15. This was six times what could be realized from author's royalties.

Self-publishing would allow the fellowship to have a measure of control over its growth. It seems almost comical, given the difficulties that were subsequently encountered in selling the *Big Book,* but a great worry at the time was the possibility of a runaway best-seller. The fear was that such an event would generate requests for help in numbers that would totally overwhelm their ability to reply to them. Thousands of alcoholics and their families would be left to conclude that they had been the victims of a cruel moneymaking scam, and the resultant bad publicity would destroy all the forty had hoped to accomplish.

"I don't think any of us really believed in Hank's charts," Lois said. "But we did feel that Exman was right. AA *should* publish its own literature."

WORKS PUBLISHING

The Alcoholic Foundation was supposed to be a governing body, with a substantive role in making decisions concerning the fellowship as a whole, and the foundation opposed the idea of self-publishing. The Rockefeller people pointed out that neither Bill nor Hank nor any of the other members knew anything about publishing, and such ignorance was the reason most self-publishing ventures failed. Furthermore, Harper Brothers was one of the most prestigious names in publishing, and its imprimatur would provide credibility to what was, after all, an incredible story.

When Bill wanted to take a job at Towns Hospital and the New York alcoholics did not think it was a good idea, he abided by their decision. When he decided that hospitals, paid representatives, and literature were called for, he discussed it with Bob and then put it before the Akron and New York groups. Similarly, the decision to form the Alcoholic Foundation was taken after much discussion, and the board included representation from Akron and New York. By contrast, the decision to self-publish seems to have been made in a heartbeat. When the trustees said no, Bill and Hank simply bought a pad of stock certificates and began issuing stock in a new company called Works Publishing.

Each certificate was inscribed with a par value of $25.00, which would be about $300 today, and signed by Hank as president of the concern. Eighteen hundred shares were issued. Hank got one-third of them or six hundred shares, with a par value of $15,000. Bill also got six hundred shares. The remaining six hundred were to be sold to other members. Checks could be made payable either to the Alcoholic Foundation or Hank. The $15,000 from the sale of stock to other members was to pay the expenses of the Newark office, which included Ruth Hock's salary, and to support Hank and Bill while they worked on the project. The fellowship at large was to profit from the enterprise through the payment of author's royalties to the Alcoholic Foundation.

No one seems to have seen clearly the implications of this scheme, including, from the evidence, Hank and Bill themselves. Surely, the two of them did not have the right to assume ownership and control of what would be the fellowship's only tangible asset. If self-publishing would realize a return that was six times what could be had from author's royalties, why should the Alcoholic Foundation profit only to that extent?

The other members may not have understood what was going on, but neither could they be interested in buying the stock. Hank and Bill decided that further evidence was needed that Works Publishing would provide the financial returns they were projecting. On the strength of Harper's positive response, they obtained a meeting with an editor at *Reader's Digest*. When the editor said the magazine might run a story about the fellowship when the book was published in the spring, Bill and Hank interpreted this expression of interest as a commitment.

Two hundred shares of stock were sold at $25.00 a share. Some members bought as little as one share, on an installment plan of $5.00 down and $5.00 a month. One member bought twelve shares. In addition to the $5,000 raised through the sale of stock, Charlie Towns lent the company $2,500 and $1,500 more later. Altogether, they raised $9,000.

When, in 1940, members took a closer look at Works Publishing, a furor arose. The groups eventually decided that *all* book profits should go to the Alcoholic Foundation, Hank and Bill were to turn their stock over to the Foundation, and members who had purchased stock were to sell it to the Alcoholic Foundation at par value. The fellowship, not Hank and Bill, would own and control the *Big Book* and all future publishing projects.

So that Bill and Bob might continue to devote themselves full-time to the affairs of the fellowship, they were each to receive author's royalties, with the exact percentage to be determined later. The royalties were an expression of the hope that the book would be the answer to the Smiths' and the Wilsons' financial plight.

Bill turned his Works Publishing shares into the foundation immediately. Hank, who by this time had started drinking again, refused to do it. Others refused, too. Further controversy arose when Bill made a seemingly unilateral decision to pay back Charlie Towns. Money was raised for this purpose by issuing still more Works Publishing stock, *preferred* shares valued at one hundred dollars per share. The fellowship had expanded by this time, and several well-to-do newer members bought the stock.

The problem of Hank's stock was solved when he showed up drunk at the AA office one day, seeking payment for his office furniture. By this time, the Honor Dealers office was closed, and the office for the Alcoholic Foundation was in New York. Hank had been paid for his furniture at least once before, but Bill agreed to pay him again if Hank would turn in his stock. Although Hank would later claim that Bill had taken advantage of his drunken state, he accepted two hundred dollars for the furniture and turned in his stock. Loans the foundation obtained from the Rockefeller dinner-list people made it possible to retire the rest of the outstanding shares.

The financing of the *Big Book*'s publication would continue to be a source of discontent in AA circles for years. Even today, grumbling can be heard in some quarters about AA's founders having gotten rich from the profits they made on the *Big Book*. Nothing could be further from the truth. In her nineties, Lois became quite well off, a result of the explosive growth in book sales AA experienced in the 1980s. But this was more than forty years after it was published. Both Bob and Anne Smith had been dead thirty years by then, and Bill, ten years.

Book royalties actually proved to be an inadequate way for AA to support its founders. The price of the book was itself a source of controversy, with many members of the opinion that the book should be sold at cost and others maintaining that it should be free. There was also a movement to put out a paperback version, which would sell for $1.00 a copy, versus the $3.50 for the hardcover.

What these members seemed to ignore was that AA's survival was dependent on the profits from the book. These profits, not member contributions, were what made it possible for AA to stop soliciting aid from the Rockefeller dinner list in 1945. Profits from literature sales still make up the shortfall in member contributions toward the expenses of AA's world headquarters and its national and international conferences.

Beginning in 1940, Bill was paid one hundred dollars a month in book royalties. Bob Smith was to get one hundred dollars a month as well, but for the first three years, there wasn't enough money to pay Bob's royalties. In 1944, the back royalties owed Bob were caught up. (Bob's financial situation was by then no longer so desperate, and he gave much of this money to Bill.) With the book selling for $3.50, instead of a fixed amount each month, Bill and Bob were each assigned royalty payments of 10 percent, or forty-five cents, per book.

The *Big Book* was never free, and a paperback edition was not published until 1986. The pressure to make it more affordable did result in the price of the book, measured in current dollars, being allowed to drop steadily. It took until 1955 to sell the first three hundred thousand books. By then, the price was $4.50, about $26.50 in today's dollars. In other words, between 1939 and 1955, the value of Bill's royalty per book sold decreased 65 percent. By the time of his death in 1971, the failure of the price of the *Big Book* to keep up with inflation had lowered the value of his royalties by more than 80 percent.

All this was, of course, far in the future in 1938. As the writing proceeded, drafts of each succeeding chapter circulated in Akron and New York. There were arguments among the members about how to describe the process of recovery and whose personal recovery stories to include. The biggest challenge seemed to revolve around how to characterize the spiritual transformation, which was at the heart of the program. Even when the total membership was made up of just forty sober alcoholics, their views on this subject ranged from fervent belief that the entire program was divinely inspired to adamant agnosticism or atheism. For the most part, the Akron members greeted the drafts coming out of New York with enthusiasm, but there was much dissension among the New York members over the religious references.

As is still true today, the New York membership included many agnostics and atheists. New York members also provoked a confrontation over the use of the word *God* in the Twelve Steps, with Hank and Fitz M. taking opposite sides. Hank, who wasn't religious, wanted to leave God out entirely and instead refer to the "spiritual nature" of the recovery the steps were designed to bring about. Fitz, whose father was a minister, thought the steps should reflect explicitly Christian doctrine. Everyone agreed that the change they had experienced was essentially spiritual. It was also most emphatically a change for the better. This may seem so obvious as to be pointless, but it has important implications.

As AA sees it, alcoholism is neither a curse nor a punishment. Nor is it a sin or the product of a weak, debased, or immoral character. Alcoholism is a malady that, in its essence, is a soul sickness, one that causes a kind of spiritual eclipse. Relief can come suddenly, as in Bill's case, or through a gradual process, which is the path AA's Twelve Steps attempt to define. Healing is characterized by a reconnection with one's spiritual, and benevolent, nature, coupled with an awareness of the universe as a spiritual place, to which we are all profoundly and positively connected.

Bill Wilson seems to have been ideally suited to bridging the divide between what, at the extremes of the debate, were the God lovers and the God haters. The Congregational Church stands between the inn where Bill was born and the Griffiths' simple white-clapboard home where he spent most of his childhood. Although Bill attended Sunday school, neither the Griffiths nor the Wilsons were religious, and he did not feel that he had been raised in any particular faith. The discord between his parents and their lack of empathy for him, followed by their divorce and their abandonment, were not the sort of experiences that lead to a view of the world as a benevolent place. By the time Bill was in high school, he seems clearly to have believed that anything he would ever get from life—including love—would be an uphill struggle.

Bill said he was an agnostic at the time of his spiritual awakening, but an agnostic is someone who does not know whether there is a God or not. Wilson also said many times that before he stopped drinking, he did not believe there could be a God in a world filled with horrors. This isn't agnosticism, it's atheism. In 1934, atheism based on the incompatibility between the seeming godlessness all around one and the notion of a loving creator was far from uncommon.

With the much greater horrors of World War II now nearly fifty-five years behind us, it is hard to imagine the effect World War I had on people's belief in God. The First World War, known then as the Great War, was the first major conflagration to be fought with products of the Industrial Revolution, and it killed, maimed, starved, and destroyed on a scale previously unimaginable. Bill did not see combat, but he knew men who had, and as he struggled in the war's aftermath to find a place for himself, the scale of its devastation became known to him.

If the war were not enough to destroy the prevailing late-nineteenth-century optimism, the world was to suffer through another cataclysm in its aftermath: the Spanish influenza epidemic. A particularly virulent strain that had incubated in trenches and overcrowded hospitals during the war, this flu attacked its victim's lungs, rendering them useless. Virtually everyone who contracted the Spanish Flu died a horrible death by slow asphyxiation. The epidemic killed between 20,000,000 and 40,000,000 people worldwide. The 700,000 people who died in the United States represents a death toll greater than the number of Americans killed in World War I, World War II, the Korean War, and the Vietnam War combined. What's more, although the flu usually attacks the very young and the very old, this virus focused on people in the prime of life: men and women in their twenties died at a much higher rate than did infants and the elderly.

The war, the influenza epidemic, and the growing impersonality of modern life combined to cause millions of people to give up on hopefulness. The Roaring Twenties is most frequently remembered as a gay and devil-may-care time. Yet it was a frivolity with a blind, mad face; a "dancing in the streets" punctuated with the violence of organized crime.

Criminal syndicates were virtually the sole purveyors of the ocean of booze consumed during a time when Prohibition had made its sale illegal. People exchanged tides of money for this alcohol, no small part of which was produced so carelessly as to cause blindness, death, or insanity. The money was used to corrupt the criminal justice system to an extent hardly imaginable today.

Much of the gaiety of the twenties was actually a manifestation of a nihilism previously unknown to Americans. A belief system had been shattered. People were living for the moment, madly, destructively, because it did not matter. Nothing mattered. It was in this spirit that Bill Wilson, the product of two long lines of thrifty Vermonters, could routinely spend his wallet empty in the course of drinking his way from bar to bar on his way home from work.

The Crash and the Great Depression seemed for many to be the final blows: God, if there was a god, had clearly abandoned the world. Civilization, if a world of dust bowls and breadlines could still be called that, was dead.

There may have been a moment, sitting with Lois on the cliffs of Bedford, Massachusetts, when Bill felt himself to be a part of some greater whole. Before leaving England for France, he also felt for a moment a spiritual presence in Winchester Cathedral. But long before the stock market crashed in 1929, the pessimism and negativity he had battled since childhood had hardened into a militant, angry agnosticism.

The more we examine Bill Wilson's background and the events he experienced leading up to his fourth drying out in Towns Hospital, the less he seems like a candidate for a spiritual conversion experience. No one could have felt more unprepared for such an experience, or be more impressed by the results, than Bill was himself. Afterward, whether in a letter to a friend or the manuscript of a book, while addressing a crowd of thousands or in conversation over a cup of coffee, Bill could make frequent and easy reference to God. For him, God was the source of the goodness and guidance alcoholics could rely on to help them put an end to their drinking and restore wholeness to their lives. He would never again doubt the existence of a god who united humankind in a spirit of benevolence, and he thought that those who did so were standing with their backs to the light.

Yet there are also ways in which Bill never stopped being the man he was before that event. His belief in God might have become unshakable, but he could never embrace any theology or even the divinity of Jesus, and he went to his grave unable to give his own personal idea of God much definition. In this sense, he was never very far removed from the unbelievers.

Bill may have included some heavily Christian wording in his early drafts of the *Big Book*, but he had not forgotten his own feelings about God during the last years of his drinking. As the arguments continued over the references to God in the Twelve Steps and throughout the manuscript, Bill could empathize with both sides.

The term *God* is used in the Twelve Steps and throughout the *Big Book*, but open-ended, even deliberately vague references, such as "higher power" or a "power greater than ourselves" or to "God as we understand Him" are also used. (The felicitous phrase "God as we understand Him" was suggested by Jimmy B., a New York AA member.) Weasel wording the "God stuff" made it possible for people of widely varying beliefs—and even nonbelievers—to embrace AA's process of *spiritual* transformation. Refraining from specifically Christian references has also made possible AA's acceptance in such non-Christian countries as India, Japan, and China.

Wilson did not want to impose his views on the others. However, the compromises he brokered about how to characterize the role of God in AA's program for spiritual conversion clearly reflect his thinking on the subject.

Over the next thirty-three years, Wilson's writing and speaking would be characterized by a continuing refusal to introduce Christian doctrine to AA. Bill took care in everything he did and said to convey an open, welcoming attitude toward avowed agnostics and atheists. Ironically, many AA members have observed that often the member most eager to give AA Christian overtones is someone whose initial agnosticism would have disqualified him for membership in a fellowship that insisted on such specifically Christian interpretations of its doctrine. Bill's quiet, consistent insistence that AA be a *spiritual* program instead of a religious one is one of his greatest contributions to the fellowship's enormous success.

18

FROM MANUSCRIPT TO BOOK

In January 1939, four hundred copies of the *Big Book* manuscript were distributed for comment. A psychiatrist familiar with the Oxford Group said that he found the book to be "pure Oxford Group." He was expressing his reaction to the insistent tone Bill had used in outlining AA's program of recovery. In response, Bill went through the text and changed the pronoun "you" to "we," and the "musts" to "ought" or "should." Concerns about the reception the book might receive in medical circles were addressed by "The Doctor's Opinion," an endorsement supplied by Dr. Silkworth, who had by this time published an article on AA in a Philadelphia medical journal entitled the *Medical Record*.

The book does not include an endorsement from religion. Dr. Henry Emerson Fosdick, highly regarded minister of Riverside Church and close associate of John D. Rockefeller, Jr., was willing to provide one. Already fearful that the book's religious overtones would provoke condemnation by the Catholic Church, Bill did not want to give Catholics anything else to object to.

The Catholic response was actually better than anticipated. Morgan R., a newly sober member, gave the manuscript to the publications committee for the New York Archdiocese of the Roman Catholic Church. (Morgan knew someone on the committee.) The archdiocese's response was highly positive. Upon reading the manuscript's characterization of the life alcoholics could find through AA as "heavenlike," one committee member laughingly reminded Morgan that this was something the Church was promising Catholics much later in the journey. Although the comment seemed lighthearted, Bill decided not to take any chances, and the reference to heaven was cut.

The prepublication copies were themselves responsible for two recoveries. A young man in California read the manuscript and stopped drinking. He was the first alcoholic to stay sober solely by following the program as it was outlined in the book. The man's letter describing his experience was so powerful that Bill obtained his permission to include it in the published manuscript.

Marty Mann, the first woman member to achieve lasting sobriety, also stopped drinking as a result of reading one of these prepublication copies. Marty was a patient at Blythewood Sanitarium in Greenwich, Connecticut, and Dr. Harry Tiebout, a psychiatrist at Blythewood, had received one. Her initial response to Tiebout's attempts to get her to read the manuscript included throwing it out the window, but after a while, she did read it. Then, in the middle of a rage so all-consuming she was literally seeing red, the words "we cannot live with anger" seemed to stand out on a page of the manuscript, and the rage left her. She felt free of it, and of the need to drink as well. Marty would go on to help hundreds of women find sobriety in AA. She also founded the National Council on Alcoholism and Drug Dependencies.

The manuscript's last stop before publication was the desk of Tom Uzzell, a friend of Hank P's. Uzzell was an editor at *Collier's*, at the time a very popular magazine, and he taught writing at New York University. Bill asked him to settle the controversy over the title, and he enthusiastically approved *Alcoholics Anonymous*, the title Bill had long favored. Uzzell's professional opinion served to put an end to the debate about which of the more than a hundred suggested titles should be used. (Among them were *One Hundred Men, The Empty Glass,* and *The Way Out.*)

Bill also left a number of other controversies for Uzzell to settle: according to various reports, the manuscript Bill gave him was at least six hundred, and perhaps as much as eight hundred, pages long. The manuscript that emerged from under his pencil was four hundred pages. Most of the cuts came from the personal stories, which had already been edited by Bill and Hank in New York and by Jim S., a member who was also a journalist, in Akron. The use of an outsider, who could be said to have both the professional skills and the objectivity that might be lacking in a member, was a technique Bill would employ in later AA writings, as well.

The book finally went to press in April 1939. By then, though, the money Works Publishing had raised was gone. The printer, Cornwall Press, was persuaded to set the type on the strength of a five-hundred-dollar down payment, but loans had to be secured from a member who owned his own tailor shop and Fitz M.'s sister before Cornwall would release the finished volumes from its warehouse. For a long time after the book was published, Bill and the others had reason to wonder why they had bothered: it didn't sell.

The *Reader's Digest* editor seemed not to remember his earlier conversation with Hank and Bill, and no article was forthcoming. Almost simultaneously with the publication of the *Big Book,* the Wilsons were evicted from their home. Now they had no home, no money, and almost no work. They were so poor they often fell behind on the twenty-dollar monthly storage bill for their furniture. Even so, Bill would later say that these were the happiest years of his life.

The book may not have been selling, but there were some small victories on the AA front. The fellowship was still growing, and more people were getting sober on the strength of the book alone. Harry Emerson Fosdick wrote a glowing review, and its appearance in religious journals and other religious publications garnered AA some extremely positive recognition. Even so, virtually no books were sold. Then Morgan R., an old friend of the radio personality Gabriel Heatter, got himself on Heatter's nationally broadcast program.

The show was one of the most popular in the country, and Heatter was going to interview Morgan about his alcoholism and his subsequent recovery in AA. By way of assuring that they would receive the maximum result from the broadcast, Hank P. came up with the idea of a mailing to doctors. The money to pay for the mailing was solicited from two well-off newer members, who received promissory notes from Works Publishing, signed by Hank and Bill, in return for their five hundred dollars. All the doctors east of the Mississippi were sent information about the upcoming broadcast and asked to buy a copy of the book.

The interview came off without a hitch, and expectations for what the show would produce couldn't have been higher. When, several days after the broadcast, Bill and Hank went to the post office box to which Heatter had urged his audience to make their inquiries, they brought along empty suitcases to collect the responses. To their astonishment, there were only twelve replies, and only two of them were book orders.

Both Hank and Bill were certainly capable of great enthusiasms and grand visions, and they were willing to work prodigiously hard to realize them. Even today, one can hardly imagine physicians responding to a solicitation to purchase a book written by a nonprofessional purporting to offer a cure for alcoholism. With all the doctors Bill and Bob Smith knew, it surely would have been possible to determine in advance the likelihood of such an approach succeeding, but there is no evidence that such research was undertaken.

On June 25, 1939, *Alcoholics Anonymous* received a favorable review in the *New York Times*, but it didn't sell any books. Unlike perhaps 99 percent of the books the *Times* reviews, the *Big Book* wasn't available in bookstores. Perhaps because the self-publishing venture was in large measure motivated by the fellowship's desire to control its own literature, no effort seems to have been made to obtain distribution to bookstores. Then Charlie Towns convinced Morris Markey, a feature writer of his acquaintance, to do a piece on AA.

Markey's article became AA's first successful attempt at publicity. He sold the article to Fulton Oursler, who at the time was the editor of *Lib-*

erty, a popular magazine with a religious orientation. Oursler later went on to write a number of successful books on religion. He also became a good friend of Bill's and served as a trustee of the Alcoholic Foundation. The article appeared in the September issue of *Liberty,* and it generated hundreds of inquiries from around the country. This time, about 350 books were sold.

In October, the Cleveland *Plain Dealer* ran the first of a series of articles on AA, backed with editorials praising the organization. Clarence S., a Clevelander who had been a member of the Akron group, had started Cleveland's first group in May of that year. Clarence's story appears in the *Big Book* under the title "The Home Brewmeister." The *Plain Dealer* articles produced hundreds of responses in the greater Cleveland area, and within a year there were several hundred alcoholics staying sober through AA in Cleveland. In February 1940, reviews in *Newsweek* and *Time* also produced some inquiries and sales, though they remained modest.

HOMELESS

By the time the Cleveland articles appeared, the Wilsons had been six months without a home. As hard as it was on them, even their homelessness produced good things for AA. The Wilsons' first move after Clinton Street was to Hank's home in nearby New Jersey. The AA meeting that had begun in their Brooklyn home was transferred to Hank's house, and by the time Bill and Lois had moved on, there were AA meetings in Montclair and South Orange. The Wilsons' stay with AA friends Meg and Bob V. in Monsey, New York, produced an AA meeting there as well. It also attracted the interest of Russell E. Blaisdale, M.D., a psychiatrist who was the director of nearby Rockland State Hospital.

Until the advent of Alcoholics Anonymous, the patient populations of most mental hospitals included many people whose primary diagnosis was alcoholism. Dr. Blaisdale let AA members come into Rockland to work with patients, and he let patients leave the hospital to attend the AA meeting in Monsey. Soon a bus was also taking Rockland State patients to AA meetings in Montclair, South Orange, and New York City. By December 1939, Rockland State had become the first mental hospital to have its own AA group.

Bill remembered this period with great cheer, and Lois always spoke of the excitement and joy with which they greeted each small success, but it was very hard on them. Lois also wrote about the day in February 1940 when she sat down on one of the marble staircases in Grand Central Terminal and cried her eyes out. She and Bill had been crossing the terminal's great concourse, en route to temporary shelter at the home of yet another AA acquaintance, and the woman whom nothing had ever been able to stop suddenly found that she was incapable of going on. The precipitating event actually occurred a day or so earlier, when Lois had come home to their latest temporary dwelling place and was greeted by the sight of her husband eating cold tomato soup straight from the can.

As they sat on the steps of Grand Central, Bill had all he could do to keep from crying, too. In time, they got up and boarded their train, but only after resolving that from then on, wherever fate deposited them, they would spend at least some time looking for a home of their own. They still had no money, and no way of ever realizing what by this time seemed like an impossible dream for this once prosperous couple with solid, upper-middle-class roots. After that, everywhere they went they consulted with real estate agents and looked at apartments and houses.

By December 1940, the Wilsons, still no closer to a home of their own, were renting a room barely big enough to hold a double bed above AA's first clubhouse on East Twenty-fourth Street. There were actually two rooms above the clubhouse, but the other was occupied by the club's AA caretaker, a "down and outer" recently released from Rockland State. Dependent as they were for shelter and clothing on such charity as friends and AA members were able to extend, Bill and Lois were about a half step from being down and outers themselves.

The positive energy Lois was able to put forth under these circumstances is remarkable. She tailored the clothes people gave them so that they fit properly and didn't seem too out of style, and she somehow found the strength to make the best of their room. Even with the walls and woodwork painted in cheery colors and the curtains she made for the window and the front of the orange crates that served as their dressers, it was a wretched existence. As far as Lois was concerned, the worst thing about it was exactly what many members liked best about the arrangement: because this wasn't their home but AA's first clubhouse, they were considered available to meet the needs of others twenty-four hours a day, seven days a week.

By the end of 1940, Hank P. was drinking in earnest. The man who had so enjoyed being sober had started drinking the year before, after more than four years without a drink. Hank had been the first alcoholic in New York to respond to Bill's efforts, and he was the virtual cofounder of the New York contingent and one of Bill's closest friends.

With the book written, the collapse of Honor Dealers could no longer be postponed. Hank's return to drink was preceded by a period of increasing anger, depression, and paranoia, during which his life fell apart. He took a job in western New Jersey he didn't want, and his alienation from Bill and the others seems to have begun when he tried to take the Alcoholic Foundation's office, and Ruth Hock, with him. Ruth didn't want to go, and no one wanted to see the office moved.

A confrontation with Works Publishing stockholders soon followed. As an executive in a major oil company, Hank had become accustomed to a very good life, but his years of sobriety were haunted by financial desperation. Hank had been in charge of Works Publishing's finances, and when he was called upon to make an accounting, he was unable to produce any records to indicate where the money had gone. Precisely how it was spent isn't known, but the most likely scenario is that no clear lines were drawn between Honor Dealers, Works Publishing, and Alcoholic Foundation expenses, or even between expenses Hank incurred in conjunction with his Works Publishing activities and his personal ones. Certainly, some blurring of lines must have occurred in respect to Ruth Hock.

During this period, Ruth was Hank's mistress. In addition to having an intimate relationship with Hank, Ruth was simultaneously working for Honor Dealers, Works Publishing, and the Alcoholic Foundation, which were all headquartered in the same office. Fearful that whatever he had managed to achieve for himself since stopping drinking was about to slip away, Hank began lying. He even tried to explain the absence of records by claiming that someone had broken into the office and stolen the books.

Bill and other members Hank had been close to tried to talk to him, but Hank's response was simply to withdraw further. His relapse was a great shock to everyone who knew him, but no one was more affected by it than Bill. Even after reports began to come to him that Hank was drinking, he seems not to have really believed it. When one day he discovered Hank soused to the gills, it shook him to the core.

Ebby had gotten drunk, too, but Ebby got sober through the Oxford Group, and he was never involved in a meaningful way in helping Bill to realize his vision. Ebby also got drunk after moving back to Albany, not right under Bill's nose. Powerless to stop it, Wilson had to bear witness to the emotional deterioration that preceded Hank's return to alcohol. Also, Ebby had been sober two years, seven months, not four years. Until Hank's relapse, it seems likely that neither Bill nor the other members thought someone who had so thoroughly made the program his life for four years *could* get drunk again.

Bill was a very loyal friend, and he tried repeatedly to reach out to Hank, but as far as Hank was concerned, Bill was too much a part of the problem to ever again be associated with the solution. As Hank saw it, the controversies surrounding Works Publishing, the breakup of his affair with Ruth Hock, whom he had hoped to marry, his messy divorce from his wife, Kathleen, and moving the foundation office from Newark to New York all had Bill's fingerprints on them.

Hank felt unfairly scapegoated in the publishing venture, which had, of course, proceeded with Bill's knowledge and participation. He also felt that Bill was at least partly responsible both for Ruth's rejecting him and the failure of his marriage. But while others may have felt Hank to be more responsible than Bill for the publishing venture's excesses, there's no evidence that Bill ever acquiesced in this view or tried to play down his own role. Bill also seems to have had nothing to do with Ruth's deciding to end the affair.

As for Hank's divorce, if his affair with Ruth weren't reason enough for his wife to want leave him, there was also his violent temper. Dr. Silkworth regarded Hank as potentially dangerous even before he started drinking again, and when Hank got drunk, Bill and Lois heeded the doctor's opinion and moved from the state of New Jersey, so that Lois could avoid being subpoenaed to testify for Kathleen in Hank's divorce. Bill was in favor of moving the Alcoholic Foundation's office to New York, but he was hardly alone in this, and Hank's drinking was itself a prime motive for wanting to put as much distance as possible between him and the Alcoholic Foundation.

Losing Hank's support and friendship was a terrible blow, but Bill was to endure much worse from his former business partner and AA stalwart. Hank's bitterness over Bill's imagined role in his disintegration was such that he seemed to go on a campaign to discredit Bill. Traveling to Cleveland, he actually accused him, at a time when Bill was homeless and frequently unable to pay storage charges on his furniture, of getting rich off his Rockefeller connection. Baseless as the charge was, it was exactly the sort of thing Clarence S., Hank's brother-in-law and the founder of the first Cleveland Group, was only too ready to hear. Clarence spent many years putting himself forward as the true founder of AA. He also spent years bedeviling the AA office, and Bill personally, about imagined financial irregularities.

Hank's behavior, and later Clarence's, was not only hurtful to Bill, it was also deeply divisive to AA. Bill's reaction to all this is a sterling example of how deeply he had absorbed one aspect of the First Century Christianity lauded by the Oxford Group: he simply refused to fight. Instead, Bill did all he could to keep the door open to Hank. He also went to Cleveland frequently to visit Clarence, and Clarence was often an invited guest at Stepping Stones. Although Clarence was never really to recant on either his charges against Bill or his claim to have been the true founder of AA, Bill always maintained a cordial relationship with him.

19

ALONE

Bill handled Hank's loss, and the turmoil that followed it, with sensitivity and finesse, but the events clearly took their toll. Soon it was evident that he, too, was moving away from the fellowship. By the beginning of 1940, the one hundred members who had published the *Big Book* had become eight hundred, and by October there were more than fourteen hundred members and AA groups in more than forty cities, but Bill wasn't very good at giving himself credit for any of this. He focused instead on the fact that the fellowship wasn't growing at the speed he and the others had expected and the speed he and Bob Smith desperately needed it to, if royalties from book sales were ever to provide them with a decent living.

His father and both his grandfathers had been financially successful. His father had ceased to provide for him after his parents divorced, but his maternal grandfather, the only man his mother seems to have fully approved of, had been an excellent provider. This wasn't something that could ever be said of Bill, and it bothered him terribly. Even when he was making large sums on Wall Street, he spent money with so little thought to the future that the Crash left the Wilsons worse off than they had ever been.

Apartments were plentiful and cheap in New York during the Depression. It was so much a renter's market that it was common for landlords to offer such incentives as several months' rent free in order to attract tenants. Yet, by the end of 1940, the Wilsons had been more than a year and a half without a home, and an end to their plight was not forthcoming. It seemed more than time for Bill to become "just another member," one with a job, maybe even a career, but there was also something else behind his decision to seek employment.

Lois's family home on Clinton Street had been more than the first AA meeting place. It was a comfort stop that included beds, meals, maid service, and shoulders to cry on. When Bill and Lois were forced to move at the end of April in 1939, the New York membership seemed unanimous in its desire to have Bill available to meet their needs on a full-time basis. To this end, a "Bill and Lois Improvement Fund" was established, but the name makes it sound like more than it was. Although a hat was passed for their benefit at the end of the meetings they attended, most often the yield was pitiful. Neither Bill nor Lois ever complained about the lack of support, but Lois said later that it was very, very hard on them both, and she thought that it was especially hard on Bill.

In the summer of 1939, Bill wrote a letter to the Guggenheim Foundation appealing for a three-thousand-dollar grant for Robert Smith, saying that he didn't see how Smith could go on without it. The request has been seen by some as a sterling example of the kind of selflessness Bill was capable of, but what's more likely is that, recalling his experience with Frank Amos, he felt that Bob's was the stronger case. If he succeeded in obtaining help for Smith, he may have hoped that, as had been the case with the Rockefeller people, his own efforts would be recognized as well. The appeal failed, as it might have been expected to, since the Guggenheim Foundation's resources are dedicated to aiding the arts, but the rejection still contributed to Bill's feeling unappreciated.

Bill had wanted to go back to work ever since *Alcoholics Anonymous* was finished. He held out through the summer of 1939, hoping that something would happen with the book. When nothing had by fall, he decided to cut back on his availability to AA and find full-time employment. The New York membership responded to this news by writing him a letter expressing their heartfelt gratitude for all he had done. While acknowledging that their debt to him hardly gave them the right to ask more, they implored him not to become just "another member," characterizing the impact the loss of his leadership would have on the fellowship as nothing less than disastrous. There were more than fifty signatures; virtually every sober alcoholic in New York had signed.

Bill acquiesced. Being asked to remain at his post was deeply gratifying, and the New York members pledged to do whatever they could to ease his financial strain. When the hat went around, though, nothing had changed. All this made the response to Rollie Hemsley's anonymity breaks that much harder to take. A major league baseball player from Cleveland, Rollie in the spring of 1940 went public about his AA membership. As the baseball season unfolded, newspapers and magazines articles and radio interviews about his miraculous transformation accompanied his travels around the country. By fall, he seemed to have attained the status of a national hero.

Rollie was appreciated, and in spades. What's more, the gobs of publicity for AA produced new members and new groups. If a baseball player could get so much credit for stopping drinking, why not a stock analyst? Especially if it was the stock analyst who was responsible for the rest of them getting sober. As Bill later told it, he started giving interviews and making public appearances in response to what Rollie was doing. Headlines were generated, and throughout the early 1940s, Bill enjoyed the attention.

But it was actually a couple of years after Rollie went public that Bill first broke his anonymity, and Bill exaggerated both the number of breaks and the length of time during which he allowed his full name and photograph to be used in conjunction with his AA activities. Bill's recollection of the matter later may have been a reflection of his state of mind in 1940. Perhaps the biggest objection AA members have to anonymity breaks is the way it sets apart people who break their anonymity from the rest of the fellowship. It seems more than a coincidence that during the time Bill recalled breaking his anonymity, distanced was very much the way he was feeling.

Bill Wilson had had a lot to say on the importance of anonymity, but now he seemed to be saying "anonymity for you, but not for me." He answered the objections by saying that he wasn't doing it for himself, but for the greater good of the greater number. The others weren't buying it, though, and they seem to have been right. Most AA members would still agree that anonymity is Alcoholic's Anonymous's most essential underpinning, even though anonymity breaks have become so common that the *New York Times,* once among the most consistently cooperative media outlet on the issue, seems to reveal AA affiliation as a matter of routine.

Although Bill later admitted the error of his ways, the criticism didn't make him feel any better about the way things were working out between him and the organization he had founded. By June 1940, the *Big Book* still wasn't selling enough to offer the prospect of an adequate royalty income. With the Rockefeller dinner and the solicitation that followed behind them, it seemed clear that neither the Smiths nor the Wilsons were going to receive major financial assistance from the wealthy.

Bill took a job as a wholesaler's representative for a firm that sold rope. He tried all summer to make inroads for his product with the maritime industry in Brooklyn, but he was a miserable failure. He just couldn't make the transition from helping people rebuild shattered lives to selling a product he knew little about to an industry about which he knew even less.

As time passed, the contrast between the words of grateful appreciation constantly being heaped upon him and the poverty in which he was forced to live became increasingly unbearable. Bill may have been disappointed and impatient about the pace at which AA was growing, but it *was* growing, and the bigger it became, the fewer were the number of people who would tell him he was wrong.

Although Bill was still in great demand, by the fall of 1940, Bill's alienation was profound. Whenever he spoke, he had always talked about whatever was on his mind, and now his remarks sometimes had a very negative and angry tone. After a talk in Baltimore in which he put major emphasis on the horrors and isolation of the alcoholic, a young clergyman told him that the gloom seemed overdone. Why, the man wondered, wasn't he placing more emphasis on the positive?

Bill had to wonder, himself. He could feel himself slipping down further and further. Just as he had thought, after his spiritual experience, that he was permanently immune to the desire to drink, he had also thought that his awakening marked the end of his battles with depression. His sudden conversion experience had brought about a release of energy that had carried him along for six years, but now that energy was ebbing, and there didn't seem to be anything he could do about it.

He didn't, of course, need to guess as to what might happen next. Hank had provided a roadmap. Bill hadn't yet isolated himself from the other members the way Hank had, but neither was he talking to anyone about what was troubling him. With Hank gone, though, who was there to talk to? Fitz M. would just tell him to pray, and he could hardly go crying to Smithy, who was enduring the same difficulties he was and more: the Smiths had children to support. As for Lois, more than anything, Bill wanted to keep what was happening to him from her. She had so wanted him to be well, and she had given so much of herself to that end. How could he disappoint her—again?

Along with his growing awareness of the shape he was in and how powerless he was to do anything about it came a new appreciation for his position vis-à-vis the program he had created. To his dismay, AA seemed to have become an organization that could help everyone but him.

THE ONE-WAY STREET

The Great Depression notwithstanding, that Bill Wilson should be forced to live like this hardly seems credible. The only possible explanation seems to be that somehow people just didn't realize how bad off the Wilsons were. When we look at how this could be, given the starkness of the evidence, we get to the essence of Bill's relationship to Alcoholics Anonymous.

It is significant that he referred to his own story of recovery, which he was expected to relate virtually every time he spoke, as the "bedtime story." He had been sober longer than anyone and he had just written a book that painted life after stopping drinking the AA way in the most glowing terms. For the other members, believing the program's promises was essential to feeling equal to the challenges in their own lives. Bill was supposed to be the ultimate source of reassurance.

No matter how bad off he may have been, there was never anyone available to tuck Bill Wilson into bed, filled with hopefulness, his belief in the miracle of recovery restored. Never anyone who could truly register how far he could be, physically, mentally and spiritually, from the recovery miracle he was supposed to be the prime example of. Bill was not only expected to always be there for them, he was supposed to *want* to do it. John D. Rockefeller, Jr., thought that AA members were practicing First Century Christianity because of their empathic response to the sufferings of others. As the founder and, even in 1939 and 1940, someone who was sober years longer than most of them, Bill's role was to be the prince of empathy.

Father Edward Dowling, an aging, lame Jesuit from St. Louis, relieved Wilson's deepening spiral of despair. Dowling's climbing the stairs to the Wilsons' room over the AA clubhouse has been characterized as an angel coming in out of the dark, cold, and rainy night. Bill was lying on the bed in their tiny room. Lois wasn't home, and he was so depressed that he was having a recurrence of the psychosomatic stomach complaints that had plagued him after the death of his high school sweetheart.

Dowling's coming to Bill at this moment had nothing to do with any awareness of his situation. In the spring, an alcoholic the priest had been trying to help had invited him to attend an AA meeting in Chicago. Dowling was favorably impressed. He purchased a copy of the *Big Book*, and he was struck by the parallels between the AA Steps and the Spiritual Exercises of St. Ignatius Loyola, essential components of Jesuit ideology.

Father Dowling wrote the AA office in New York, enclosing a dollar for any additional literature it might be able to send him that would be of help in writing an article about the program for a Catholic newsletter he edited. By the time church business brought him to New York and he had taken the opportunity to investigate AA at its source, Father Dowling had started the first AA group in St. Louis.

When the club's janitor told Bill there was "some bum from St. Louis" downstairs, he hardly expected anything good to come from the encounter. Dowling, on the other hand, couldn't have been more excited at the prospect of meeting a civilian with such a profound understanding of the basic principles underlying his own way of life. When Bill admitted that he had never even heard of the Spiritual Exercises, the priest wasn't discouraged in the least: for him, Bill's having arrived at his understandings from a different route only seemed to confirm that he was an extraordinary man.

Wilson was hardly in the mood to be flattered. He responded by giving the priest the full benefit of his view of what life at the top was really like. After listing his complaints, Bill asked (some thirty years before the Rolling Stones) whether he was ever to get any satisfaction, and Father Dowling answered, "No. Never!" In the shape he was in, Bill found the priest's certainty astounding, but Dowling was merely elucidating a central tenet of Christianity (or any moral system) that extols selflessness: virtue must be its own reward; we cannot expect any satisfaction for doing what we know we must.

This was the life he had been trying to lead since his awakening. It is doubtful that at first Bill was much cheered by the priest's message. But the realization that the program he had created had the power to bring this priest to him out of the night, filled with the sort of enthusiasm for helping drunks that had gone out of his own efforts, was restorative. As the evening wore on, it became clear to Bill that in the priest he had found someone to whom he could speak freely and be understood. Dowling's very presence seemed like a much-needed reward for his efforts.

At the time Bill met Father Ed Dowling, he had already come to know Harry Tiebout, the psychiatrist at Blythewood Sanitarium who had given the manuscript of the *Big Book* to Marty Mann. Tiebout is thought to be the first psychiatrist to incorporate the AA view of alcoholism into his practice. He also wrote a number of seminal articles for medical journals, exploring from the psychiatric viewpoint the theoretical underpinnings of the AA process of recovery.

Harry Tiebout was an enthusiastic supporter of AA and a good friend of Bill Wilson's. They had had many conversations about the psychology of addiction, but at this point Wilson was not interested in psychotherapy. According to Robert Thomsen, an earlier biographer, Bill later said that "there was no way to describe what Ed [Dowling] did for him, the doors he flung open before him. After absorbing the impact of their first encounter, he awakened to a new reality, a totally altered view of himself and his place in the world. And with this he felt he was entering a new relationship with AA."

Wilson came to refer to Father Dowling as his "spiritual" sponsor. According to Lois, the potential double entendre was indeed intentional. As the priest had on the night they first met, he seemed charged with the task of lifting Bill's spirits as much as with counselling him on spiritual matters.

Eventually, Father Dowling did write his article on AA, which constituted the first Catholic endorsement of the fellowship. Dowling also wrote many other articles on the subject of Alcoholics Anonymous, and he worked tirelessly to promote awareness and acceptance of AA by the

Catholic Church, as well as personally counseling a great many alcoholics. In time, alcoholics he had helped started AA groups in cities throughout Missouri and Iowa. And through it all, he was a good friend to Bill Wilson, someone who was always willing to listen and offer encouragement, sympathy, and advice. Perhaps most important, he was the kind of friend AA's "head man" had found to be in short supply: Ed Dowling never wanted anything from him in return.

RENEWAL

Much as Grandfather Griffith's interest in opening an automobile dealership had helped to end an earlier depression, meeting Ed Dowling seems to have gotten Bill going again, and the timing couldn't have been better. The big publicity break everyone had been hoping for was about to occur: The *Saturday Evening Post* had assigned a reporter to do a feature story on Alcoholics Anonymous. The *Post* was the largest general circulation magazine in the country, and it had learned about AA in perhaps the best possible way. Jimmy B., the New York member who suggested the phrase "God as we understand Him," had moved to Philadelphia in February 1940 to take a new job. Before he left, Bill gave him the names of several Philadelphia alcoholics who had purchased *Big Books*, and Philadelphia soon had its own AA group.

The group quickly came to the attention of Dr. A. Weise Hammer, a prominent Philadelphia surgeon whose enthusiasm for AA has seldom been equaled. Hammer introduced AA to Philadelphia General Hospital. With the endorsement of Dr. John Stoufer, chief of psychiatry, and Dr. William G. Turnbull, the hospital's superintendent, it wasn't long before inpatient care and a clinic for alcoholics were established. Dr. Hammer and Dr. C. Dudley Saul, chief physician at Philadelphia's St. Luke's and Children's Hospital, also introduced AA to a friend of theirs: Judge Curtis Bok, one of the owners of the Curtis Publishing Company, the *Post's* parent corporation.

When Bill had first learned of the *Post's* interest, he was elated. He saw immediately that a *Post* article could unleash on a national scale the kind of explosive growth the *Plain Dealer* series had created in Cleveland. However, by the evening of Father Dowling's visit, he was so far down that the prospect meant little to him.

Nevertheless, the Bill Wilson that *Post* reporter Jack Alexander came to know over the next several months was AA's "poster boy" at his best. Although Alexander had approached the assignment with a high degree of skepticism, he was totally charmed and, like the Rockefeller men, was soon numbered among AA's staunchest supporters. Alexander wrote a highly favorable article and a second, equally positive, piece about the fellowship some nine years later. He also wrote articles for the *Grapevine*,

AA's monthly magazine, helped Bill edit the AA book *Twelve Steps and Twelve Traditions,* and served a stint as a member of AA's board of trustees.

As Wilson took Alexander first around New York and then around the country, so that the reporter could come to know AA in various locales, his own enthusiasm for the progress AA was making was renewed. Nevertheless, by January, he was again looking for a job, this time as a fundraiser for the American Bureau for Aid to China. In the letter he wrote to the director of the organization listing his qualifications, Bill referred to the upcoming *Post* story as evidence of his ability to attract favorable attention to a cause, and he enclosed a copy of the article. That he was still looking for a job after having seen the glowing article Alexander had written, which was scheduled to be published in February, is cause to wonder whether he'd had second thoughts about the impact it would have.

While Bill later talked about the response to the article as though it had caught AA unaware, this is another example of his willingness to modify the facts to make a better story. Well before the article's anticipated publication date, Lois was organizing anyone who could type into squads and scheduling those who couldn't to answer telephones, in preparation for the expected deluge. When the publication date was pushed back, the extra time was used to become better prepared: by the end of the month, Lois had even typed up a formal "Plan of Action."

The key to why Bill was looking for work may be the letter he wrote to his father a few days before getting in touch with the American Bureau for Aid to China. Although he had had little contact with him in years, he seems to have learned that his father was suffering financially. In fact, with the Depression having brought building virtually to a halt, and the quarry business along with it, for what seems to have been the first time in his life, Gilman was truly in need. Bill enclosed some money with the letter that, given his own financial state, he must have borrowed from someone, and he promised to provide further assistance in the future.

Bill hadn't seen his father since they were both in Florida at the same time in 1927. Gilman was cutting rock for the Overseas Highway linking the Florida Keys to the mainland, and Bill had just returned from Cuba, where his drinking had prevented him from learning anything of value about the sugar industry. Gilman Wilson had always worked as a quarryman. Since leaving his family, he had spent most of his time in Canada, and in 1941 he was living in a small town in Alberta.

Bill wrote him a very positive letter, minimizing the suffering he had experienced as an active alcoholic and painting a bright picture for the future of AA, which he acknowledged himself to be the founder of. Bill characterized the money he was enclosing "as a small token of gratitude." Whatever pain his father's behavior after the divorce had caused him seems to have been overcome by Bill's desire for a family. It was something he would pursue the rest of his life. He even arranged to have his father and his father's second wife, his half-sister, Helen, and his mother buried in the same family plot in the cemetery in East Dorset, where he and Lois would be buried.

Bill's desire to be of financial assistance to his father and Christine, his step-mother, may have been the reason he was looking for work. Given the controversy bubbling about the price of the book and the supposed riches flowing into his pockets, he may have felt that even if the *Post* article had the impact he anticipated, his royalties would not be enough for him to be able to support them.

In March, even before the full impact of the *Post* story could be known, Bill felt compelled to write an open letter to the fellowship outlining the compensation he had received in the prior year. What is perhaps most interesting about this is that in 1940 the groups were not yet contributing to support the work of the Alcoholic Foundation and the AA office. Beyond purchasing copies of the *Big Book*, the people who were demanding an accounting of his personal income could not be considered to have been contributing to it.

Stressing that the money came from outside sources (John D. Rockefeller, Jr., and his dinner guests), Bill reported his salary as $120.00 a month. His AA income in 1940 included $500.00 from Works Publishing, which was 20 percent of the $2,500.00 the Alcoholic Foundation had acknowledged as due him from the sale of the *Big Book*. Bill also listed $100.00 the foundation gave him toward the past-due balance on the storage for his furniture and $75.00 it gave him to pay a dentist's bill, making his income from the Alcoholic Foundation $675.00. His total income in 1940 from AA and Rockefeller sources combined was $2,115.00, which would be about $24,000.00 today.

The $500 from *Big Book* proceeds, like the money paid for his dental work and the overdue storage charges on his furniture, were funds received to relieve conditions of extreme duress. While reference had been made to Bob Smith and Bill receiving "author's royalties" from *Big Book* sales, the terms hadn't been fixed, and the foundation didn't have enough money to pay him (or Dr. Bob), run the office and meet the expenses of the foundation.

While it had its humiliating aspects, the open letter did quiet some of the concern about Bill's possibly taking advantage of his position as AA's penultimate leader to line his pockets, but the relief was short-lived. In his letter to Bureau for Aid to China, he cited, as evidence of his ability to convince people to part with their money, his success with Pennick and Ford, the small company whose stock he had been manipulating. He did not mention, of course, that most of them were wiped out in the 1929 Crash. Bill also mentioned John D. Rockefeller, Jr., and the other wealthy men who attended the Rockefeller dinner for AA, but he didn't reveal that they were only supporting AA to the extent of about three thousand dollars a year.

Even with these omissions, he didn't get the job, but when word got around that the letter had included a copy of the *Post* article and made reference to his role in AA and his Rockefeller connection, he was accused of "using the program for personal gain." There are still AA members who think Bill should not have made mention of his AA work. But since he had devoted virtually all his time and energy to trying to help alcoholics for more than six years, not to make reference to AA would mean leaving the most recent six years of his résumé blank. This is tantamount to insisting that he must depend solely on whatever compensation the fellowship was willing to provide him.

That Bill should acquiesce in Father Ed Dowling's "never!" to such an extent wasn't what most AA members wanted for their founder. It might not have been what any of them wanted, had they fully understood the implications of their objections. One of the great strengths of AA has been the willingness of the majority of its members to accommodate the concerns of the minority, in the interest of preserving AA unity. It was a principle Bill believed in wholeheartedly, and even though it was many years before royalty payments provided him with an adequate income, he never again sought other employment until after he had officially retired from his role as AA's "head man."

ON THE MAP

The *Saturday Evening Post* article, titled "Alcoholics Anonymous" but known in AA circles as the "Jack Alexander" article, was published in the magazine's March 1, 1941, issue. Unlike the fellowship's previous media hits, this time the response exceeded anyone's wildest expectations. Within days, meeting attendance doubled. Within weeks, these newcomers were being sent out on Twelve Step calls to other prospects. Answering the letters and telegrams that poured in kept AA secretaries Ruth Hock and Bobbie Berger, along with Lois and her volunteers, busy day and night for the next five or six weeks. Between October 1940 and the end of February 1941, the membership had grown from fourteen hundred to two thousand. By the end of 1941, AA boasted eight thousand members.

The response was due in part to the vastness of the *Post's* readership, but it was also because the article couldn't have been more favorable if Bill had written it himself. It so well conveys the spirit of the fellowship, and it so clearly and succinctly describes what AA is and what it does, that it could well serve as a condensed version of the *Big Book*. This may be why, nearly sixty years later, Alcoholics Anonymous is still reprinting the Jack Alexander article as a booklet.

The article gives the impression that AA's 2,000 members in 50 cities were 200,000 members in 500 cities. It describes a membership dominated by Main Street's, if not society's, movers and shakers. The professions represented include lawyers, engineers, salesmen, insurance men, buyers, manufacturers' reps, advertising executives, publicists, newspaper editors and reporters, and retail store managers. The reader is given the impression that all of them have left behind lives of ruin and are now enormously successful.

John D. Rockefeller, Jr., is credited with helping to defer AA's start-up expenses and having "gone out of his way to get other prominent men interested." The Oxford Group, which by this time had fallen badly out of public favor, is mentioned only as the milieu that brought AA's cofounders together. They are said to have quickly withdrawn from the Oxford Group because of "its aggressive evangelism," thereby nicely making a distinction between AA and OG on this point.

That AA was itself not a religion was driven home by characterizing its belief in a "higher power" requirement as something that could be satisfied by a belief in one's "Inner Self." If this seemed too difficult, believing in "the miracle of growth, a tree, man's wonderment at the physical universe, the structure of the atom, or mere mathematical infinity" would also do. To further make it clear that AA posed no threat, the article states that most AA members raised in an organized religion become "regular communicants" again.

Except for Dr. Bob, no doctors are described as members for fear of alienating a profession the fellowship was still trying hard to win over as advocates for the AA approach. Yet the many quotes from and references to endorsements by physicians and psychiatrists make it seem as though AA already had achieved the level of acceptance by the medical community it would not attain until many years later. The article states that AA's success rate is 100 percent with all "non-psychotics" who sincerely want to stop drinking. As Alexander portrayed it, getting sober and staying sober the AA way is a pleasant and struggle-free experience, with relapse virtually unknown and no mention of suicide or of any strife either within the fellowship or in the families of its members.

Alcoholics Anonymous is described as a strictly voluntary affair, "self-operating and self-multiplying," and there is no indication that anyone in the medical profession or the clergy has had a role in starting groups or recruiting members. Bill and Bob are identified only by pseudonyms, and their roles are greatly deemphasized, as is that of the New York office and the Alcoholic Foundation, and there is no mention of the role the Rockefeller men were still playing in AA affairs. The dire financial plight of its founders is alluded to, but the impression is given that there is no longer much for them to do. They are described as anxious to move "to the fringe of their movement" so that they can concentrate on meeting their own needs.

Perhaps the most unexpected thing about the article, given its many omissions, exaggerations, and elisions, is how well it succeeds in capturing the true flavor of the organization. The piece conveys wonderfully the excitement of salvaging wasted lives and the joy and energy released by the lifting of the obsession with alcohol. The bond of goodwill based on shared experience between members and between sober alcoholics and those who still suffer is vividly portrayed. The positive environment AA provides, complete with a social milieu, focus, purpose, and a system of rewards is all there. The reader can readily understand why AA members feel good about not drinking.

That Bill was able to have the story go so much AA's way is a coup that would make the career of any PR flack. Jack Alexander was no pushover. He was, on the contrary, one of the *Post's* top reporters. As Alexander later described it, upon first encountering AA, he found it too good to be true and Bill Wilson too good to be true as well. To Alexander, Wilson seemed too open and honest. He was sure there had to be a catch. But the reporter's skepticism was no match for Bill, who by this time had had more than six years' experience convincing skeptical drunks that both he and AA were for real.

Jack Alexander's initial contact with the fellowship began with four members, well-dressed, successful professionals handpicked by Wilson, who called on the reporter at his home. Alexander met Bill Wilson for the first time the next day, and Bill seems to have been by his side throughout the rest of Alexander's tour of the fellowship. He saw what Bill wanted him to see, in the light Bill wanted him to see it. By the end of the tour, Alexander had been thoroughly converted. As the article took shape, the correspondence between Jack Alexander and Bill suggest that the reporter had come to see himself as having been charged with an important task. He was introducing his readers to something of vital, even lifesaving importance, and he was relying on Bill to help him do it in the best possible way.

About the only point Bill failed to persuade the *Post* on was AA's need for anonymity. Alexander seems to have been on Bill's side, but the magazine's position was firm: without pictures, there would be no article. Bill relented, but all the photographs were staged, and at least some of them included nonmembers posing as members—Lois and Ruth Hock are clearly identifiable. Only Bill and two other members are seen full face, and some of the others actually have their backs to the camera. The names used in the captions and throughout the article are pseudonyms. (The AA reprints of this article do not include the photos.)

Like Works Publishing, the decision to allow the pictures in order to have the article was made without consulting the membership at large. In doing so, Bill risked a permanent rift with the fellowship's more conservative members. Unlike Works Publishing, though, the decision was not made in haste, and the positioning of so many members in unidentifiable ways and the use of pseudonyms seemed the best possible compromise. Also, just how to consult with what was now two thousand members in fifty cities was an issue that had not yet been addressed.

Bill succeeded with Jack Alexander because, in spite of his growing feelings of alienation from the fellowship and his unhappiness with the financial bind the membership had put him in, his confidence in and enthusiasm for Alcoholics Anonymous remained unshaken. Alcoholics Anonymous worked: it could help virtually anyone. If more people knew about it, the thousands it had helped would become tens of thousands, hundreds of thousands, millions. In time, the ripple effect of this would change the entire world. This was the essential AA story, and the truth of it was as evident to Bill then as it is to all of us today. He never lost sight of it, and he made sure that Jack Alexander didn't, either.

THE MOUNTAINTOP

The *Post* article brought about enormous change for AA. It also meant big changes for Bill and Lois. Within a month of its publication, Bill's income had nearly doubled, and the Wilsons had a home of their own. The Alcoholic Foundation authorized payment of twenty-five dollars a week to Bill Wilson from the proceeds of *Big Book* sales. The same amount was also authorized for Bob Smith, although payments to him did not begin immediately. Since the thirty dollars a week from the contributions made by Rockefeller and his dinner guests was to continue, this meant that Bill was now making fifty-five dollars a week.

The membership expressed its gratitude in other ways as well. Joan C., a real estate agent in Summit, New Jersey, had a friend named Helen Griffith (no relation to Bill), who was very grateful for Joan's sobriety, and Helen owned a house in northern Westchester County. It had been built as a summer home, at a time when northern Westchester was still more rural than suburban, and it came with 1.7 acres, but almost none of it was level. The house certainly had drama: it was perched on top of a steep hill, and it could only be approached on foot from some two hundred feet below, but it hadn't been lived in for some time and the roof leaked and it was generally in poor repair. It was also far from well built: there was no basement under most of the structure, no insulation, and no provision for heat except the fireplace in the living room. There was also very little electricity and an inadequate water supply.

Besides the drama, what the house did have was windows. Every room had at least two of them, and one wall of the large living room was composed of three sets of French doors that opened onto a lovely, screened porch. The room was dominated by a large stone fireplace, and the fireplace and the wooden beams on the ceiling made the room seem strikingly similar to the large back room in the Wilson House in East Dorset. It was a great room, and Lois and Bill could immediately see their furniture in it. It was also an even better place to hold AA meetings than the parlor floor on Clinton Street had been, and the Wilsons could see the furniture pushed back and the room filled with people.

The location also offered a unique combination of privacy and ready access to New York. There wasn't another house in sight, yet the train station was within walking distance. Joan C. and Helen Griffith wanted the Wilsons to have the house. They set terms that could hardly have been more attractive: $6,500 and 100 percent financing, with an interest rate that amounted to little more than carrying charges. Their payments would be $40.00 a month for fourteen years, for a total of $6,720.00. (The Wilsons had been paying $20.00 a month to store their furniture.)

There were still moving expenses and overdue charges for furniture storage, but another AA member volunteered to take care of both. A third member sold Bill and Lois a car for thirty dollars. Before the deal for the house could be completed, something happened that seemed to be further confirmation of the old saw that nothing succeeds like success. Lois was invited on a six-week cruise to South America as the guest of the mother of another AA member whose family owned a large shipping company. (The continuing response to the Alexander article made it impossible for Bill to get away just then.)

Because of the cruise, the Wilsons were allowed to move in before the closing, and a few days later, Lois and her friend were off. The two of them were the only passengers on a freighter, the captain of which was an old friend of Lois's host, and they were shown a royal time. Left alone to finish the unpacking, Bill did not fare very well. It was April, but still cold enough to require heat, which the house didn't have. Between the chill and the dampness and the stress of the chaos he was surrounded by, Bill came down with a cold. It settled in his chest, which sent him to the drugstore for cough syrup.

Instead of taking the cough medicine as directed, Bill simply started sipping. About halfway through the bottle, he found himself thinking that what would really cure the cold was some whiskey and, with him alone in the countryside, no one would ever know. Alarmed, Bill examined the label on the bottle, and learned that the cough syrup contained a high percentage of alcohol. He poured the rest of the bottle down the sink, and nothing further came of the incident.

When Lois told me this story, which she also related in her memoir, *Lois Remembers,* it was clear that, some forty-five years later, she still felt guilty about having left Bill alone. Except for the summer in Akron when he lived with the Smiths, it was the first time he had been without her for an extended period since he was in the army.

SETTLING IN

As the Wilsons set about making their new house a home, they found that it had something in common with the room they had just vacated above the Twenty-third Street clubhouse. It made the fellowship feel good to have them there, but it wasn't easy to live in. Most of its drawbacks could have been overcome, if they had the money, but an income of fifty-five dollars a week did not provide the wherewithal for capital improvements.

They hoped they had found a way to heat the place when Bill spotted a coal furnace on the sidewalk in front of a local saloon. The owner was throwing it out until Bill expressed an interest, when it suddenly was for sale. The price was only twenty dollars though, something even they could afford. After the furnace was purchased and hauled home, there was still the question of how to install it. Because there wasn't even a crawl space under most of the house, a system of ducts that might deliver heat to each room was impossible. Instead, a large hole was cut in the floor directly above the furnace and covered with a register grating. Smaller holes were made near the bottom of the walls between the rooms downstairs. The idea was that the heat that drifted up through the hole in the floor above the furnace would circulate between the rooms downstairs and up the staircase to the second floor.

The Wilsons soon learned why their furnace had been on the discard pile: it was smoky and sooty, and it didn't produce much heat. Not long after Bill and Lois moved to Stepping Stones, Bill's half-sister, Helen, came to New York, and in the fall she moved in with them. (Bill would later get her a job at the AA office.) Helen's bedroom was on the first floor in the part of the house that had a basement and Bill rigged the furnace with a series of pulleys and weights and a line that came up through a hole in the floor and terminated next to her bed. When Helen awoke, she pulled on the line, setting in motion a chain of events that opened the damper on the furnace, rekindling the banked fire. Even so, long after Helen had restarted the fire, the house was still so cold that none of them wanted to get out of bed.

Bill would eventually acquire storm windows and insulation, and an oil burner would replace the coal furnace. Even so, very little heat ever undertook the journeys expected of it. Lois seems not to have minded it too much, but Bill, whose circulation was impaired by his smoking, spent the winter months in his heaviest wool suit, supplemented by long underwear, sweaters, a watch cap, and even gloves. He was also known to get up in the middle of a conversation and curl up like a cat on the grating over the furnace.

Bill also took an inventive approach to the problem of how to augment the water supply. The well was down at the bottom of the hill, hundreds of feet below the house. A better pump was needed, but the cost was prohibitive, so Bill got hold of a cattle trough capable of holding hundreds of gallons of water and installed it in the attic. Since the attic was only accessible through a trapdoor in the ceiling, and there were no stairs, getting the thing up there must have tested all of his Vermont-bred self-reliance. Later, Bill put his talent with ropes and pulleys to use in making it easier to get up to the attic. When he finished, releasing two ropes wound around a turn buckle mounted on the wall swung open the trapdoor, lowered a ladder, and turned on the attic light.

Once the trough was in place, Bill altered the plumbing so that the trough acted like the pressure tank found on top of tall buildings: water was pumped into the trough first and flowed from there to the rest of the house. Bill put a float in the trough and wired it so that when the tank was full, a bell would ring down in the kitchen, signaling that it was time to shut off the pump. Wiring the float so that the pump shut off automatically may have been something he was planning to do, but the delay proved to be the system's undoing.

One day, with company coming for the weekend, Bill turned on the pump. Then other friends stopped by and invited the Wilsons to go for a ride. By the time they returned, water was cascading down the front steps. The disaster affected Lois much more than Bill, for while he tackled projects like the furnace and the water supply, she seems to have done most everything else. Lois had painted the now ruined ceiling and personally scraped and stained the waterlogged floors.

Lois also made the house's curtains herself. Before they could afford to buy the fabric to make curtains, she had painted swags on the walls around the windows. She also reupholstered and restained the antiques she had inherited. The bucolic impression Stepping Stones made on visitors was Lois's doing as well. With no money to spend at nurseries, she dug up wild flowers from roadside and field or started plants from cuttings and seeds. She also traipsed through nearby woodlands and in Vermont as well, and when she spotted a likely sapling, she dug it up, carried it to the nearest road, and tied it on top of the car.

Since grass seed and weed killer were out of the question, Lois created lawns through mulching and assiduous weeding. The result was a look that gave the place a special charm: with lawns that resembled mowed fields, it was impossible to think of Stepping Stones, which was named for the stones on the steep path leading up to the house, as a Westchester estate.

The Wilsons' combined ingenuity, plus Lois's design talent and sheer hard work, turned Stepping Stones into a place filled with a sense of beauty and peacefulness. This was especially true some years later, when they were able to acquire several adjoining parcels and more land that was horizontal. To visitors, Stepping Stones seemed an embodiment of the life the *Big Book* promised to alcoholics who thoroughly followed the AA path of recovery.

Close friends knew better. They marveled that Bill and Lois could manage to live there at all. Because there was no money for proper repairs, much of the furniture was held together by wire, twine, and tape. The house was cold and drafty in the winter, inadequate water, sewage, and electrical systems failed frequently, and no matter how often the roof was repaired, it leaked with every hard rain.

"We feel so comfortable here," visitors would say on even the coldest days, as they sat near the blazing fireplace.

"You're supposed to," Lois would reply triumphantly. "Bill and I always wanted everyone to feel like Stepping Stones was their home, too."

If there was a theme to Lois's decorating, it would seem to have been just that: a desire to create an inviting, nonthreatening atmosphere. Besides the family heirlooms and antiques, there was furniture from Macy's, the makeshift dressing table, and the ad hoc sewing nook. There were also the AA (and later Al-Anon) photographs and memorabilia: homely reminders of meetings, conventions, and conferences combined with handmade tributes sent by AA groups or individual members. In time, they covered nearly every surface and lined the walls above the bookcases in the big upstairs room that served as a library. There were also the quirky things that happened to strike the fancy of Bill or Lois. Lois's collection of glass insulators from light poles was arranged on a stand in front of one of the French doors, as though it was Tiffany. Hanging on the wall in the kitchen was an army field telephone, which served as the only communications link to Bill's studio he would ever allow.

Holiday parties and large gatherings on Thanksgiving Day and Christmas were regular features of life at Stepping Stones. Family members, people from the AA (and later the Al-Anon) office, and AA friends mixed with neighbors, tradesmen, and virtually anyone, drunk or sober, who didn't have anywhere else to go for the day.

Picnics, open to all AA members and their families, were an early tradition. Bill also used Stepping Stones to promote unity within the fellowship. Picking a fight with him virtually guaranteed an invitation to spend the weekend there. If you were very mad at him, you got to stay a week, and if at the end of the week you were still convinced of his villainy, you could count on being invited back.

SURVIVING SUCCESS

Alcoholics Anonymous's first New York office was located on Vesey Street in the financial district, and while Lois shouldered the lion's share of the effort to make Stepping Stones livable, Bill commuted to New York three or four days a week. The Vesey Street space was one good-size room, with a partial partition that created an office for Bill. The staff which consisted of Ruth Hock and the more recently hired Loraine Greim, worked in the bigger half of the room, answering correspondence and filling book orders. It was not long before a third staff member, Eileen Lucy, joined them. (None of these women was an alcoholic. While in time AA members would also be hired to work in the AA office, the staff has always included nonalcoholics.)

The *Big Book*, which had been dross on the market for nearly two years, was selling. Orders were coming in for as many as half a dozen or even a dozen books at a time. There was money now, money from book sales and, with the Depression ending as the country geared up for war, money in the land. The improved economic climate, plus the fact that AA was beginning to get to people earlier in their battle with alcoholism, meant that the financial condition of the average AA member was improving as well. To Bill, it was a good time to ask the groups to support the AA office so that it could continue to field inquiries from people wanting to know more about AA. An appeal went out and, while not all the groups responded, many did, with the result that AA had made a beginning toward becoming self-supporting.

The impact of the *Post* cover story seemed to grow by the day, and as time passed the article's greatest significance seemed to be the effect it had on the media itself. The *Post*'s decision to do a feature story on Alcoholics Anonymous would have been enough for editors all across the country to find the fellowship newsworthy, but the *Post* did more than that: it didn't just report on Alcoholics Anonymous, it endorsed its effectiveness. And while the article emphasized the number of professionals and business people who had found that AA could help them stop drinking, it also made it clear that AA had helped all sorts of people—including journalists.

We have so long been able to take for granted the existence of a multimillion-strong phalanx of sober alcoholics that it is hard to imagine the sheer excitement this generated. Alcoholics Anonymous members were in demand, and feature stories on AA became commonplace. Because the *Post* portrayed AA as a phenomenon that was sweeping the country, the establishment of an AA group in a city that didn't yet have one was more than a newsworthy event; it was an indication that the city had arrived in some important way.

An AA group can be started by anyone at any time any where. It's not officially an AA group until it registers with a central office, but there is no way to compel a group to register, and no "charter" to lift if it doesn't. Yet it was important for the New York office to know where there were AA groups if it was to be able to effectively field the inquiries that were still flooding in. One day, Bill realized that he could put the publicity AA was getting to good use in keeping track of AA's growth. He hired a national clipping service, and it was soon feeding him a steady stream of articles about new AA groups being formed.

Personally, things were better for Bill, and it may have been true that Father Ed Dowling had helped him to see his relationship with AA in a new light, but in Cleveland, Clarence S. was still working to foment dissent. Aided by the Cleveland *Plain Dealer* stories in 1939 and the publicity Rollie Hemsley, who played catcher for the Cleveland Indians, generated in 1940, by 1941 there were more than twenty AA groups in Cleveland and more than six hundred AA members. In October, Bill was invited to the "Smith Dinner," an AA celebration Cleveland AA was hosting to honor Dr. Bob. It was quite an event, with nearly one thousand AA members in attendance from a number of Ohio and Michigan groups.

Clarence S. met Bill at the train station, and when he happened to mention that he and Bob were getting royalties on *Big Book* sales, Clarence was furious. He did not raise the issue at the dinner, which was a great success and marked the beginning of the AA custom of large commemorative gatherings. Then, a short while after Bill returned to New York, both he and Bob were invited to come to Cleveland to speak at another dinner. As Bill recalled it, this one was not very well attended, and after the dinner, they were escorted into a hotel parlor where they were asked to explain, in the presence of a CPA and an attorney, precisely what income they were deriving from AA and on whose authority.

Since Bill had sent a letter to the groups in February covering the same ground, he could not help but wonder why anyone felt this was necessary, but apparently tipped off in advance, he had come prepared. After a review of the certified audit Bill had brought with him detailing AA's finances from the inception of the Alcoholic Foundation forward, the chairman of the committee the Cleveland groups had formed to conduct their investigation apologized to Bill and to Bob. He also promised to do what he could to try to set the record straight, but the controversy, which Clarence seemed prepared to rekindle at every opportunity, never really went away.

Many of the things Bill did during this period were motivated by his concern that AA stay together. The letter he sent about his personal income, the clipping service, and the appeal to the groups for support of an office that could represent them on a national (and even international) level are all examples. The decision Bill made, because of the Cleveland brouhaha, to make formal financial accountings to the groups on a regular basis, was also prompted by his concern for unity.

Looking back on it, they seem like natural things to do for anyone concerned to build a national and perhaps even an international movement, but people who knew Bill during these still very early days of AA seem unanimous in their awe of his foresight.

To an extent perhaps unimaginable today, the lives of early members were taken up with the struggle to stay sober and live sober, something most of them, men and women in their forties or fifties, had no adult experience of. From Lois's diaries and from the comments of early members, it is clear that in the 1940s (and even in the 1950s) many people relapsed. When they did, other members rushed to their aid, baby-sitting, nursing, tapering them off, and helping to square things with family and employers. When it was necessary, they often provided financial support or a place to live.

Even if members with a period of good sobriety didn't succumb to life's challenges, most of them had in their lives someone who spent more time drinking than not drinking. Such people were likely to be in need of some kind of assistance on a regular basis. It made for a chaotic, crisis-ridden existence, and the embrace of religion by so many former agnostics and atheists seems to have had something in common with foxhole conversions. The amount of time members spent engaged in prayer and meditation may not be so much a measure of their devotion as it is the desperation of their quest for some emotional stability.

Bill Wilson certainly had his own life problems after he stopped drink-

ing, and Ebby was not the only AA member he found himself being asked
to help on a recurring basis. There may have frequently been a sense of
crisis permeating his life, but he never seems to have lost sight of his ultimate goal, which was to create an organization that would always be there
when alcoholics anywhere wanted help.

"We used to think he was crazy," more than a few early members have
said. There were days when it seemed like you could not find a couple of
hundred sober members in the whole New York area. All we can see is
the water pouring in the basement, Bill is talking about the need to make
provision for things that would only be a problem if we were ever to get
the damn thing up as far as the 100th floor."

A concern of Bill's that virtually bordered on an obsession was the
need to continue to find ways to make sure that AA was being run from
the bottom up. He always had ideas for AA, and most often, they were big
ones. He was willing to campaign vigorously for a change he believed AA
needed to make, but ultimately, he wanted the decision to be made by the
fellowship as a whole. One consequence of this (in combination with his
own insecurities) was that Bill always felt that he was serving only at the
group's pleasure. If they did not want him, he had to be ready to step
down.

Bill had handled the Cleveland situation well, but the angry question-
ing of his honesty and integrity was not the only thing about his relationship with AA that he found hard to take. There was also the meager
income, the lack of appreciation for the work of the New York office,
and the work he himself was doing in trying to keep up with AA's rapid
growth.

Within a few months of the Cleveland debacle, Bill Wilson was trying
to reenlist in the army to help fight World War II. At forty-six, he was too
old for combat, but he received a recommendation from a colonel in the
army's supply service, and he was offered the rank of captain by the
brigadier general in charge of the army's quartermaster depot in Philadelphia. By this time, though, chronic ulcers had replaced Bill's imaginary
stomach ailment, and when he took the army's physical exam in March,
he was rejected.

Alcoholism was apparently no bar when the army was considering
AA's head man, but other members who tried to enlist were rejected on
these grounds. Bill tried to persuade the army to change its mind. He
wrote General Lewis B. Hershey, the head of the Selective Service, and
tried to convince him that sober alcoholics could be assets to the war effort. When Hershey did not agree, Bill took up the argument with Sam

Rayburn, Speaker of the House of Representatives. He offered to help the army establish AA groups for the officers it was losing to alcoholism, but Rayburn was not interested.

Bill's interest in rejoining the army no doubt had its patriotic element, but there also may have been in it a desire for the kind of glory that AA's anonymity principle was denying him. He may have been struggling to get along on fifty-five dollars a week in a house that needed thousands of dollars' worth of work, but he was rapidly becoming famous in a subterranean way. If AA members were in demand, the outfit's head man was that much more so. The *Post* article's inclusion of dramatic recovery stories was also widely imitated, and there could hardly be a more dramatic recovery story than his own.

CELEBRATED

Bill didn't live very well when he was at home, but when he traveled to visit an AA group, he was a celebrity of the first order. Alcoholics Anonymous may have spread from one drunk to another, and its growth was greatly aided by newspaper and radio publicity. Physicians, psychiatrists, and members of the clergy may have been responsible for introducing AA to a number of new cities, and the proselytizing work of individual members, like Clarence S. in Cleveland, may have been largely responsible for developing AA throughout entire regions of the country. However, as far as most AA members were concerned, they owed their lives to Bill Wilson.

Between 1941 and 1943, Bill and Lois made a number of extended trips to visit AA groups, and everywhere they went, Bill was mobbed. Whenever he spoke, the rooms were filled to overflowing, and people hung on his every word. More often than not, the press was there, too, eager to accord him the level of media attention commensurate with the excitement his presence was creating.

"Bill the Broker," as he was commonly identified, seemed very happy to accommodate them. Wherever he went, Bill granted interviews, complete with full name and pictures. When AA members criticized his seeming thirst for publicity, his answer was that, as AA's founder, he should be an exception. People responded to leaders. Every organization had them, and AA would be more effective if he accommodated this expectation.

The predictable consequence of this was that soon other members felt that AA would be more effective if they, too, broke their anonymity. Then some of these publicly known AA members got very publicly drunk, and the same media outlets that had trumpeted the news of the AA-assisted triumph over alcohol were often just as eager to spread the word about how thoroughly the fellowship had failed them. One of these anonymity breakers did not rely on others to get out the bad news: dead drunk, he took to the airwaves himself, denouncing AA and blaming it for his drinking problem.

Bill got the message. By the time he undertook his last major trip in this period, a 10,000-mile cross-country tour in 1944, he was talking reporters out of taking his picture and using his full name.

In the 1940s, with air travel limited and the western states less populated than today, California seemed much farther away from the East and the Midwest. Although AA got started in Los Angeles in 1939, it had been a small and struggling effort until the publication of the Jack Alexander article. By the time Bill and Lois arrived on the West Coast in 1943, Los Angeles had more than a thousand members. The fellowship was so well established there that Los Angeles AA members raised twenty-five hundred dollars to pay for their trip; they even bought the Wilsons luggage and clothes.

While in California, Bill spent some time with his mother in San Diego. Emily had helped with some of his medical bills during the last years of his drinking, but it was the first he had seen her since getting sober. Bill's mother was more than seventy now. Her second husband was dead, and although her son, her daughter, and her grandchildren were all living in the Northeast, Emily was living by herself.

Bill's mother had had quite a life since she and Gilman had separated. According to her grandson, Leonard W. Strong, 3rd, also known as Bud Strong, Emily had trained as a medical doctor before becoming interested in osteopathy. When she and Charles Strobel, her second husband, who was an M.D., moved to San Diego in the 1930s and set up a joint practice, she found that most of the patients wanted to see the other Dr. Strobel. Bud told me Emily's response was to go to Vienna, where she tried to become a student of Freud's. When Freud didn't return her telephone calls, she instead studied with Alfred Adler. (Adler moved to the United States in 1935.)

By the time of Bill's West Coast trip in 1943, Emily was no longer practicing osteopathy or psychoanalysis, but she wasn't exactly retired, either. She was still playing the stock market, an interest that seemed to have developed in parallel with Bill's. Unlike Bill, though, her success was long term. Bill called her a second "Hetty Green," but according to Lois, unlike the original Hetty, most of Emily's gains disappeared in bad real estate investments. At the time of Bill's visit, though, she still owned several apartment buildings, on which she did most of the repairs herself. Bill Wilson's mother may have been the first woman in California to have her own set of plumber's tools.

Emily came to Los Angeles for Bill's big evening at the American Legion, where more than a thousand AA members crowded in to hear him speak. According to Lois, his mother was surprised to see so many people making such a fuss over him. She also thought that Emily seemed jealous of the attention Bill was getting, and that Bill was disappointed by this reaction. Lois said that Bill always wanted his mother's approval, but he never felt as though he had it, and that he and his mother never really got along very well.

After traveling north to San Francisco and other California cities, the Wilsons went to Portland and Seattle before heading south again to spend Christmas and New Year's with Emily in San Diego. It was the first holiday she and Bill had been together in more than twenty years, and it doesn't seem to have been a very comfortable experience. Bill's mother seemed to have turned miserly. The owner of several apartment buildings was living in a hotel under circumstances that Lois characterized as "pathetic."

San Diego must be about as far as one can get from Vermont in the continental United States. Emily lived there alone until age eight-five when, at her children's insistence, she returned East, where she lived briefly with Dorothy before entering a nursing home in Dobbs Ferry, some ten miles south of Bedford Hills. When Emily died in 1961 at the age of ninety, she left an estate valued at $100,000. In trying to understand Bill's mother, it seems relevant that Lois always described Bill's maternal grandmother as being so self-effacing you wouldn't notice her being in the room. For Emily's mother, the duties of a wife and mother seemed to leave room for nothing else, not even a personality, and it may be that Emily could not conceive of domestic life in any other way.

Bill's mother frequently reminded him of the pain she had endured at his birth, which had been difficult and required a protracted, forceps-aided delivery. As she told the story, the ordeal had brought her near death, and she characterized the delivery as a great sacrifice she had made on his behalf. Emily seems to have taken pleasure in saying these things in front of other people, without ever noticing how excruciatingly painful Bill found her performance to be. A curious letter she wrote to Bill in her later years indicates that Emily was not entirely insensitive to the difficulties of their relationship. In it, she said that she was aware of and there was the implication that she was perhaps even saddened by her self-imposed estrangement from her son. She alluded to "circumstances" that had kept them apart in this world and expressed her hope that they would become closer after both of them were dead.

After New Year's, Bill and Lois returned to Los Angeles. Their tour had included stops local AA groups had arranged in hospitals, psychiatric institutions, and prisons where AA had won acceptance. In Los Angeles, the Wilsons were also able to do things reserved for celebrities. A Hollywood AA member arranged a private tour of Universal Studios, where they visited sets and ate in the commissary. They also visited Trabuco Collage, located southeast of Los Angeles. According to Orange County historian Jim Sleeper, Gerald Heard, Christopher Isherwood, and Aldous Huxley founded Trabuco College in 1942. The school functioned to provide a place for metaphysical research and meditation. Heard and Huxley would both become friends of Bill's. It was with them that Bill first experimented with LSD and other psychedelics, and both Heard and Huxley would write articles for the *AA Grapevine*.

THE BLACKNESS RETURNS

When Bill returned to Stepping Stones after his triumphal cross-country tour, he plunged into a crippling depression that rivaled in severity the depressions he had suffered in reaction to his parent's divorce and the sudden death of his high school sweetheart. It would prove to be the first in the series of depressive episodes that would plague him for most of the next ten years.

In spite of the way Bill was feeling, he somehow managed to write a report to the groups about the trip. It took a tremendous effort, but he saw the report as a way of helping AA members to know that they were part of a greater whole. Conversely, were he to say nothing to the groups about what he had seen and experienced, it would be tantamount to declaring that there was no greater whole the individual member need be concerned with.

As word got around that Bill was sick, some members reacted as though one man's personal health crisis was a threat to the stability or even the validity of the entire program. For Bill Wilson to be less than a personification of the sober life promised by the *Big Book* shook their worldview to its core. While many members were sympathetic, others felt that he had betrayed them. Those who were most disturbed went on the attack: Bill was accused of not working the program and of secret drinking or pill taking. Some members called for his resignation, overlooking the fact that he had never held any AA post he could resign from. Angry letters were sent to the New York office, and Bill was even subjected to vindictive accusations hurled at him by members who traveled to the AA office or even to Stepping Stones for the purpose.

The depth of Bill's dedication to AA was perhaps never more clearly demonstrated than during this period. He endured these attacks in silence; there is no indication that he ever uttered an unkind word in retaliation. He continued to work to keep AA together. As the fellowship grew and expanded to other cities and other countries and continents, he tried to build a structure that would help it to stay together, focused on helping alcoholics stop drinking and open to anyone who wanted its help.

Writing the report on his cross-continental trip marked the first of the many instances in his battle against depression when, through a sheer act of will, he pulled himself together enough to provide AA with something he thought it should have. His output during these years might lead to the conclusion that perhaps he wasn't so sick after all, but a number of people provide compelling confirmation of both the severity of his incapacitation and the determination many of the things he did manage to accomplish required. There were days when he would sit for hours with his head on his desk, trying to summon the will to focus on the project at hand.

Like alcoholism, for many people depression would seem to be a multifactorial illness, and this seemed to be the case for the depressions Bill suffered from the mid-1940s to the mid-1950s. His long cross-country trip had certainly been exhausting, but it had also been an unqualified success. Nowhere did he meet with the dissent he had known in Cleveland. To the contrary, the enthusiasm with which he was greeted and his astonishment at seeing how far his dream had come had carried him from city to city on a wave of elation.

However, the trip did have elements of a vacation, and returning to New York meant returning to the problems he had left behind. By 1944, the fellowship could be found virtually anywhere in the United States, and most inquiries from alcoholics seeking help were being directed to the central offices that were springing up in cities and regions across the country. Reflecting this change, the mail coming into the New York office now was primarily from AA members concerned about the way their group (or central office) was functioning.

Bill later said about these years that it seemed like all disputants to every controversy wrote New York on a regular basis. It was enough to make the staff long for the time when all it had to do was fill book orders and provide the address of the nearest AA group or AA loner. Answering the letters from members involved in an AA-related dispute was primarily Bill's responsibility, and it was not easy. He neither had nor wanted the authority to tell an AA group what to do or the power to enforce any decision he might make in the course of trying to resolve a controversy. This was enough to make responding a delicate matter, but the hardest part was trying to understand what had prompted each letter. Sometimes it was clear that the people writing were making valid points, but in other cases, it was just as clear that he was being asked to intervene in a personality clash. At a minimum, he wanted to understand what was really going on well enough that his response would not make matters worse.

Returning to New York also meant having to again take up the "Cleveland problem," which was essentially the "Clarence S. problem," with a drinking Hank P. behind the scenes. No matter how ridiculous his charges or annoying his personality, Clarence could not be ignored. He was the undisputed leader of AA in Cleveland, and the members heading up AA contingents in other Midwestern cities were in many cases people Clarence had helped in their recovery. Although many Cleveland members took pains to distance themselves from him, he continued to insist that Bill was behaving improperly, and Bill was constantly stretched to find ways to defuse Clarence's criticisms without seeming to challenge his authority or undercut his dignity.

Coming home meant again facing the debts accumulated as a result of the 1929 Crash and the years of unemployment and underemployment that had followed. It also meant trying to live on a small salary in a house with a seemingly endless need for repairs and improvements.

Bill appears never to have made a connection between the way his parents seemed to feel about him and the way he felt about himself, but some people have speculated that this depressive episode may have been precipitated by his unsuccessful visit with his mother. After he stopped drinking, Bill's letters to his mother don't express the pathetic longing that's evident in the letters he wrote in childhood and as a young man, but it is apparent that he was still looking for her approval.

Surely, this is why he invited her to Los Angeles to witness the tribute paid him by one thousand sober alcoholics. He could hardly help but find crushing the reaction he received instead. Bill Wilson was adored by AA members the world over. A once hopeless alcoholic, he had now gone ten years without a drink. The vision he had had of one alcoholic helping another forming a chain all around the world had been realized to the extent that there were already thousands of people who felt that they owed him their lives. Yet his mother seemed to have almost no reaction to the fact that he wasn't drinking, and as for what he had accomplished, she told him that she didn't think it worth "all the fuss" being made over him.

A NEW LIFE

Whatever the cause or causes of the depression, ten years after he stopped drinking, the man whose sobriety had been characterized by such boundless energy now found that there were days when he couldn't get out of bed. When he did manage that, it was all he could do to bathe and dress. Walking had been a mainstay of Bill's existence, but now it sometimes required all of his will just to put one foot ahead of the other.

The most hopeful explanation was that he was suffering from nervous exhaustion brought on by the trip, but the days turned into weeks and he still wasn't feeling any better. Bill's travels to visit AA groups came to an abrupt halt, and he withdrew from the day-to-day operations of the New York office. His energy now had to be focused where it could do the most good. In the spring of 1944, a time when he could hardly have been feeling much worse, Bill was invited to address the annual meeting of the Medical Society of the State of New York. He accepted the invitation and hoped for the best. As the date approached, there was no improvement, but on May 9, 1944, Bill showed up looking every bit the picture of health he was expected to be and delivered an impressive accounting of the "Basic Concepts of Alcoholics Anonymous." Like everything else that went out under his name, he had written the paper himself. In this room full of doctors, he made no mention of how sick he was.

Over the next ten years, Bill made significant contributions to AA's growth and development. However, as had been true of alcoholism earlier in his life, depressive illness now had first claim on his time. In 1944, the New York office moved to a larger space on Lexington Avenue, near Grand Central Station. In June of the same year, the *Grapevine*, AA's monthly magazine, published its first issue. Although Bill approved of both events and was consulted frequently as they went forward, they were largely the work of other New York members.

One consequence of his withdrawal was to make clear the extent to which the fellowship had taken on a momentum of its own. According to the statistics kept by the New York office, at the end of 1944, AA had 10,000 members in 360 groups. By the end of 1945, there were 560 groups and 15,000 members; a year later, there were close to 30,000 members and nearly 1,000 groups.

GET UP

Lois always possessed extraordinary inner resources. She had never been depressed for as long as an entire day in her life, and she could not fathom what had happened to Bill.

"I couldn't understand why he didn't get up," she said, referring to the onset of the depression Bill suffered in 1944. "It seemed to me that staying in bed was the reason he was depressed, and not the other way around. I would bring him food and try to make sure he ate, but I wasn't very sympathetic."

Bill's closest AA friends, like Marty Mann, who suffered from depression herself, were understanding and concerned, but when the rumor started that he was drinking again, it spread like wildfire. As preposterous as this rumor was, it had the effect of lending credence to the notion that he wasn't "working the program." In the *Big Book,* Bill had written a glowing description of what life was like after stopping drinking the AA way, and he said it was what anyone could look forward to who had "thoroughly followed our path." Therefore, if Bill was unhappy, then it must be because of something he was, or was not, doing.

In a sense, Bill set himself up for this. The glowing terms he used in writing about living sober the AA way lend themselves to misinterpretation. It is easy for sober alcoholics to overlook the fact that the *Big Book* was written for people who were seeking relief from their obsession with alcohol. Even for someone who has been through it, reconstructing the mindset of a late-stage alcoholic can be like trying to recall the worldview that accompanies a raging toothache after the tooth has been filled or extracted and all traces of the agony it caused have faded away.

Bill had not claimed that following AA's Twelve Steps would provide entrée into a level of existence superior to anything anyone has ever known before. This is much more than the Oxford Group, at least in its original "religious enhancement" phase, ever claimed. Following Oxford Group prescriptions was supposed to bring people the experience of God in their lives others had found through the practice of their religion alone. And neither the Oxford Group nor Alcoholics Anonymous ever claimed to be providing the solution to all of life's problems, something only the most radical religions have ever put forward.

Some have accused Bill of deliberately painting an overly rosy picture of what would be in store for anyone who stopped drinking the AA way, but the life he described is in fact common enough. People who are not living in a state of permanent crisis engendered by having to live with a chronic, untreatable, degenerative, ultimately fatal illness generally have happy lives. If we make allowance for the sweeping style that infects the *Big Book* as a whole, it seems clear that, as far as Bill was concerned, he was making a true report. We have only to think of Hank P. standing up in his convertible as he drove down Park Avenue, crowing about how wonderful life is, to get a sense of how exhilarating the freedom from the need to drink can be for an alcoholic.

Hank P. may not have reacted in the best way when life began dealing him lemons, and Bill may not have done everything he could to help himself when he first experienced a recurrence of the severe depressions that had plagued him earlier in his life. Years later, he would write about discovering that, no matter how depressed he was, he *had* to get out of bed and keep moving. He would also tell about his trying to find relief from sources other than the AA program. These included psychotherapy, dietary modification, thyroid supplementation, osteopathy, walking and breathing exercises, vitamin B-12, male hormones, ACE (an extract of the adrenal gland), and niacin. While none of these avenues produced a cure, he seems to have found them all to be of some benefit.

MEA CULPA

It wasn't only other people who thought that Bill Wilson was himself to blame for his depressions. Bill felt this way much of the time, too. It is, of course, common for people suffering from depression to blame themselves for their illness. With their long history of blaming themselves for their inability to control their drinking, it is something alcoholics suffering from depression may be especially prone to.

Even after Bill had found ways to minimize the worst effects of a depressive episode, he would attribute his depression to a lack of faith. He often pointed to Robert Smith as someone who was doing a much better job of working the AA program. In a letter written to a fellow AA member in 1956, Bill said that Bob was "made of better stuff" and that he "always came much closer to spiritual achievement." By contrast, Bill saw himself as "a shopper at the theological pie counter."

Robert Smith was an immensely fine man. It is true that he seems always to have been a steadier personality, and from all the evidence, he led the best life he knew how to after he stopped drinking. Yet, by his own admission, he never knew, even for a day, the kind of thoroughgoing relief from the desire to drink the *Big Book* promises those who thoroughly follow the AA path. But Dr. Bob was never accused of not working the program. Some of this must have to do with Bill's role as AA's poster boy. It was Bill who wrote the *Big Book* and represented AA publicly. It was Bill who toured the country, telling his "bedtime story" and promoting the joys of living sober the AA way; he was the one AA members mobbed, and it was to him that members he hadn't even met felt they owed their lives.

Alcoholics Anonymous has never claimed that it had the only approach to alcoholism that works. Other members for whom AA did not provide complete relief from their obsession with alcohol have found psychotherapy, exercise, dietary modification, and vitamin supplementation to be of benefit. Dr. Bob, too, might have been accused of not working the program, had he sought "outside relief" from his desire to drink.

OUTSIDE HELP

In 1939, when Bill first came to know Harry Tiebout, the tremendous energy he had experienced since his spiritual conversion experience was beginning to diminish. He toyed with the idea of becoming a patient of Tiebout's then, but in 1940, he met Father Ed Dowling. Dowling didn't think he needed psychotherapy and he didn't accuse Bill of not working his own program, either. Instead, he compared Bill's malaise to that of the saints, and he told him that it was a symptom not of spiritual shallowness but of spiritual growth. By 1944 though, the depths to which Bill had plunged seemed anything but saintlike, and he sought Tiebout's help.

In the 1940s, many sober AA members sought further growth through psychotherapy and psychoanalysis. According to a number of New York AA members I have spoken with from that era, it sometimes seemed that every other New York member they knew was in therapy. Yet when word was spread about Bill Wilson seeing a psychiatrist, the reaction from many members was worse than it had been to the news that he was suffering from depression.

As these members saw it, Bill's seeking outside help was tantamount to saying that the AA program did not work. There are AA members today who still feel this way about seeking "outside help," whereas others do not see any contradiction in believing that following the AA program can relieve the need to drink, yet not be the answer to other problems like depression.

The depth of the reaction in AA circles to Bill's seeking psychotherapy can perhaps be gauged by the fact that when I knew her some forty years later, Lois would maintain that while Bill found his conversations with Tiebout helpful, he was never really "in therapy" with him. Bill was indeed in therapy with Tiebout, and he never tried to hide it. He saw him twice a week, in Tiebout's office in Connecticut, and said that he found it helpful in dealing with his depression.

Pass It On, the AA book about Bill W., acknowledges that Bill did seek psychological help, yet it also conjectures that he didn't learn anything from it, and it suggests that Tiebout may have learned a great deal from Bill. Some AA members I have spoken with have even insisted that Tiebout must have gotten as much from seeing Bill as Bill got from seeing Tiebout. By 1944, though, Tiebout had been in practice many years. He had been treating alcoholics at least since the early 1930s, and he had first embraced the AA approach to treating alcoholism in 1938.

By 1945, Bill was in treatment with another psychotherapist, Dr. Frances Weekes, a Jungian. Bill saw her once a week. Lois consistently denied that Bill had had this experience, as well, but he was still seeing Weekes in 1949. All that's known about the insights Bill may have gotten from his sessions with her is a letter he wrote in which he said that Weekes felt the demands of his AA position were causing him to neglect his own needs.

The demands on Bill were extraordinary at times, and perhaps nothing was more draining than the fellowship's seeming insistence that he devote himself to it totally, despite its inability or unwillingness to meet his financial needs. Because the groups did not adequately support the New York office, the office had to rely on the profits from book sales to meet its expenses, leaving less than enough for the fellowship's founders to live comfortably. Bill and Lois were treated royally in their AA travels, but when they returned home, it seemed to be a case of "out of sight, out of mind." The adulation never translated into enough heat or a roof that did not leak.

Given what we know of Bill's history, it isn't surprising that he would find himself relying on people to meet his needs who weren't able or willing to do so. Weekes must have at least wished to explore some of this with her patient. Bill would say later of his psychotherapeutic experiences that they helped him to understand and deal with his depression, but they did little to prevent the depressions themselves.

OTHER EXPLANATIONS

Others who knew Bill saw his depression in terms of energy. John Norris, M.D., was a nonalcoholic trustee of the Alcoholic Foundation, later known as the AA General Service Board, and for many years its chair. "Dr. Jack," as he was known in AA circles, was the medical director of Eastman Kodak when he first met Bill in the early 1940s. Norris thought that Bill's depressions were caused by an overreliance on being the center of attention. According to Norris, the energy focused on Bill would buoy him up. Then, when the attention was no longer there, it would leave him feeling depleted, diminished. When I asked him why he thought Bill was this way, he seemed to think the question pointless. Like many physicians, Norris seemed quite hostile to the idea of psychotherapy.

Tom P. is an AA member who knew Bill from the early 1940s. Tom told me that Bill was his sponsor, and he and Bill were both close personal friends and colleagues for many years. A former journalist and advertising executive who later wrote several books on spiritual living, Tom was hired by AA to help Bill edit the AA book *The Twelve Steps and Twelve Traditions.*

He also edited the new stories added to the second edition of the *Big Book* and did other writing and editing work for AA.

As Tom saw it, Bill had several reasons to be depressed. Unlike Jack Norris, he felt that when Bill traveled to visit groups around the country and later, around the world, the energy flow was all going the other way. Everywhere he went, there was a constant stream of people who wanted something from him, and his overfull days often continued late into the night. They also included nearly constant smoking and endless amounts of coffee. Tom said that Bill would return from these trips more dead than alive.

While Bill seemed to get a lift from the adulation focused on him, at the same time, the life he led when he was traveling, or even at home at Stepping Stones on a busy weekend, was certainly depleting. All too frequently, there were too many people wanting too many things. Little was offered in return, except the satisfaction of knowing that he might have helped someone. In fact, the demands made on him at Stepping Stones, which was supposed to be a place where he could retreat from all that, eventually grew so extraordinary that Bill and Lois acquired another "retreat" farther upstate. They so tightly guarded the privacy this place afforded that, more than ten years after Bill's death, Lois would only talk about its location in the most general terms.

But even taken together, Jack Norris's "adulation theory" and Tom P's "depletion theory" don't add up to an understanding of why Bill's first major depression after he stopped drinking lasted more than two years. Nor do they explain ten years of severe depressive episodes. Everyone who attains some level of celebrity knows what it's like to be held in an esteem no one could possibly live up to and to have people want more from you than you could possibly provide. Most people in very demanding positions learn to set limits that are well inside what would leave them so depleted as to negatively affect their health and happiness.

Whatever else Bill Wilson might have been, he was certainly a very good man. Much of his irresistible charm flowed from a childlike sweetness, and there would certainly seem to be a sense in which Bill never grew up. The image he had of himself as starting so far in the hole that getting anywhere required a superhuman effort never seems to have left him. According to Nell Wing, who worked with him for more than twenty-three years, when Bill was intently involved in a project, he frequently became convinced that he was "alone against the world." In one of these states, he would actually go around the AA office moaning, "Oh, poor Bill. No one cares what happens to him."

Nell also pointed out that Bill began trying to quit smoking in the early

1940s. He was already showing signs of smoking-induced respiratory impairment: frequent colds that all too often became nasty bouts of bronchitis. Most of his early attempts to stop had a humorous side to them: Bill would stop buying his own cigarettes and instead rely on OPBs (other people's brands). Nell said that the staff at the AA office, his most frequent victims when he was on the mooch for a smoke, always had a good laugh about this. Bill would laugh good-naturedly along with them before giving up entirely and going back to buying cigarettes again, but Nell thought that his failures bothered him more than he let on. It seems incredible to think that the man who helped show so many people how to overcome addiction could not overcome his own to nicotine.

That there might be a genetic component to Bill's depression is something no one seems to have focused on during his lifetime, but as a young woman Bill's mother had suffered from emotional difficulties that had kept her apart from her family. She had periods of emotional imbalance later in life, as well. In 1949, she suffered an episode of depression that included mood swings and distorted thinking severe enough for Bill and Dorothy to fear that she might take her own life. Dorothy flew to San Diego to be with her mother until the crisis passed. In her middle years, Dorothy herself suffered from emotional problems severe enough for her to seek the services of Harry Tiebout.

Perhaps unsurprisingly, given the way Bill's psyche seems still to be regarded as public property in AA circles, it seems that at one time or another virtually every known cause of depression has been offered to explain Bill Wilson's. I spoke with a number of people who, pointing to his capacity for wild enthusiasm about a project or idea he was particularly keen on as evidence of the sort of "manic" swings the depressions were the inevitable couterpoint to, stated authoritatively that he suffered from bipolar illness. Yet none of those who offered this opinion possessed both the professional qualifications and the intimate knowledge of Wilson such a diagnosis would require.

Throughout the period from 1944 to 1953, Bill was seeking help for depression, writing about it, and trying to help others suffering from it. Besides the days when he struggled to focus on the task at hand, there were also times when he fought desperately to keep his despair from descending into an uncontrollable hysteria. Then there were occasions when he was simply immobilized, unable to do anything of consequence, and they endured for anywhere from a few days to a couple of months. Bill described them as times when he was "drawing a blank," because it captured exactly the way he felt.

Another person on a journey of personal growth who thought he had arrived, only to discover that there was still ground to be covered, might have accepted the news with equanimity. But Bill was often harder on himself for being ill than the most critical of AA members. Besides berating himself for what he perceived as a lack of faith, he was given to describing himself as an example of "compulsive madness," a "psycho," and "insane." It was as though, as far as he was concerned, the depressions were the *real* Bill Wilson and the rest a fraud, with his undeniable achievements mere flukes. In between bouts of depressive illness, he used these terms to describe himself in a more light-hearted manner, but he still used them. It was clear to those around him that his inability to handle his disability with more equanimity itself undercut his self-esteem.

That his experience was not unique—many AA members shared with him their own struggles against depression—did not seem to lessen his self-condemnation. This was at least in part because depression again began to play a major role in his life precisely when, at least officially, he seemed to have the least reason to be depressed.

PEELING THE ONION

It may have been easier for Bill to be publicly hard on himself for being depressed than it was for him to acknowledge something that he saw as a major reason for his depressions. According to Tom P., when he was working with Bill on the *Twelve Steps and Twelve Traditions,* Bill was frequently overwhelmed by the guilt and remorse he felt as a consequence of his infidelities and the turmoil his affairs were causing within the Fellowship.

I spoke with Tom P. in 1999, over lunch at the East Ridge Organic Country Store and Organic Restaurant, which is run by the East Ridge "Addicts Helping Addicts" community Tom founded in 1961. Tom's interest in organic food had already been long-standing when, in 1977, he was diagnosed with lung cancer. He underwent the Gerson treatment, a medically supervised detoxification and rejuvenation therapy based on organic foods and vitamin and mineral supplementation, and he is now eighty-eight years old and cancer free, hale, and hearty. Tom said he would frequently tell Bill, "You need to change your behavior."

According to Tom, trying to write about the need for alcoholics to practice "rigorous honesty," take "searching and fearless" moral inventories, admit faults, make amends to those they had harmed, and become ready to have God remove character defects left Bill feeling terribly fraudulent. The result was those days others have also described when he was so despondent he literally could not pick his head up from his desk.

"All the while we were working on the 'Twelve and Twelve,'" Tom said, "I would argue with him about this. 'Bill,' I told him, 'you're killing yourself. And think about what you're doing to Lois!'"

While other people I spoke with insisted that Lois never knew about Bill's affairs, Tom insisted that "Lois knew everything and she didn't have to guess about it, either. A lot of people tried to protect her, but there were others who would run to Stepping Stones to tell Lois all about it whenever they saw Bill with another woman."

I asked Tom how Bill reacted when Tom would insist that Bill's guilt over his infidelities was responsible for his depressions.

"I think that was the worst part of it," he said. "Bill would always agree with me. "'I know,' he'd say. 'You're right.' Then, just when I would think we were finally getting somewhere, he would say, 'But I can't give it up.'

"When I would press him as to why the hell not, he would start rationalizing. What would really kill me is when he'd say, 'Well, you know, Lois has always been more like a mother to me.' Which somehow was supposed to make it all right for him to cheat on her."

Tom himself had also been sexually compulsive even after he quit drinking, and he found it very hard to change his behavior. "Compulsive sex can be just like alcoholic drinking or drug abuse," he said. "It's just like gambling, or spending money you don't have, or eating yourself into a stupor. It's all supposed to be a lot of fun, but when the party's over, you feel worse about yourself than you did before, and so you go out and do it all over again."

Tom said that it took him five years after he quit drinking to change his behavior in this area, and for five years after that, he tried to get Bill to change, too. "Besides what he was doing to the women he was chasing and to Lois, his behavior was a huge source of controversy in AA," Tom said. "He could be very blatant about it, and there were times when it seemed like the reaction to a particularly flagrant episode would end up destroying everything he had worked for. But then people would scurry around and smooth things over, or cover it all up."

According to Tom, Bill's behavior caused some of his most ardent admirers to break with him. Eventually, Tom broke with Bill, too.

"I told him that I still considered him to be my sponsor, but that I didn't want to work with him anymore. I said that I still hoped that we could be friends, but I didn't want to have anything more to do with him publicly. I just couldn't go on feeling as though I was in any way supporting what he was doing to Lois—and to himself.

"Bill said, 'Fine. I feel the same way about you, too,' and we shook on it. As though it were some mutually agreed upon parting of the ways, with fault on both sides. Which was a real switcheroo, you know. I think he knew that I saw right through it, but I guess it made him feel better not to have to take responsibility for destroying what had been a very enjoyable and productive working relationship."

Before having lunch with Tom, I was shown around East Ridge, and I noted in the meeting room that a much-enlarged version of my favorite photograph of Bill and Lois held a place of honor. The picture was taken in 1954 in the wildflower garden at Stepping Stones. Bill is wearing a suit, but the jacket is open, the first couple of buttons of his shirt are undone, and his clothes look as though he'd slept in them. At the same time, his beaming, picture-of-health smile makes him seem anything but slovenly. He's in fact dressed the way men often dressed (but were seldom photographed) in the nineteenth century when working at home. Lois's long skirt and her shirt and jacket also seem both casual and workman-like, and she too seems relaxed and very happy.

When at lunch I told Tom that the photo had always been my favorite of them, he said he felt the same way about it, which was why he had had it blown up and placed in the meeting room "where everyone would be sure to see it." Then he said something I couldn't hear to Lisa, one of his granddaughters, who was sitting with us, and she excused herself and left the table. A few minutes later, she was standing next to me with the portrait. "Tom wants you to have it," she said.

I was deeply touched, and after I had thanked him, I looked at the photo more closely and noticed that Bill had autographed it to Tom, "with deep affection and gratitude."

"You were a great admirer of Bill's," I said.

"I still am," said Tom. "I never stopped loving the guy. He was a great man, and a good man, really. And somehow, when it came to AA, his thinking was always crystal clear. He was an absolute genius at organizing things and at getting people to work together."

"It must have been very hard for you to break with him," I said.

"Oh, it was terrible. Terrible," he replied. "But I just couldn't take anymore of it. Lois was like a sponsor to me, too. I loved them both too much to continue to have any part of it."

Sexual fidelity does not seem to be something Bill was capable of. His father wasn't faithful, and it was not something he had been brought up to consider a value. As the AA office staff expanded in the 1940s, Bill seemed to take an active part in its recruitment efforts. One longtime AA member told me that at first she didn't know why in 1946 Bill hired her and another young woman AA member. "Neither of us could type or take dictation," she told me. Then, one night soon after they were hired, Bill took both women to an AA meeting. He sat between them and, all during the meeting, he had a hand on one leg of each of the women.

There was also a young woman Bill had begun an affair with whom he subsequently hired for the AA office. She worked at the office from about 1948–1950. She seems to have been very much like Bill's mother, a strong-willed, stubborn woman who was very insistent about having her way. Because everyone knew she was Bill's mistress, she expected to get it. Apparently, she did not appreciate the extent to which AA is a democracy. Bill's recommendation might have gotten her the job, but her behavior became so disruptive that in 1950 the AA trustees told Bill that she could no longer work there.

While Bill often seemed to feel free to take advantage of whatever opportunities were available to him as AA's head man, a number of people who were close to him told me that there were times when he was painfully aware of the threat his philandering posed to everything he had worked for. Barry Leach, a longtime AA member who was a close friend of Bill's for more than twenty-five years, Jack Norris, and Nell Wing all said that Bill had let them know how badly he felt about his unfaithfulness to Lois. That he nevertheless was seemingly unable to control himself filled him with despair and self-loathing at times and left him feeling unworthy to lead AA.

SPIRITUAL EXPLORATIONS

There are surely many reasons for AA's success, but one of them has to be the way its head man was capable of embracing more than one view of a particular issue. For all that Bill was willing to try and even advocate a number of "outside" approaches for other members suffering from depression, he returned again and again to the view that his own depressions were caused by a lack of faith. Since his belief in God and in the spiritual nature of the universe was unwavering, it is hard to know exactly what he meant by this, but it seems most likely that he was referring to his seeming inability to accept the tenets of any religious doctrine.

At the same time that Bill was seeing Dr. Weekes, he was also meeting with Monsignor Fulton J. Sheen. Sheen was later anointed a bishop, and he achieved great popularity with his own television program in the 1950s, but he was already well known in the late 1940s. He had a radio program with an audience estimated at a million people, and he had converted a number of public figures to Catholicism.

Others have reported that the purpose of Bill's visits with Monsignor Sheen was to take instruction in the Catholic faith, but Lois seemed to bristle at the notion that Bill could need to take instruction from anyone. According to her, Bill and Sheen were friends, and their discussions were more like debates than conversations.

I pointed out that in 1947 Bill met with the monsignor every Saturday for nearly a year, and that after he stopped meeting with him, he told people that he had decided against converting to the Catholic faith. He said he was concerned about the impact his conversion would have on AA, if people were to conclude that the fellowship had become associated with a specific religion. Lois claimed that Bill had said those things because the AA rumor mill had circulated the story that his conversion to Catholicism was imminent. According to her, Bill didn't say that he had never had any interest in becoming Catholic because he didn't want to be seen as insulting the Catholics or their popular priest.

The formal nature of Wilson and Sheen's get-togethers would suggest otherwise, but whether Bill ever seriously considered converting to Catholicism may never be known. He made many statements indicating that there was much about the Catholic Church that attracted him, but he is also on record as having told Sheen and others that he wished the

Church would open a division for fellow travelers, which was where he thought he would feel most at home.

The biggest reason why Bill felt that he lacked faith may have to do with his admission that he was never "able to receive assurance that He [Christ] was one hundred percent God." He attributed this to his not receiving any formal religious training in his childhood. It's hard to know what he meant by this latter statement, since Bill is also on record saying that he attended Sunday School at the Congregational Church in East Dorset until age eleven. He said he quit because he was asked to sign a temperance pledge, but Bill later signed numerous pledges in the family Bible to stop drinking. His stopping Sunday School may have had more to do with the fact that age eleven is also when his parents divorced and went their separate ways, leaving Bill and his sister in the care of his maternal grandparents.

Rather than a lack of religious training, it is more likely that Bill's inability to fully accept that Jesus was "one hundred percent God" was a product of his insistence on a scientific approach to things mystical. Given that he felt this way about Christianity, it does not seem likely that he would ever have given serious thought to converting to Catholicism, with its doctrine of papal infallibility. Yet it is hard to imagine a lay Protestant with no personal interest in Catholicism journeying to the office of a prominent Catholic priest every Saturday for a period of months simply to argue theological propositions. While the monsignor and most observers might well have been under the impression that Bill was taking religious instruction, there may also be something to Lois's view of the matter. Bill's intellect was profound and wide ranging, and the depth at which he was exploring Catholicism does not rule out the possibility that he saw his sessions with Sheen as another instance of his "window shopping at the theological pie counter."

Many people, including more than a few AA members, regard AA as a quasi-religious organization, but Wilson was adamant in his insistence that AA existed to help people stop drinking, and a belief in God was not and should never be a requirement for membership. He felt that he had received nothing from his sudden conversion that could not be accomplished gradually, through deliberate, conscious effort. He thought that the benefits of sudden transformational spiritual experiences were fleeting, and that alcoholics who had them also needed to take AA's Twelve Steps to sustain the relief from the need to drink that the experience had provided.

Unlike many people, Bill did not see any conflict between science or medicine and religion. He never doubted that his "hot flash," as he referred to it, gave him a glimpse of the Divine, but the further he was away from it, the more he leaned toward a psychological explanation of the phenomenon. He thought the ego was a necessary barrier between the human and the infinite, but when something caused it to give way temporarily, a mystical experience could result. After the experience, the ego that reasserts itself has a profound sense of its own and the world's spiritual essence. This is why the experience is transformational. The terms Bill came to use in explaining the source of his mystical experience are those used by Harry Tiebout in explaining, from a psychological viewpoint, the way AA's Twelve Steps work.

Bill was interested in all sorts of spiritual phenomena, and some have seen in this a personal quest for spiritual mountaintops. There were (and there still are) some members who would put Bill himself on a spiritual mountaintop, but he never seems to have felt as though he had gained any special insights from his spiritual explorations. Lois and others who knew him well thought that this interest, like so many things in his life, was motivated by his overwhelming desire to help alcoholics stop drinking.

The AA Steps, particularly as described in the AA book the *Twelve Steps and Twelve Traditions,* outline a process that can be undertaken by anyone seeking to remove impediments to experiencing the essentially spiritual nature of life, but many people don't accept the idea that life is essentially spiritual. Bill thought one reason for this had to do with most people's lack of familiarity with spiritual phenomena. It was his contention that the mystery could, and should, be removed from mysticism. He wanted to "democratize" experiences that had always been regarded as rare and ineffable so that, stripped of its elitism and inaccessibility, the benefits of mysticism could be available to everyone. It wasn't spiritual mountaintops that Bill was seeking but easier access to "spiritual kindergarten," which is the way he always characterized AA, for those alcoholics who had trouble accepting a spiritual solution to their problems with alcohol.

It was Wilson's scientific interest in spiritual things that made him an intellectual cohort of Aldous Huxley, but his quest for an understanding of the mystical realm was shared by other early AA members as well. Many believers have regarded an interest in psychic phenomena as heretical, but the Wilsons and the Smiths don't seem to have seen any conflict between their belief in God and a curiosity about the world of the spirits. When the Smiths were visiting the Wilsons at Stepping Stones, they joined Bill and Lois in the séances the Wilsons usually referred to as "spooking sessions."

These events, during which attempts were made to contact the spirit world, were held on an irregular basis at Stepping Stones and at the homes of some of the Wilsons' Westchester friends throughout the 1940s and into the 1950s. According to Lois, various participants, Bill prominently among them, sometimes thought they had succeeded in receiving messages from the other side. My office at Stepping Stones was in the bedroom that was most commonly used for these sessions, which also included demonstrations of automatic writing. The table the participants gathered around was still there. According to Lois and others who had attended these sessions, they had succeeded in levitating this table on a number of occasions.

Bill seems to have become well practiced in making way for spiritual experiences. Twenty years after the experience of the Divine that struck him sober, he wrote that in the intervening years he had been "subject to an immense amount of psychic phenomena of all sorts." Wilson believed that the cumulative weight of these phenomena validated his belief in humanity's divine and therefore immortal nature, and he wanted every alcoholic to be able to say, as he could, that their belief in God was "no longer a question of faith" but "the certainty of knowledge [gained] through evidence."

LSD

Bill's interest in helping alcoholics find relief from the need to drink was also what motivated him to explore the possibilities presented by LSD. Humphrey Osmund and Abram Hoffer, the founders of orthomolecular psychiatry, are perhaps best known for their work in treating schizophrenia and alcoholism with niacin, a B-complex vitamin, but they were also among the first researchers to experiment with LSD. In the 1950s, LSD was widely thought to have psychotherapeutic potential. Research in this area was then funded by the National Institutes of Health and the National Academy of Sciences, and it was undertaken by some of the most prestigious medical and scientific institutions in the country.

Some of the first LSD researches were conducted with schizophrenics and alcoholics who were unable to stop drinking. Many of the early experiments involved patients with both diagnoses, since these patients' schizophrenia was thought to make it impossible for them to benefit from a spiritual conversion approach to their alcoholism. According Dr. Hoffer, the initial intention was to induce a psychic experience akin to delirium tremens, or DTs, in the hope that it might serve to "shock" alcoholics out of their dependence on alcohol.

As anyone who had experienced or even witnessed DTs will attest, there are few experiences in life more horrifying. Wanting to induce a DT-like state may seem cruel and sadistic, but it should be remembered that this was at a time when electroshock therapy was also an experimental treatment for alcoholism. LSD was considered as a last resort, to be tried with otherwise unreachable alcoholics. The hope for a positive outcome was based on the observation that in the aftermath of the DTs, some alcoholics with whom all intervention efforts had failed were capable of understanding the desperation of their condition and responding to treatment.

The candidates for these experiments were people who seemed irreversibly engaged in drinking themselves to death. Physical restraints were provided and steps taken to prevent seizures, but to the researchers' surprise, instead of a DT-like assault, the LSD produced a profound and beautiful experience. It also seemed to dramatically improve recovery rates: 15 percent of the patients who were given LSD recovered, versus 5 percent of those who were not.

Though 15 percent is still not very high, it represented a threefold improvement, and any protocol that demonstrated such a gain with desperately ill patients would generate excitement and interest. Wilson's first reaction to hearing about LSD experiments with alcoholics was entirely negative, but when he learned of the results being achieved, his interest was piqued. Even Father Ed Dowling was convinced of its effectiveness, and by the mid-1950s, Dowling had had more than twenty years' experience in working with alcoholics.

When Bill took LSD, use of the drug was legal. He first took it as a participant in medically supervised experiments with Gerald Heard and Aldous Huxley in California in the 1950s. Lois also participated in the first LSD experiments in California. At Bill's insistent urging, she took LSD herself but always claimed later not to have felt anything. Bill insisted that she did too feel something and that she in fact had a very pleasant time. Nell Wing, who took LSD herself during one of these sessions and was there when Lois tried it, tends to believe Lois. She explains LSD's lack of impact on Lois by noting that she took much less than the others had. Father Ed Dowling was among the people who accepted Bill's invitation to join him in these early experiments. Bill also invited Jack Norris, medical director for Eastman Kodak and long-serving nonalcoholic chair of AA's General Service Board, but Norris declined.

It is hard to appreciate today the enthusiasm with which LSD experimentation was initially greeted. Aldous Huxley wrote Father Thomas Merton that LSD might even be the SOMA he had written about in his futuristic novel, *Brave New World,* and that it was deserving of the most serious and thorough scientific research. Sam Shoemaker wrote to Bill about the wholehearted endorsement of LSD experimentation by an

Episcopal bishop, and Wilson wrote to Carl Jung, praising the results obtained with LSD and recommending it as a validation of Jung's spiritual work. (Word was received of Jung's death, and the letter was never sent.)

Wilson is thought to have continued experimenting with LSD well into the 1960s. Lib S., a longtime AA member who lived in New York for many years, told me that she participated in LSD experiments with Bill in the late 1950s in New York. Marty Mann, Helen Wynn, and others participated in the New York experiments, which were supervised by a psychiatrist from Roosevelt Hospital. Lib S. said that the alcoholic participants in the New York researches were all sober. The purpose was to determine whether the drug might produce insights that would serve to remove psychic blocks that were preventing people from feeling more spiritually alive. Each participant had to agree to undergo extensive debriefing, and all were urged to make detailed notes about what they were experiencing.

Bill agreed with Huxley's assessment of LSD's power to open the "doors of perception." He described his first experiences of the substance's effect as being akin to what he had experienced in Towns Hospital the night his obsession with alcohol was lifted. Nell Wing told me that her own LSD experiences were something she has always valued. Although Nell denies that Bill ever went this far, other people who knew him during this period said that his initial enthusiasm for LSD was so great that he thought it should be available to all alcoholics. This still falls far short of wanting to distribute the substance at AA meetings, as some have claimed.

In the immediate aftermath of his experiences with LSD, Bill did feel that the information gathered at the sessions he participated in should receive the widest possible dissemination. Bill was often wildly enthusiastic about a new discovery and eager to share his excitement with others. Yet he seems never to have given serious consideration to making available to other AA members the results of these sessions, and the man who was concerned about the effect his conversion to Catholicism might have on the fellowship never publicly advocated the use of LSD by other AA members.

MAKING CHANGES

The depressive episode that felled Bill in 1944 made it clear that he could not continue the pace of his AA activities. When he was feeling somewhat better, Bill and an AA friend put up a concrete block structure on the highest point of the Stepping Stones property, several hundred yards beyond the house. It had no plumbing and no telephone. Later, a chemical toilet was installed, and an army field telephone permitted communication with the main house. The cottage, which Bill referred to as his studio, had a fireplace, a kerosene stove, and, like the main house, a lot of windows. A studio couch and the desk and chairs he had purchased from Hank completed the furnishings. Nestled in the trees, it was a beautiful, peaceful spot.

It was here that Bill would, as his health permitted, work on a set of guidelines for how an AA group ought to act in its relations with its own members, other groups, and the outside world. The fruit of these efforts was first published in the *AA Grapevine* in April 1946 as "Twelve Points," though Bill subsequently called them AA's "Twelve Traditions." They were so named in the hope that they would become the accepted standard for group conduct. The toll Bill's depressions were taking can be seen in the fact that it was not until December 1947 that the explanatory essays for each Tradition began to appear in the *Grapevine* on a one-per-month basis.

The Traditions are sometimes referred to as the "Twelve Steps for the groups." Like the Steps, they are twelve in number. They were also presented in the context of "this is what we have found works best for us," rather than, "this is what you have to do if you want to be an AA group." Just as AA members are not required to take the AA Steps, AA groups are not mandated to abide by the AA Traditions.

The AA Traditions cover many topics. They stress the need for anonymity, group autonomy, self-support, and nonaffiliation with other causes. One of them even states that AA itself should not be organized, meaning that it should never acquire a central authority with the power to impose its will on the groups.

There are many remarkable aspects about the governing style outlined by AA's Traditions, but perhaps what makes them most unique is that they represent a thoroughgoing renunciation of the power and glory many (though not all) AA members were only too ready to bestow on its founder. People who knew Bill the longest all agreed that he never wanted to be glorified. "Because he had been around so long," Lib S. said, "he thought he was well-suited to the job of putting whatever was going on at the moment in the best perspective. But he always saw himself as subject to what the majority of members wanted."

WHO'S A MEMBER?

One of the Traditions addresses the issue of membership requirements, something many groups had felt duty bound to promulgate. Bill often said later about this that if each group were to impose all the membership requirements the groups had come up with, virtually no one would be eligible to join AA. Some of the rules were designed to exclude women or young people or African Americans, but most of them centered around attempts to identify the "real" alcoholics as opposed to the heavy drinkers or even the occasional social drinker hoping to make new friends. By stating that the only requirement should be a desire to stop drinking, Tradition Three effectively rejected the rules that some groups had promoted. In the essay on this Tradition, Bill went further. Anticipating the question of who gets to decide whether someone has a desire to stop drinking, he stated flatly that anyone was a member who said he was a member.

Nothing about the issue of membership requirements was more vexing to Bill than questions about race and sexual orientation. In 1940, he invited two black men to attend AA meetings in New York City, and he found himself widely castigated for it. Many members felt that he had no right to make such a decision unilaterally. Bill was sincerely flabbergasted by this response: it had not occurred to him that there was any decision to make. He had founded Alcoholics Anonymous for people who were alcoholic and wanted to stop drinking, and these men qualified on both counts.

When the question was put this way, even the most ardent segregationist admitted that the men had as much right as anyone to see if they might benefit from AA. Yet, there were still members who could not agree with the idea of socializing with Negroes. Bill resolved the issue with what proved to be a historic compromise: the men were allowed to attend AA meetings as "observers." Bill urged AA groups everywhere to admit black members. If the group couldn't do that, he urged it to "make a superhuman effort" to help the black alcoholics who came to its attention by letting them attend meetings as observers and then helping them to start their own group.

This policy did make it possible for some black alcoholics to get sober. The first black group was started in the mid-1940s in Washington, D.C., and the group founder's story can be found in both the second and the third editions of the *Big Book* under the title "Jim's Story." The group received a lot of assistance from white alcoholics, who helped to pay the rent on the group's meeting place when there were still only two or three people in attendance.

When Bill visited Akron in 1947, he and Smithy again endorsed what they hoped would soon be AA's universal practice regarding blacks in AA. The two cofounders made a point of visiting a black alcoholic at St. Thomas Hospital who wasn't allowed on the alcoholic ward. In 1948, Sister Ignatia and Dr. Bob successfully petitioned the hospital to change this policy. In the last years of his life, Dr. Bob frequently attended the AA meetings of Akron's first interracial AA group.

From AA's earliest beginnings, Bill also promoted an open-door policy for gay and lesbian alcoholics. Marty Mann, the first woman to stay sober in AA, was a lesbian, attending her first meeting in April 1939. When she arrived, the first floor of the Wilsons' home was filled with thirty or forty people, all alcoholic men, and their spouses. Marty, who was the only woman alcoholic and a lesbian as well, hardly felt welcome.

When she went upstairs to take off her coat, she didn't want to go back down. Then Lois came up, put her arms around her, and gave her a hug. Marty would say later that she had never before felt such love from another person. When Lois said, "Why don't we go down together?" she was ready to accompany her.

Marty returned to Greenwich after the meeting and said to an alcoholic friend at Blythewood, "Grennie, we are no longer alone." The statement would become a sort of anthem in AA circles. Lois took Marty to each of her first few meetings, which were also the last ever held in the Wilsons' Clinton Street home, and Marty would credit Bill and Lois's kindness to her as being critical to her recovery. Lois told me that she and Bill were always aware of and fully accepted her sexual orientation. In describing the evening she accompanied Marty to her first AA meeting, she said that she was sure that part of Marty's reluctance to enter that roomful of people was due to her sexual orientation.

The Wilsons always numbered gay men and women among their AA friends, with Marty and her partner a regular part of their social circle for years. The Wilsons and Mann worked together in helping to establish High Watch Farm in 1940, the first institution for alcoholics based on AA's spiritual principles, and the Yale School of Alcohol Studies in 1943. They also helped Marty in her effort to start the National Committee for Education on Alcohol in 1944 (later the National Council on Alcoholism), and they stood loyally by her during the controversies some of her actions created, such as her revealing her membership in AA when fund-raising for NCA.

As an example of Bill's attitude toward who could become an AA member, Barry Leach, a longtime New York alcoholic who was himself gay, liked to tell of an incident that occurred at an AA clubhouse in New York City. It was early in 1945, and a man who was obviously alcoholic showed up one day, seeking to attend a meeting. The man was black, and at the time, New York still had no black members. He was also a self-admitted drug addict, an ex-convict, and homeless. What is more, his hair was bleached a platinum blond, and he was wearing makeup. While he might not be entirely uncommon in metropolitan AA circles today, he certainly was in 1945. After talking the situation over with several other members, Barry called Bill to ask him for advice. Bill's immediate response was that if the man was a drunk, he belonged in AA.

Barry also shared with me a tape he played as part of a presentation he made at AA's Fiftieth Anniversary International AA Convention in Montreal in June 1985 on homosexual men and women in AA. The tape was of a talk Bill gave about the AA Tradition on membership in which he indicates that there were gay men in AA as early as the late 1930s.

Bill advocated that AA be open to everyone with a desire to stop drinking—and that anyone is a member who says he or she is—with a confidence that not many members shared. Others saw diversity as a threat to AA unity. In the very early days, many male members opposed admitting women for this reason. Where others saw weakness, Bill saw strength. In his view, keeping AA open to all was more than something AA could survive. A fellowship composed of so many different people would serve to underline what they all had in common: alcoholism.

THE STEPS REVISITED

As Bill both fought and tried to find a way to live with depression, he also managed to log a remarkable string of accomplishments. He was involved in the establishment of the Yale Alcohol Studies School, founded in 1943 by E. M. Jellinek, and he was on the faculty of its alcohol studies program.

Bill also weathered the controversy caused by the fact that, along with many other prominent people, his name and Dr. Bob's appeared on the National Committee for Education on Alcohol's letterhead. The membership raised such a fuss about what they saw as an "outside affiliation" that Bill and Bob were forced to resign from the NCEA board in 1944. Bill always lamented that, unlike other AA members, he was not allowed to associate himself with alcohol-related causes, but he created another firestorm in 1945 when he endorsed Marty's decision to reveal her membership in AA in order to garner publicity for the new organization. He later admitted that he had been wrong to think that an exception should be made on the anonymity question in Marty's case.

The Wilsons' financial condition improved steadily throughout the 1940s. By 1946, AA had twenty-four thousand members in more than seven hundred groups. Bill and Lois bought a new car and embarked on a tour of the western states. By 1948, there were some sixty thousand AA members and nearly two thousand groups, with at least one group in every state and at least some AA in twenty-three countries. The *Big Book* was now selling thirty thousand copies a year. The greatly improved royalty income these sales represented made it possible for the Wilsons to acquire some additional land. The new parcels added greatly to the amount of level land, and a driveway was put in that made it possible to approach the house by car.

Nineteen forty-eight was also the year that a member died and left AA ten thousand dollars. A debate ensued about whether AA should accept the money. Bill was completely against it. He thought it would open up AA to all the potential problems with money it had so long sought to avoid. Ultimately, the bequest was declined, with the fig leaf for those in favor of accepting that the public relations value of the declination be emphasized. The press was given the story, and it made the wire services and was carried everywhere. People were much impressed by the seriousness with which AA took its vow of "corporate poverty." Much more was done for "the million who do not know" by refusing the ten thousand dollars than could ever have been done with it.

Alcoholics Anonymous's string of PR coups continued. In 1948, the *Reader's Digest* article on AA that had been hoped for in 1939 finally appeared. The six thousand letters the AA office received in response to it amply validated the excitement the prospect of a *Reader's Digest* story had generated. The *Ladies' Home Journal* also ran a very positive piece that year, and AA was featured in a "March of Time" newsreel that was shown in more than nine thousand movie theaters. Marty Mann appeared in this film and talked about alcoholism, but without revealing her AA connection.

By 1950, AA membership was approaching a hundred thousand and there were thirty-five hundred groups worldwide. In April, Bill and Lois visited AA in eight European countries. The terrific publicity continued. The April 1, 1950, issue of the *Saturday Evening Post* featured another article by Jack Alexander about AA. Entitled the "Drunkard's Best Friend," it was again a catalog of AA successes and methods. In 1953, Jack Alexander became a member of the Alcoholic Foundation's board of trustees.

In the period from 1944 to 1955, during which Bill suffered the most from depression, he authored sixty articles for the *Grapevine* and represented AA in numerous appearances before religious, medical, and governmental forums. While his travel would never again be what it was in the early forties, he still did travel extensively, including a two-month-long European tour in 1950. Bill also organized and produced AA's first international convention. It was held in Cleveland in 1950, and AA members from the world over have assembled at five-year intervals ever since. The last three international AA conventions have seen attendance of more than fifty thousand people. Even though liquor sales drop precipitously when virtually every hotel room for miles around is occupied by former drinkers, this crowd's reputation for free spending and good behavior is such that cities begin competing to host the event years in advance.

The international convention idea is an example of how Bill was able to stay on top of trends that threatened to divide AA, even as he worked toward assuring its long-term survival. Bill's enormous personal popularity was the cement that bound AA together, but it was also something others thought they might enjoy, as well, if they were to become AA's head man. By 1946, there were more than two thousand AA members in Cleveland, far more than in New York. Chicago had more than twice as many members as New York, and Detroit about as many.

There were people in these locales and others with a large AA population who didn't see why AA had to be run by Bill Wilson from New
York. By the late 1940s, state and regional AA conventions were plentiful,
and Texas, among others, was ready to hold its own international convention, quite independent of the New York office and the Alcoholic
Foundation. In a display of Disraeli-like diplomacy, Bill told the Texas AA
members he thought it would be all right if they invited whomever they
wanted to their planned 1952 convention, but he counseled against calling it an "international" convention because this could inspire other states
to do the same.

Bill then worked to organize an international convention of his own,
to be held before the planned Texas event. Three thousand people attended the first international AA convention, held in 1950 in Cleveland
at the end of June. It was the only one to be attended by AA cofounder
Robert Smith. His wife, Anne, had died the year before, and Bob himself
was very ill with cancer.

The convention was held in Cleveland to make it possible for Dr. Bob
to attend, but Cleveland was also a good choice for other reasons. It was
the home turf of Clarence S., and it had one of the largest and earliest
concentrations of sober alcoholics. Its proximity to Akron, where AA was
born, gave it great historical significance. Convention preparations also
required a lot of contact between Cleveland, Akron, and New York,
which served to ameliorate friction between the three camps.

Bill, who was always searching for symbols to help people keep in perspective the significance of the greater whole to which they were joined,
opened the convention wearing a lei over his right shoulder. He explained
to the assembly that it was a gift to all of them from a group whose members would never attend any AA gathering but their own. The AA group
at a leper colony in Hawaii had sent it.

By the time of the convention, Bob's cancer was most painfully advanced, and he spoke very briefly. Even so, the experience exhausted him,
and he left the convention early and was driven home to Akron. Robert
Smith died on November 16th.

Bill used his time on the platform to express his concern that AA unity
be emphasized above all else. The conventions were always emotionally
draining for Bill, and none was more so than the first one, because it was
the first, because Smithy was so ill, and because of the business Bill hoped
to conduct. He wanted the convention to approve the AA Traditions, and
he wanted it to agree to put into place the AA system of representation
known as the AA Conference.

His efforts to see established a democratic process through which local or regional desires could be transmitted to the whole of AA was motivated by his concern for unity, but it was also a way of ensuring that AA would never stray from its primary purpose. If AA's direction were ultimately determined at the group level, Bill felt confident that staying sober and helping other alcoholics to achieve sobriety, which is what an AA group must do if it is to survive, would always be the fellowship's focus.

For years before the convention, Bill worked to drum up support for the AA Conference whenever he traveled to AA groups around the country. Not all AA members were in favor of democracy. Dr. Bob was among those who weren't sure that the conference was a good idea. A few days before Smithy's death, Bill visited him for the last time and obtained his approval for the establishment of a representative structure to govern AA.

Before AA had a leadership structure, it still had leaders. Most often, some of the people who started the first group in a given city were ultimately responsible for the growth of AA throughout an entire region, and they became the head men for that part of the country. There were also the members who organized and ran the intergroup offices, structures set up to coordinate activities between the groups in a large metropolitan area, who became the leaders of the area the intergroup served. There were entire states, like Texas, where there were individuals generally recognized as being "in charge." The problem, as Bill saw it, was that all these AA leaders were de facto. As were the trustees of the Alcoholic Foundation, and for that matter, AA's cofounders. Any of these people could try to take AA in whatever direction they cared to, and while others could refuse to follow, there really was no way to hold them accountable.

Bill's faith in the will of the groups, also known in AA parlance as the "group conscience," to keep AA on course was of the same stuff as his position on membership requirements. Both were based on the notion that the requirements for staying sober were AA's best protection against straying far off course. Bill trusted the group conscience because it was at this level that the membership would always be made up of alcoholics in early recovery, which would mean that their priorities were ordered by the need to stay sober.

Although Bill's intention wasn't to replace AA's local leadership but to legitimize it, many longtime AA members did not see it that way. At least some of the opposition to the conference idea seems to have come from people who wanted to do exactly what the scheme was supposed to prevent: take AA in a different direction. Not all members were happy with AA's nondenominational nature or with its commitment to always remain a "spiritual kindergarten." The fellowship's commitment to spiritual progress rather than spiritual perfection troubled members who, having achieved relief from the need to drink, had set their sights on higher goals. They wanted the fellowship's focus to change with their own.

During at least some of Bill's travels in support of the conference idea, forces opposing it were also on tour. They were led by, among others, Henrietta Seiberling, the woman who years before had introduced Bill and Dr. Bob. The countercampaigns had their effect. In spite of both his and Bob's endorsement of the idea, the best Bill could obtain from the 1950 convention was approval to try his conference scheme on an experimental basis. Seiberling's campaign against the conference system of representation included charging Bill with having taken complete leave of his senses, but Bill seems never to have borne her any ill will. Henrietta spent the last years of her life in New York City, and she and Bill saw a lot of each other.

In 1951, the year following the convention, Bill and Lois embarked on a tour of AA cities to promote the conference and encourage members to participate in selecting delegates. The tour resulted in their bearing witness to the selection process in many cities, something Lois said they both found to be a most gratifying and thrilling experience.

Also in 1951, AA was chosen to receive the Lasker Award, given by the American Public Health Association for outstanding achievement in the fields of medical research or public health administration. Although AA wasn't in either field, with one hundred thousand sober alcoholics to its credit, it had obviously made an enormous contribution to the public health. The decision about whether to accept the award marked the first time that the AA conference would be making a decision affecting AA as a whole. The one thousand dollars that came with the Lasker was declined, but at Bill's urging, the award itself was accepted, on the grounds that it would enhance the fellowship's prestige among public health administrators.

In 1952, a wealthy AA member who learned that Bill was still working to pay off the debts he had incurred during the last years of his drinking tried to give him sixty thousand dollars. Bill did sometimes accept gifts from members, including two automobiles from some wealthy Texans, but he turned down this and all similar offers of cash.

A year later, AA published the *Twelve Steps and Twelve Traditions*. Referred to by AA members as the "Twelve and Twelve," the book contains the essays on the AA Steps Bill had struggled with all through the late forties and early fifties, along with the essays he had written on the AA Traditions. Written when his depression was often at its worst, the Steps essays were greatly informed by the experience: they are still full of hope, but they do not even refer to the promises outlined in the *Big Book*. Some members attacked the essays as a dilution of the program. Even today, there are members who insist that the Twelve & Twelve is "soft AA" and that the "real" program can be found only in the *Big Book*.

The Step essays are also informed by the intervening years in another way. By the late 1940s, it was becoming clear that there were a great many more women alcoholics than there had seemed to be ten years earlier. The Twelve & Twelve recognizes this by not blatantly assuming that all alcoholics are male heads of household.

Alcoholics Anonymous was also finding that alcoholics of all ages could stop drinking. From the essay on the First Step onward, an attempt is made in the Twelve & Twelve to deviate from the characterization of an alcoholic as someone who finds himself at midlife bereft of all he has accomplished. There were still members who felt that alcoholics must suffer as they themselves had suffered in order to reap the benefits of AA, but Bill made specific, positive reference to the "young people who were scarcely more than potential alcoholics" who were joining the fellowship.

THE OTHER WOMAN

In the mid-1950s, when Bill was in his early sixties, he began an affair that was different than any he had had before. The woman's name was Helen Wynn, and she was in her early forties when Bill met her. Helen and Bill were together some fifteen years. They saw each other regularly in New York and later in Pleasantville, a town fifteen minutes south of Bedford Hills, where Helen bought a home.

Helen Wynn was a former actor and a very attractive woman. Yet, according to Lib S., an AA member who thought of Helen "as a sister," people were so taken by Helen's personality that her looks were not something they took particular note of. Helen had an outspokenness and bravado that must have reminded Bill of his mother. She also had a keen interest in adventure.

Helen was born in 1913 in Gold Springs, Utah, a mining town her father had founded along with several other prospectors. In spite of its optimistic name, Gold Springs proved not to have "springs" of gold or anything else of value, and the town disappeared.

At age seventeen, Helen was living in Duluth, Minnesota, and managing a bookstore; and it was while working in the bookstore that she became interested in child psychology. With her parents' support, she and two of her friends went to Vienna to study with Alfred Adler, the psychoanalyst Bill's mother would study with in the mid-1930s. Since Adler lectured only in German, which none of them spoke, they studied instead with a Dr. Wexeburge. When at the end of a year Wexeburge told Helen and her friends that he thought them poorly suited to careers as psychoanalysts, they spent what was to have been the following year's tuition on skiing, bicycling trips, opera tickets, and beer gardens.

When the money was gone, Helen gave her friends a series of letters to be mailed to her parents at regular intervals and moved to New York, where she got a job at Macy's. Eventually, the letter-writing ruse was discovered, and her father sent her the money to return to her family, which was now living in Phoenix, Arizona. It was while living in Phoenix that Helen read in a gossip column that a Dr. Berthold Viertelhome, who was someone she had known in Vienna, was now in Hollywood producing German adaptations of American films.

Helen moved to Hollywood and took a job as Dr. Viertelhome's assistant. After working at a number of other jobs in the film business, she again went to New York where, armed with letters of introduction from Hollywood acquaintances, she began acting in summer stock. By the mid-1930s, Helen was a founder of the Surry Players, a New York–based theatrical production company.

Shepperd Strudwick, an actor who bore a striking resemblance to Joseph Cotten and who would go on to have a long and distinguished career on both stage and screen, was also a member of the Surry Players, and in 1936 Helen and Strudwick were married. The ceremony took place in the St. Martin of Tours chapel in the Cathedral of St. John the Divine. The chapel was designed by Ralph Adams, who was Strudwick's uncle.

In 1939, the Surry Players opened a production of Chekhov's "Three Sisters" in New York. While some reviewers had good things to say about the acting, including Helen's portrayal of Olga, the production itself was nearly universally panned, and the play closed after only nine performances. The "Three Sisters" production marked the end of Wynn's stage career. In 1945, she and Strudwick had a son, Shepperd Strudwick, 3rd They divorced in 1946.

Many people told me Lois never knew about Bill's affair with Helen Wynn, and an AA member who was one of Helen's intimates told me that she didn't think that Helen and Bill were ever more than friends. Yet Bill seems never to have been circumspect about his affairs, and there is little doubt that his relationship with Wynn was both intimate and public.

Bill's womanizing was common knowledge in New York AA circles. Many members who joined AA in New York long after his death told me that among the first things they learned about the program's illustrious founder was that he was a ladies' man and a bad sponsor.

The stories about Bill being a bad sponsor seem to have as their basis his inability to say no to people. All of the people who knew him well seem agreed that you could not have a better friend. As evidence of the personal help he extended to alcoholics, we have a rhyme Lois wrote and Scotch taped inside the first copy of the *Big Book*. Based on the nursery rhyme about the old woman and the shoe, it describes a "funny man" who "had so many drunks around he didn't know what to do. He nursed some, he razzed some, he taxied some to Bellevue. But the funniest thing about him was, he really fixed a few."

The poem refers to their life on Clinton Street after Bill stopped drinking, but Bill actually spent the next thirty years nursing, razzing, and taxiing drunks. Yet there was only so much of him to go around: many a dazzled newcomer, after a ten-minute conversation with Bill at an AA meeting, would ask him to be their sponsor, and invariably, Bill would agree. Soon the newcomers would find that, compared to other people's sponsors, theirs was hardly ever available.

The impression that he was a ladies' man seems to have come from the way he sometimes behaved at AA gatherings. When Bill wasn't accompanied by Lois (or later, Helen), he could often be observed engaged in animated conversation with an attractive young newcomer. His interest in younger women seemed to grow more intense with age. Barry Leach, who knew Bill nearly thirty years, told me that in the 1960s he and other friends of Bill's formed what they came to refer to as the "Founder's Watch" committee. People were delegated to keep track of Bill during the socializing that usually accompanies AA functions. When they observed a certain gleam in his eye, they would tactfully steer Bill off in one direction and the dewy-eyed newcomer in another.

Given the openness of Bill's pursuits, that anyone who was a friend of Helen's and part of Bill's inner circle could not be aware of the affair seems hardly credible. However, in spite of his natural and unassuming manner, many people were unable to see Bill clearly. Even today, many AA members believe that alcoholism had them in a death grip, and they talk unself-consciously about the miracle of their recovery. During Bill's lifetime, it would seem that nearly all AA members felt this way, and a great many saw Bill Wilson as a miracle worker. For every member who criticized Bill for his depressions, there was at least one member ready to deny that Bill was ever depressed. For anyone concerned about the effect of Bill's smoking on his health, others were ready to insist that he didn't smoke that much, or if he did, it certainly wasn't bothering him.

Bill Wilson and Helen Wynn had an intimate and, at least in the early years, a passionate relationship, but they seem to have had more than that. At age sixty, Bill Wilson may have found a soul mate.

Bill and Helen seem to have met at an AA meeting. Soon after their affair began, Bill got Helen, who had been sober only a short time, a job at the *AA Grapevine*. Most everyone who worked at the AA office at the time Helen was hired seemed to know that she was Bill's girlfriend. They were frequently seen together when Bill was in New York, and Helen sometimes accompanied him to AA-related events. Unlike some of the other women Bill had recommended for jobs at the AA office, Wynn proved to be a valuable asset. Starting with a part-time, provisional position, she worked her way up over a period of years to become the magazine's editor.

After Helen left the *Grapevine* in 1962, Bill contributed to her support, though when he wanted to direct a portion of his royalty income to her, the AA trustees refused to do it. Bill was furious, and Helen was terribly hurt. In 1963, though, prompted by his worsening emphysema, Bill and AA executed a new royalty agreement that called for Helen to receive 10 percent of his book royalties, and Lois 90 percent, after his death. Bill also added a codicil to his will in which he referred to this agreement and confirmed that the allocation of royalty income it provided was indeed his desire.

A CONTRASTING PERSONALITY

We may well wonder how Lois could have remained ignorant of her husband's fifteen-year affair with another woman. Tom P. and several other people were sure that, given the plethora of tattletales running to Stepping Stones, she must have known, but those who knew her best insisted that she did not. By the time Bill and Helen met, Lois had been long practiced in ignoring her husband's peccadilloes.

From all the evidence, Bill never stopped loving Lois. He seems always to have sincerely enjoyed her company and to have sought and respected her opinion. He never stopped believing that he owed his very life to her loyalty and support. He was also deeply aware that, without her, there might not have been an Alcoholics Anonymous. According to Lib S., Lois and Helen were friends, and Helen seems to have held Lois in the highest regard.

During the years Helen and Bill were together, Lois seems always to have had first call on Bill's time and to have participated in his life as much as she cared to, but their return from their first cross-country tour in 1944 marked a change in Lois's attitude toward AA. She never stopped being one of AA's biggest boosters, but she went to New York and the AA office as little as possible. Lois didn't want Bill going there, either, and she came to resent the demands the office made on her husband's time.

Lois's enthusiasm for exploring psychic phenomena was also limited. She went along with the spooking sessions. She liked to brag about Bill's psychic powers, the visions he had and the instances of his seeming to receive automatic writing; but none of it had the significance for her that it did for Bill.

Helen Wynn was twenty-two years younger than Lois. She was also a quite different personality. The two women were bright and bold, attractive and accomplished, but where Lois seems always to have been self-sufficient and rock steady, Helen could be mercurial and needy. Like Bill, she seems always to have possessed a restlessness that couldn't be more than temporarily slaked.

Helen was a willing and enthusiastic participant in Bill's New York life. Until he became too ill with emphysema in the mid- to late-1960s, Bill came into New York several days a week. He didn't return to Bedford Hills at night but instead stayed at the Washington Hotel in New York. Bill's days would be spent at the AA office, and his evenings with a circle of close friends that included people who worked at the office and other AA members.

Bill used this group as his sounding board, holding forth on a regular basis about whatever was on his mind. Lois's enthusiasm for Bill's monologues was less than it might have been. In part, this was because they were ideas he had already discussed with her, but it was also because Bill liked to hear himself talk, and Lois, who prided herself on her brevity when speaking or writing, found his verbosity embarrassing.

Whenever Bill was in New York, he would regale this group with his plans for AA. He also liked to talk about the conclusions he was drawing from his spiritual investigations. Bill thought he was learning a great deal about the spiritual world and humankind's relationship to it. Much of what he was learning he felt could have important implications in the treatment of alcoholics. Most alcoholics, he was increasingly convinced, had turned to alcohol as part of a misguided but well-intentioned and necessary spiritual quest. Wynn, an AA acolyte many years Bill's junior, listened rapturously.

There was another aspect of Bill's bond with the younger woman. Like Bill, Helen suffered from depression. All during the years of Bill's drinking, Lois had been empathy itself. She never stopped believing in him as a good and potentially great man, and she dedicated her life to finding some way to help him in his battle with alcoholism. But Lois didn't set out to find a cure for Bill's depressions. She even found it hard to believe that he was sick. When Bill talked with Helen about depression, she knew exactly what he was talking about and she was therefore able to provide him with the understanding Lois could not provide.

Beginning in the late 1960s, Bill's emphysema had progressed to the point where he often wasn't getting around very well. Helen visited him at Stepping Stones, and she was sometimes accompanied by her son, Shepperd Strudwick, 3rd. In 1968, with Bill's growing infirmity making it harder for them to spend time with one another, Helen bought a house in Ireland. She and Bill stayed in contact, though, and near the end of Bill's life, when his emphysema was much progressed and he was on oxygen full-time, she returned to the United States and visited him in the hospital.

WHAT DID IT MEAN?

In its duration, intensity, and scope, Bill Wilson's relationship with Helen Wynn was of a different order than his other affairs. One AA member told me that Jack Norris himself confirmed to him the story many others reported to me about Jack having stayed up all one night to talk Bill out of divorcing Lois so that he could marry Helen. A number of people thought that, given the strength of his feelings for Wynn, only his sense of obligation toward Lois kept him from going through with it, but others I talked with seemed sure that Bill never seriously entertained the proposition. Tom P. told me that an understanding of what Bill was really after is possible only by taking note of the movement afoot to force him to give up either Helen or his leadership position in AA. As Tom saw it, this is another instance of Bill arguing for more than he wanted. By seeming to allow himself to be persuaded by Norris, he succeeded in winning AA's acceptance of his affair.

As for Lois, even if she was somehow able to believe that the tales of his previous escapades were solely the product of malice, it seems impossible that she knew nothing of his affair with Helen. If nothing else, there is the evidence of her husband's will and his royalty agreement with AA providing for Helen. Yet Lois was never known to give any indication to anyone that she thought her husband was ever less than faithful. Those who knew her best believe that, if this was true, it was because she never let herself know.

Wilson himself seems never to have entertained other people's highly idealized view of him. He rejected all impulses to turn AA into a personality cult, and he set up a system of governance for the organization designed to safeguard against it ever degenerating into one. In his public speaking and in his writing, he went out of his way to portray himself as a flawed human being struggling toward the light. Bill Wilson was forever insisting that many people were further along the path of spiritual enlightenment than he was. He also took great pains, when talking or writing about the honesty requirements of AA, to caution that a desire to unburden oneself should not lead to revelations that would injure innocent people.

When it came to other people, Bill was invariably tolerant of their differences and forgiving of their foibles. Some people, feeling unworthy of their responsibilities, attack others in an attempt to shift the focus of a scrutiny they imagine themselves to be unable to withstand. Bill never did this. Even when attacked by others, he refused to respond in kind. As for the sanctity of his writings and even the AA Steps, according to Lois and to Nell Wing he began each day prepared to tear it all up and start over, if he should discover that there was a better way to help alcoholics.

At the same time there is no evidence that his behavior ever caused him to feel so morally compromised that he could not fight for a principle he believed in. Throughout his long involvement with AA, there are numerous examples of crusades he led to persuade the fellowship of the wisdom of a particular course. There are no examples of his ever failing to take up the challenge.

Beginning at least as early as the publication of the Twelve and Twelve in 1953, some AA members have felt that the program no longer had the moral rigor or spiritual purity of its earlier days. Always, there have been attempts to lay the blame for this alleged "dilution" of the AA program at the feet of Bill Wilson. It is true that his spoken and written comments about AA became more laden with nuance over the years. There were fewer claims that the AA approach will result in miraculous changes in an alcoholic's life and character, a greater willingness to acknowledge that an individual's struggle with character defects might be lifelong. There were also explicit admissions that alcoholics who are not drinking can still have emotional health problems.

But from a review of the program's literature, it would seem that Alcoholics Anonymous never claimed to be about anything other than helping alcoholics to achieve sobriety, and Wilson's harshest critics have never contended that he ever wavered in his contention that AA can make it possible for alcoholics to stay away from alcohol. Many outside factors certainly played a significant role in the fact that AA's success rate is many times higher than it was in Akron, Ohio, during the summer of 1935. Changes in AA itself have certainly played a role as well. These include the growing number of AA meetings, the establishment of morning, noontime, and even midnight meetings, and the formalization of the sponsor relationship. They also include the creation of beginner's meetings, young people's groups, special interest groups for gays and lesbians, and Spanish-language groups. The meetings devoted to the particular concerns of various professions from health professionals to clergy to police have made a contribution. The willingness, albeit with some grumbling, to accept the dually addicted into the fold has certainly been a factor. Many of these changes in AA were begun during Bill's lifetime with his encouragement and support. As for the others, there is little reason to think they are anything he would have opposed.

Bill's personal behavior was certainly painful for and may have had a detrimental effect on the recovery of at least some of the women he behaved inappropriately with. He also had ample reason to feel bad about his betrayals of Lois.

Beginning with the reinvigoration of the women's movement in the 1960s and 1970s, many women have been critical of AA's "maleness." A focus of this criticism has been AA's unwillingness to revise its literature to change pronoun references or to excise its instances of blatant "little woman" sexism and the fact that women are not to be found in AA leadership positions in proportion to their representation in the membership. It is worth remembering that Bill was raised almost a century ago, and while he could justifiably be accused of possessing sexist attitudes, he was also capable of treating the women who worked with him with dignity and respect.

When Bill wrote the literature now being objected to as sexist, he was reflecting the prevailing attitude of his time. Nell Wing worked more closely with him for a longer period than anyone did. She has always said that from the time she first met him in 1947, the relationship he cultivated with her was that of an older brother. Bill also expressed his confidence in the ability of women to hold executive positions in the AA office, which not all the men in the office and on the board of trustees shared.

EXPANDING HORIZONS

January 24 had a bizarre significance in Bill Wilson's life. In 1916, it was the date he was married. In 1971, it was the day he died. In 1954, January 24 was the day Lois suffered a heart attack. It is commonly thought that the worst of Bill's depressions ended with the 1955 international AA convention, which was when he officially stepped down as AA's head man. One of the methods Bill recommended for dealing with maudlin self-concern was to immerse oneself in helping others, and Lois's heart attack seems to have provided him with such an opportunity.

Her need for him seems to have acted as a stabilizing influence, thereby making it possible for Lois to follow her doctor's advice to rest for a full year. She was sixty-three when she had her heart attack. That she lived another thirty-four years is the best indication of how completely she recovered from it.

Three weeks after Lois became ill, Bill's father died. Bill had last seen Gilman the year before, when he visited them at Stepping Stones. By then, Gilman was suffering from dementia caused by hardening of the arteries, and he found it very difficult to talk. Some have speculated that his mental impairment may have been related to his drinking, but according to Lois, like many people, as Gilman grew older, he drank progressively less.

Gilman Wilson died penniless in Vancouver, British Columbia. His financial reversal was so severe that he ended up working as a night watchman in a quarry he had once been part owner of. Although Bill only saw his father perhaps a dozen times between 1906 and 1948, he always maintained a cordial relationship with him, and beginning in 1941, he contributed to his support. When Gilman's health deteriorated, Bill wanted to move him east, but it would have meant giving up the pension his father received in Canada, and Gilman and Christine, his second wife, were looked after by Vancouver AA members.

Nineteen fifty-four was also the year Bill carried on a death-row correspondence with Caryl Chessman, a convicted mugger, kidnapper, and rapist. Chessman had committed many crimes, but he was bright, articulate, and insightful, and he claimed to have had an awakening of sorts. He was also a jailhouse lawyer of the first order, winning for himself a series of stays of execution that kept him on death row for twelve years. Chessman became a nationally known figure in the early 1950s after the publication of his autobiography, *Cell 2455, Death Row*, in which he chronicled his descent into what he characterized as criminally insane behavior.

In his book, Chessman compares the criminal psychopath to an alcoholic, and this prompted Jack Alexander to wonder whether people like Chessman might find the AA Steps useful. Alcoholics Anonymous had been helping alcoholics in prisons since 1940, when the first prison group was formed in San Quentin. Alexander's thought was that if the Steps could produce a spiritual conversion in alcoholics, they might also be able to help people who engaged in criminally insane behavior.

Although Chessman and Bill exchanged a number of letters, the question of whether the AA Steps might be able to help criminals who were not alcoholics was never addressed. Their correspondence was cut short when Chessman's extended letter-writing privileges were again restricted to family members, but Bill's letters to him are still remarkable. In one of them, he told Chessman that society reacted similarly to alcoholics and criminals: it wanted to punish them or kill them off. One is at a loss to know what Bill could have meant by this.

Public drunkenness was illegal in the United States in 1954, but it was hardly a capital offense. Every local jail had its "drunk tank," where the intoxicated were held overnight and then released. Longer sentences were reserved for northern climes and imposed with the onset of winter, with release dates coincident with the arrival of warmer weather. Incarceration was certainly no substitute for medical treatment, but putting homeless alcoholics in jail to keep them from freezing to death can hardly be construed as punishment.

Bill's letters to Chessman express in stronger terms the concerns about blind and soulless amorality he makes reference to in the AA book *Twelve Steps and Twelve Traditions*. According to Bill, both the alcoholic and the criminal were sick, but society made them sick. Society itself was nearly as sick as the people it regarded as its least desirable elements. The pursuit of money, power, and prestige was dominating virtually everyone's behavior; they were the only things that counted, and no one could be happy without them. Consequently, the people who failed to acquire these things suffered from depression and overpowering feelings of rebellion and revenge. As Bill saw it, a society that put such a high premium on these values was doomed.

It wasn't only society that he was concerned would destroy itself. In addition to philosophers and social scientists like Gerald Heard and Aldous Huxley, Bill numbered among his acquaintances the nuclear physicist Robert J. Oppenheimer. Oppenheimer played an integral role in the development of the atomic bomb, but he later became an opponent of nuclear weapons. Bill shared Oppenheimer's concern about the danger of a total nuclear conflagration, and he also believed that AA, which urged people to live life on a spiritual basis, had the power to save the world.

Wilson's politics are hard to categorize. He seemed to deplore rampant materialism, but his support of free markets never faltered. Neither did his opposition to the welfare state, although on a personal level he was the world's easiest touch. Alcoholics lived with him rent free when he hardly had two nickels to rub together, and beginning when he could ill afford it, he sent money to the same father who didn't contribute to his support after his parents divorced. Bill also helped his cousin Howard, his half-sister, Helen, and just about anyone else down on his or her luck who came his way. Nell Wing said that Bill was forever borrowing money from her so that he could "lend" it to some poor soul who happened to wander into the AA office.

Then, of course, there was Ebby Thacher, who had already run through his family money by the time he found the Oxford Group. Ebby seems perpetually to have been financially desperate, and Bill was always willing to do whatever he could for him. Ebby lived with Bill and Lois on and off for years, and Bill supported him at other times, as well.

All through the forties, the fifties, and even into the sixties, when he was well enough, Bill was personally engaged in what AAs refer to as Twelfth-Step work. While he might have been opposed to the welfare state, his idea of trying to help the still suffering alcoholic included buying someone a meal or lending him or her a few dollars. Bill doesn't seem to have done these things purely from a sense of altruism. Nor was he trying to pay back the money he owed after the 1929 Crash twenty years later because he believed that a deal was a deal. He never held Hank P. or Ebby or anyone else to this standard. Bill helped people without reference to their worth, and he paid debts that others would long before have walked away from out of the same motive: he thought they were the right things to do for his own spiritual development.

Wilson might sound radical when discussing the cause of society's ills. However, it wasn't the economic system he condemned so much as the unreasoning value society put on success. His own interest in the world of business and finance never flagged. In the 1960s, he reestablished contact with Joe Hirschhorn, and he again provided him with occasional investment advice. Bill also became interested in the work of Stanford Ovshinsky, a scientist who had discovered a new way of converting heat directly into electricity. He advised Ovshinsky to focus on commercial applications for his discovery. When Ovshinsky's Energy Conversion Laboratories of Detroit became Energy Conversion Devices, Inc., Bill served on its board of directors.

For Bill, it all seemed to be a matter of keeping things in perspective. When he could afford it, the man who believed that unbridled materialism caused both alcoholism and criminality traded for a new car every two or three years, bought his suits at Abercrombe, and vacationed in the Bahamas. He might have thought that society was in the process of destroying itself, but he also knew that its salvation lay in convincing people to embrace a life based on different principles. That Alcoholics Anonymous is composed of people trying to do just that is clearly part of Bill Wilson's legacy.

In 1954, Yale University offered Bill an honorary doctorate, with the stipulation that no photographs would be taken and there would be no publicity. Many AA members thought that Bill should accept it, and the trustees of the Alcoholic Foundation were in favor of it. Fearful of the precedent it would set of an AA member being able to earn personal recognition for AA work, Bill declined the honor. His refusal made a deep impression on the Yale awards committee, and it served to enhance AA's reputation as a morally superior organization. At Bill's request, no public announcement of Yale's offer was ever made, but copies of the correspondence between him and the nominating committee were circulated privately, in the hope that other AA members who might be tempted to accept honors based on their AA work would follow his example.

Other institutions subsequently offered Bill honorary degrees, but these, too, were declined. Bill also turned down the opportunity to be the subject of a *Time* magazine cover story, although his full name wouldn't have been used and he would have been photographed from the back.

THE SIXTIES BILL

At the 1955 International AA Convention, the AA General Conference was made a permanent institution, and Bill officially stepped down as AA's head man. However, his work for AA was far from over. He would still write AA's Twelve Concepts of Service and the *AA General Service Manual,* which together form a kind of constitution and a governmental structure for Alcoholics Anonymous. He would also write *AA Comes of Age,* a book about the history of the development of the program's governing structure.

The AA Concepts don't share the elegance of AA's Twelve Steps or its Twelve Traditions, nor are they as well known to AA members. The Steps and the Traditions are reprinted in virtually every AA publication, but only those members who become interested in the workings of the AA conference seem to be aware of the Concepts. Although many years of thought and reflection went into fashioning them, the statement of each Concept is long and convoluted, and the thoughts expressed sometimes seem tortured by Bill's felt necessity that, like the Steps and the Traditions, the Concepts should be twelve in number.

Alcoholics Anonymous's Twelve Concepts represent a unique and fascinating set of principles that derive the right of AA's leaders to speak and act for the fellowship while establishing written guarantees for individual freedom and minority rights. If the subtext of the AA Traditions is to help prevent AA groups acting as individual groups from straying from AA's primary purpose, the subtext of the Concepts is Bill's strongly felt need to establish a structure for AA that would help insure that the organization as a whole would never lose track of the fact its reason for being was to help alcoholics stay sober. As with the Traditions, his faith in the wisdom of the group conscience to keep AA on course forms the bedrock on which the Concepts are based.

The Concepts serve to protect the fellowship from becoming a top-down rather than a bottom-up organization. Both Bill's legal training and his experience in the world of finance are evident in their careful rigor. The essays he wrote to accompany them demonstrate the amazing range of his thought and powers of expression; they are also at turns as down-home and folksy as anything he ever wrote. Alcoholics Anonymous wags have commented that Bill's primary purpose in writing the AA's Twelve Concepts was to try to protect the fellowship from himself, but there were also a number of longtime AA members only too ready to anoint themselves the new head man, should anything happen to him.

Alcoholics Anonymous members often suppose an inability to let go to be a prime characteristic of alcoholics. While many AAs continued to turn to Bill for leadership, others criticized him for staying involved in AA affairs long after the convention in 1955. But that he was willing to let go at all sets AA apart from the leadership of the Washingtonians and the Emmanuel Movements to help alcoholics. It also sets it apart from so many of the male-dominated, personality-based self-help movements that have come and gone since AA's inception. Bill's attachment to the organization he founded was profound, and his interest in it was unflagging. Yet from the beginning, he seems to have been much more focused on leading AA in the direction he thought it ought to go than dominating it.

It was after stepping down at the 1955 convention that Bill put together *Alcoholics Anonymous Comes of Age,* a compilation in summary form of the talks he gave at the convention. The book serves as a brief history of the fellowship, but Bill himself thought it was dull reading, and many people agree.

After the 1955 convention, many AA members resented his continuing attempts to influence what the fellowship did, but Bill lobbied hard to encourage AA involvement in film and television productions. As he saw it, AA may have been a household word, but there were millions of alcoholics who had never tried it. He wanted AA to be involved in these productions so that the producers had the information they needed to portray AA correctly.

He also proposed and worked for the establishment of an AA World Service Conference that would link AA members around the globe. Like many of the things he wanted for AA, his interest in a conference that would link AA groups from other countries was considerably ahead of the general consensus; the first AA World Service Conference wasn't held until 1969.

As Bill's emphysema progressed in the 1960s, whatever he accomplished was done against the background of increasing disability. In 1961, he wrote Carl Jung to thank him for steering Rowland H. toward a spiritual solution for his drinking problem and he outlined the connection between that event and the formation of AA. Jung, who was age eighty-five and in failing health, replied, confirming his view that alcoholism was a product of a "spiritual thirst for wholeness."

In 1961, AA had 160,000 members and 9,000 groups, but it was still seeking justification and validation for its approach to helping alcoholics stay sober. That Jung, a leading theorist of the "enemy" camp, which was the way many AA members thought of psychoanalysis, would acknowledge the efficacy of spiritual conversion experiences in producing psychological change was seen by many as the fellowship's final vindication.

Wilson himself never seems to have had ideological enemies. He regarded Father Ed Dowling as his spiritual sponsor, and he had many theological conversations with Fulton Sheen, but he also relied on William James, the father of American psychology, to provide an explanation of what had happened in the middle of the night in Towns Hospital. Bill employed the psychiatrist Harry Tiebout's terminology in describing the changes AA's Twelve Steps were able to bring about; and he sought help for his depressions from the psychiatrists Tiebout, Frances Weekes, Abram Hoffer, and Humphry Osmond.

In 1963, AA was stung by a critical article published in *Harper's* magazine titled "Alcoholics Anonymous: Cult or Cure?" Written by Dr. Arthur H. Cain, a psychologist, the article claimed that AA had become a fanatical cult and a hindrance to research in the field of alcoholism. It also said that AA's dogmatism had prevented people from seeking a more moderate solution to alcoholism, including achieving sobriety in AA without becoming enslaved to it.

Cain also said that he had found AA hostile to criticism from any source. As if in confirmation of his point, AA members responded to the article by bombarding *Harper's* with hundreds of angry letters. Other members wrote saying that they felt the criticism was important and necessary. Some even said that the views Cain was expressing were their views, as well. Bill handled the brouhaha the article caused by writing an article in the *Grapevine* suggesting that AA might be able to learn from its critics. He also indicated in an oblique way that he felt that some of what Cain had said might be true.

The wisdom of Bill's approach to the controversy was borne out when a second article by Cain subsequently appeared in the *Saturday Evening Post*. The *Post* had by this time lost much of its circulation, and the views expressed in it were often desperately slanted toward the sensational. This article was clearly hostile to AA, and Dr. Cain actually wrote to Bill to apologize for it. He said that the magazine's editors had insisted on changes he had felt uncomfortable with. He also said that, had he known the article would be titled "Speaking Out: Alcoholics Can Be Cured Despite AA," he would not have allowed them to publish it.

Bill felt there was one more thing to be done to ensure AA's future. He wanted to see the ratio of nonalcoholic to alcoholic trustees on the AA General Service Board, formerly known as the Alcoholic Foundation, changed to give the alcoholic trustees control. At the time the Alcoholic Foundation was incorporated, there were hardly any members sober as long as three years, so ensuring that the nonalcoholic Rockefeller men would control the foundation seemed prudent. But twenty years later, Bill felt very strongly that AA's fate would not be in its own hands as long as the nonalcoholic trustees could dominate the board.

Unfortunately for Bill, he seems to have been the only one who felt this way. That he was the only one who thought it was time for a change certainly seems odd, but the issue was also less significant than it appears to be. No dispute had ever pitted the nonalcoholic and the alcoholic trustees against one another, and if one ever did, since 1955, AA's governing structure had placed the ultimate authority for AA in the AA Conference. The conference delegates could override board decisions. The delegates also had the power to change the trustee's ratio. They could even, if they saw fit, dissolve the board.

As far as Bill was concerned, though, on this issue the practical signifi-cance of his proposal was of little consequence. As he saw it, if AA was to be in charge of itself, there was no place for non-AA members to have a majority voice in its affairs.

The matter quickly became a power struggle between Bill and the con-ference. Just because AA's founder was so insistent, the conference dele-gates seem to have felt the need to demonstrate their ultimate authority by refusing to act. When the conference turned him down, Bill took it very personally. He was so hurt that, turning whiny and sarcastic, he ac-tually asked the delegates if they would still permit him to have an office at AA headquarters in New York.

Bill liked to use the analogy of parent and child when discussing the re-lationship between AA and its founders, but he didn't seem to grasp what his relationship to AA must be after it had come of age. Year after year, he campaigned for and succeeded in obtaining reconsideration of the ratio issue, but the conference always turned down his proposal. The insignifi-cance of the issue gave Bill's efforts a Don Quixote–like quality, but it was a way for him to continue on in a familiar role: leading the organization he had created in the direction he thought it should go.

Finally, in 1967, Jack Norris, the nonalcoholic chair of the board, asked the conference to change the ratio, and the conference responded immediately. The nonalcoholic trustees had had only a simple majority. As if to make it abundantly clear that the nonalcoholic's role in AA was advisory, the conference expanded the board to provide for twice as many alcoholic as nonalcoholic trustees.

NIACIN

Of all Bill's postretirement activities, none created more of a furor than his advocacy of niacin megavitamin therapy for alcoholics and schizo-phrenics. Lost in most accounts of his interest in this B vitamin is his in-sistence that he got involved in promoting its use reluctantly. Bill learned about niacin from the psychiatrists Humphrey Osmund and Abram Hof-fer, whom he had previously come to know through his interest in LSD.

Niacin, a B vitamin, seems to have a mood stabilizing effect on some of the people who take it. According to Dr. Hoffer, Bill was immediately im-pressed with the results he and Osmund were obtaining by giving niacin to alcoholics who were not previously able to maintain sobriety. Bill was even more impressed with the way niacin made him feel. Of all the things he tried in seeking relief from depression, nothing seemed to have the impact niacin did. He told many people that it was only after taking niacin that he knew what it was like to feel normal.

Hoffer and Osmund published papers on their researches in some of medicine's most highly respected peer-reviewed journals, but they had little impact. Virtually all therapeutic agents win acceptance in the medical community because of a massive effort undertaken by a pharmaceutical house. Niacin was readily available, cheaply manufactured, and, as a naturally occurring vitamin, could not be patented. As Bill saw it, the fact that such a campaign hadn't been launched for niacin was the only reason it wasn't gaining wider acceptance as a treatment for alcoholism.

According to Dr. Hoffer, Bill saw niacin "as completing the third leg of the stool, the physical to complement the spiritual and emotional." Bill's family history of depression and the immensely positive response he had to niacin would seem to support the possibility that his depressions had, at least in part, a physical cause.

Hoffer met Bill for the first time in the early 1960s at a meeting of the Parapsychology Foundation. Bill was seated next to Humphrey Osmund, Hoffer's research partner. Bill had received his invitation through Aldous Huxley, who was a strong supporter of Osmund and Hoffer's work, as was his brother, Sir Julian Huxley. Julian Huxley was the head of the UN's World Health Organization. The Huxley Institute for Biosocial Research, which Hoffer and Osmund founded to support research in the field of orthomolecular medicine, was named for Aldous and Julian Huxley.

Lois always felt that niacin had indeed helped Bill. Although Lois claimed never to have known depression, she took niacin herself every day for the rest of her life. She felt that it gave her energy and helped to protect her from colds and flu. Lois also encouraged other people to take niacin, and she continued Bill's support of Osmund and Hoffer's work by supporting the Huxley Institute.

With Bill's encouragement, Hoffer and Osmund published a book on the researches entitled *New Hope for Alcoholics*. The title aptly reflects how Bill felt about niacin therapy. He devoted the rest of his life to making alcoholics aware of the possible benefits niacin offered. He even wrote three pamphlets on the subject, the last of which was published posthumously. The pamphlets were directed to physicians, and Bill attended numerous "Doctors in AA" meetings in an attempt to interest doctors who were treating alcoholics in this therapy.

Bill also tried to get other alcoholics who suffered from depression to try niacin. Lib S. told me that her husband, Tom, who was also an alcoholic, suffered from depression. Bill got him to try niacin, but after about two weeks, Tom stopped taking it, and the depressions continued.

"One night, Bill dropped by," Lib recalled, "which was something he would just do from time to time. It was only about six o'clock, but Tom was in bed. 'What about the niacin?' Bill wanted to know. When I told him that Tom had stopped taking it, he marched right into the bedroom and talked to Tom like a Dutch uncle.

"Tom started taking it again. At first, nothing seemed to happen. Then, gradually, he started having more energy. After about three months, he turned to me one day and said, 'You know, I'm not depressed anymore.'" Tom kept taking niacin and, according to Lib, he never suffered from depression again.

Bill also helped Hoffer and Osmund in their work with schizophrenia, including advising them on how to organize Schizophrenics Anonymous Groups. He was instrumental in organizing a conference at Fordham University held to discuss the use of megavitamins for the treatment of schizophrenia and alcoholics. Hoffer also remembers Bill helping to persuade the National Institute of Mental Health to issue a grant for a study of the effectiveness of niacin in treating schizophrenia.

Unfortunately, as was often true about the things he was excited about, Bill's enthusiasm for niacin knew no bounds. He even had secretaries working in the AA office taking it. They weren't alcoholic or schizophrenic, nor had they ever suffered from depression, but Bill thought they should be taking the vitamin, so they took it. There's no evidence that it hurt them, but in urging them to take it, Bill certainly hurt himself.

He also hurt himself by using his office at AA headquarters to promote niacin. The first pamphlets he wrote on the subject were mailed from the office, accompanied by letters from Bill on AA stationery. As he had ample reason to know, many AA members were as socially conservative and close-minded as he was liberal and open-minded. That he wasn't able to anticipate their reaction to his juggernaut for a vitamin therapy seems incredible, but when the uproar ensued, he was shocked, angry, and hurt.

Many AA members thought Bill was violating the very AA Traditions he had written about not associating AA with outside causes. In his defense, it should be remembered that, by this time, he had been trying to help AA members suffering from depression for nearly twenty years, and had written countless letters on AA stationery in which he shared what he himself had found helpful in dealing with depression.

Bill had also written about depression in the *Grapevine*. In 1962, the

Grapevine even published an article about dealing with depression by the minister of the Universalist Church in Woodstock, Vermont.

To Bill, his telling AA members about the benefits of niacin took place along a continuum. But AA members are generally wary about using any substance to improve the way they feel, and many saw Bill's advocacy of niacin as part of a different continuum—that of his experimentation with LSD. Bill moved his niacin-promoting activities to an office in Pleasantville, and he no longer wrote letters singing the praises of niacin therapy on AA letterhead. But the damage he did to his prestige in AA circles was enormous.

This was especially unfortunate, because Osmund and Hoffer were terrifically impressed with AA and with the value of peer-group support in general. Niacin does seem to be an effective treatment for some people who suffer from depression or schizophrenia. Orthomolecular psychiatry, in its infancy when Bill first encountered it, now treats many mental health problems. Thousands of physicians the world over subscribe to its tenets.

GOOD-BYE, GOOD-BYE, GOOD-BYE

By the time Ebby Thacher died in 1966, a victim of emphysema, Bill had been trying to quit smoking for more than twenty years. He'd also known since the early sixties that he had emphysema himself. Smoking had begun to impair his health in the 1940s, in the form of frequent colds and chronic bronchitis, and his breathing was noticeably labored from the mid-1960s onward. Yet even when his breathing became so problematic he needed frequent doses of oxygen to get through the day, he smoked.

A number of visitors to Stepping Stones during Bill's last years report witnessing scenes in which Bill would be trying to decide whether to have more oxygen or another cigarette. Inevitably, the cigarette won out. Bill was thought to have finally quit smoking early in 1969, by which time his bouts with bronchitis had become struggles with pneumonia, but several people confirm that he was still smoking even after most everyone thought he had quit. He hid cigarettes in his car, and for as long as he was still well enough to drive, he smoked.

It seems beyond comprehension, but the evidence is inescapable. The man who pioneered the approach to addictive illness that has helped millions free themselves from alcoholism and a myriad of other addictive problems—including smoking—literally smoked himself to death.

What a different world it would be if instead of promoting niacin, Bill Wilson had quit smoking himself and spent the 1960s trying to help other

AA members do the same. But Bill had been shocked out of drinking. In a moment of complete desperation, his ego collapsed at depth and the light poured in. An event like that never occurred for him in relationship to his smoking. AA's Twelve Steps provide a gradual, yet more permanent, method for letting the light in, but it wasn't a path Bill was capable of taking to quit smoking.

Bill was seventy years old in 1965, and the emphysema was taking its toll. Many people in AA were intolerant of the changes that were taking place in the way young people dressed and behaved, feeling that those who tuned in, turned on, and dropped out deserved exactly what they got. Especially since, when hippies came to AA, it was because they wanted to stop drinking and using drugs and not out of any particular desire to change their lifestyle.

As the sixties progressed, Bill viewed with alarm what he saw as the accelerating breakdown of group conscience throughout the world, and he worried about how it might affect AA. On a personal level, he was anything but hostile to these "new" people. As far as he was concerned, what was most significant about the 1960s for AA was that the fellowship was beginning to include people in their early twenties, and even younger, in significant numbers.

When Bill found four long-haired, bell-bottomed, and mini-skirted young people in the AA office one day, he did what he often did with people he wanted to get to know better: he took them to lunch. He also reported the encounter in the *AA Grapevine*. Bill admitted that having people around who looked like that might take some getting used to. But he also let people know that the hippies he had met had impressed him with their commitment to staying alcohol- and drug-free.

Long practiced in arranging his life around his disabilities, Bill managed to keep up a good front so long that, even as late as 1970, many of the people who saw him regularly at the AA office weren't aware that he was dying. As often as possible, he took the walks around the neighborhood at Stepping Stones he had become accustomed to as part of his battle against depression, and he kept up his interest in niacin. When he was well enough, he was at work on his third article about the vitamin. It was on his desk at the time of his death.

As the emphysema progressed, Bill's nights were frequently filled with dreams and visions. Even when awake, he sometimes fell victim to hallucinations. While many of them were pleasant, others were not pleasant at all. Bill's ravings about the things he thought he was seeing turned his existence, and that of Lois, Harriet, their housekeeper, and Nell Wing, who was a regular guest, increasingly nightmarish.

By 1969, Bill was ill most of the time, but he still managed to make the two appearances that were most expected of him: the AA General Service Conference in April, and in November, the "Bill W. dinner," the annual fund-raiser for the greater New York City AA Intergroup. But in 1970, when he began his customary talk at the opening dinner of the AA General Service Conference, his breathlessness forced him to stop almost before he had begun. Nineteen seventy was, of course, also a convention year. Bill was very ill in July, when the AA International Convention met in Miami with eleven thousand in attendance, but he made a heroic effort to be there.

The trip took so much out of him, he was forced to cancel all his scheduled appearances. An ambulance transferred him from his hotel room to the Miami Heart Institute, where Ed B., an AA physician friend, attended him. Bill did speak briefly at a Sunday morning breakfast, rising from a wheelchair equipped with oxygen to do so. He left the convention immediately afterward for the Miami Heart Institute. He was at the institute for a number of days before he was well enough to fly to New York.

Shortly after returning to Stepping Stones, Bill developed pneumonia. The hallucinations were a regular feature now, and he was in and out of the hospital all summer and into the fall. In November, Lois attended the Bill W. dinner by herself. The affair had long been New York's largest sit-down dinner, and twenty-two hundred people attended in 1970.

Lois read the remarks Bill had written for the occasion. His topic was spiritual importance of anonymity to AA. At the end of his talk, Bill included something he said was paraphrased from an old Arab saying a friend had told him about: "I salute you and I thank you for your lives." It was, of course, exactly the way everyone present felt about Bill. The remarks became known as "Bill's Last Message." Lois would read it at the dinner every year for the rest of her life. The friend who had told Bill about the Arab saying was Helen Wynn's son.

Bill was confined to the upstairs bedroom at Stepping Stones through the rest of the fall and into the winter, attended by nurses around the clock. Most commonly, he would greet each day filled with dread of what lay in store for him.

It seemed just a matter of time now, but Dr. Ed B., the specialist from the Miami Heart Institute, thought a new breathing machine the institute had just acquired might be able to help Bill. Brinkley Smithers, a longtime AA friend, chartered a plane, and, accompanied by Lois, Nell, and Dr. Ed, who came north for the trip, Bill was flown to Miami.

During the flight, Bill entertained his fellow passengers with descriptions of his parents, grandparents, and his old friend Mark Whalon. They were all dead, but he could see them there with him in the plane.

After Bill was settled into his room, Lois and Nell went to dinner. The date was January 24, and it was Lois and Bill's fifty-third wedding anniversary. When Lois went to Bill's room to say good night to him that evening, he seemed comfortable and in good spirits. By 11:30, he was dead.

With AA's approval, Bill's obituary appeared on the front page of the *New York Times,* complete with his full name and a photograph. It went on for more than two thousand words, chronicling his remarkable life and AA accomplishments. By 1971, there were some three hundred thousand alcoholics staying sober in AA.

A private memorial service was held at Stepping Stones, and other services were held in major cities all over the United States and in some foreign capitals as well. The service in New York was held at the Cathedral of St. John the Divine. There were about 500 AA groups in the metropolitan New York area at the time, plus 150 groups in jails, hospitals, and other institutions.

St. John's is the largest cathedral in the world, and it can accommodate in the neighborhood of forty-five hundred people. Perhaps the greatest tribute to Bill may lay in the fact that, according to the *Times'* account of the event, only five hundred people attended the service. Long schooled in the AA dictum to put principles above personalities, AA members apparently felt uncomfortable about turning out to pay tribute to their founder and guiding light.

Fourteen years later, with AA's active membership numbering well over one million and more than five million copies of the *Big Book* in print, New York area AA members again assembled at the Cathedral of St. John the Divine. This time it was to celebrate AA's fiftieth anniversary, and the church was packed to overflowing.

Bill was buried in East Dorset in May, again in a private ceremony. The headstone makes no mention of AA. The footstone, like others in this cemetery, memorializes his military service during World War I. By the time Lois was buried next to him in 1988, the grave had become a place of pilgrimage. Many AA members still leave sobriety medallions and other mementos on top of the headstone.

In 1984, an Irish AA member wrote to Lois asking for something of Bill's. She sent him a collar pin. A couple of months later, the man wrote to say that the pin was doing a world of good. It seems they had some of their worst cases down on their knees, and they were holding the pin to their foreheads while they prayed over them.

Lois wrote back that she didn't see how Bill's collar pin could help anyone stay sober and she didn't think Bill would have approved. She went on to say that while there wasn't anything Bill could do anymore to help anyone stay sober, they could help people by practicing the AA program. The man wrote a third time to thank her for setting them straight, and he assured her that the pin would never again be put to such a use.

The Wilson House in East Dorset has been restored and reopened as an inn. More recently, the same nonprofit corporation bought the Griffith's home, located across the street on the farside of the church. Virtually all the inn's furnishings have been donated, and the staff is made up almost entirely of volunteers. Alcoholics Anonymous and Al-Anon meetings are held in the big room in the back behind the bar, and those who stay there can partake of the simple meals prepared and joined in by the staff. The inn's charges are calculated to make a stay there widely affordable.

A tour is offered, and everyone who stops by is urged to sign the guest book, but there are no mementos for sale. Ozzie L., who started the project, told me that he had planned to have postcards and much else. Then he decided that the only thing he wanted people to take away from their visit was a sense of the spirit of the place.

There is indeed a special quality about the Wilson House. Whether it has to do with the fact that Bill was born there or with the spirit in which the inn is run, one can hardly imagine it existing without Bill Wilson.

As we approach the millennium, we can hardly imagine what the world would be like without him, either. Bill Wilson has been dead for nearly thirty years. Alcoholism is still one of humankind's major scourges, but his dream of one day helping every drunk everywhere has never been closer to reality. The structure he created to replace him, then pleaded, hectored, cajoled, and fought to see put into place has worked well. Alcoholics Anonymous has carried on, one alcoholic helping another, for nearly as long as it existed with him. Its membership now numbers in the millions, and it can be found in nearly every country.

It may be too much to say that AA could ever save the world. On the other hand, the millions of alcoholics AA has helped have surely led better lives than they would have otherwise. There are also all the people Al-Anon has helped, and the Twelve-Step programs for gamblers, debtors, drug addicts, overeaters, codependents, and so on.

For all the forces still threatening to tear the world apart, there would also seem to be a new, still desperately fragile, yet growing, sense of community. And it is perhaps worth remembering that, just a few short years ago, a new century is something many people thought we would never survive to see.

Thanks, Bill.

WHERE TO FIND HELP

ALCOHOLICS ANONYMOUS

If you're looking for an AA meeting, the best way to find one would probably be to ask someone you know who is in AA. If you don't know anyone in AA or you would rather not ask them, pick up the telephone, call information, and ask the operator for the number for Alcoholics Anonymous.

There are AA intergroup offices in most metropolitan areas, and one of their main functions is to know where the meetings are and when. An intergroup office can also be helpful if you want to talk to someone about your drinking. There are usually people in the office you can talk to right away. If you want to talk further or have someone take you to an AA meeting, an intergroup office can arrange that, too.

Where the population is thinner, the operator may give you the number of an AA answering service, something you might think of as an intergroup office without the office. You will still be able to find out about an AA meeting, and you will still be able to talk to someone about your drinking or have someone take you to a meeting, but since AA answering services are usually run entirely by volunteers, it might take a little longer.

An AA Intergroup Office or Answering Service can also be a source for information about treatment programs and treatment assessment and referral services.

A worldwide directory of Alcoholics Anonymous and other information about AA can be obtained from the Alcoholics Anonymous General Service Office, 475 Riverside Drive, New York, NY 10027. Telephone: 212-870-3400. The directory and much else is also available on AA's Web site: http://www.alcoholics-anonymous.org

THE NATIONAL COUNCIL ON ALCOHOLISM AND DRUG DEPENDENCIES (NCADD)

If the operator can't find a number for AA in your area, ask her for the telephone number of the local council on alcoholism. NCADD has an affiliate in most counties. In addition to being able to help you connect to AA, the local NCADD affiliates have literature on problem drinking and drug taking and many of them also offer assessment, counseling, and treatment referral services.

NCADD also has a 24-hour referral service, 800-NCA-CALL, which it calls its "HOPE line."

A director of NCADD affiliates can be obtained from: The National Council on Alcoholism and Drug Dependencies, 12 West 21st Street, New York, NY 10010. Telephone 212-206-6770. A listing of affiliates and much else can also be found on NCADD's Web site: http://ncadd.org.

THE AL-ANON FAMILY GROUPS, INC.

Al-Anon also has intergroup offices in many metropolitan areas that offer much the same services as AA Intergroups. And like AA, where there aren't enough members to support an intergroup office there are Al-Anon answering services. NCADD affiliates can help you connect to Al-Anon as well.

A worldwide directory of Al-Anon groups can be obtained from: Al-Anon Family Group Headquarters, Inc., 1600 Corporate Landing Parkway, Virginia Beach, VA 23454-5619. Telephone: 888-4AL-ANON. The directory and much else is also available on Al-Anon's Web site: http://www.al-anon.org.

ALATEEN

As its name suggests, Alateen is for teenagers looking for help coping with a family member's drinking. Information about Alateen can be obtained through Al-Anon.

ALL ADDICTS ANONYMOUS

Based on the Twelve Steps of Alcoholics Anonymous and the Four Absolutes of the Oxford Group, All Addicts Anonymous (AAA) is a non-profit self-help group that offers help in dealing with addictions to "alcohol, drugs, tobacco, food, sex, worry, resentment, lying, depression, or anxiety." It specializes in helping people with multiple addictions who have not been able to maintain recovery. Information about AAA, including a directory of other AAA groups, can be obtained from the Upstate Group of All Addicts Anonymous, 161 Ridge Road, Hankins, NY 12741. Telephone: 914-887-4483.

MODERATION MANAGEMENT (MM)

Moderation Management describes itself as "a supportive mutual-help environment that encourages people who are concerned about their drinking to take action to cut back or quit drinking before drinking problems become severe." It also states that it is "not intended for alcoholics or for those severely dependent on alcohol."

It is a voluntary, non-profit program based on the premise that not all problem drinkers are alcoholics, a notion embraced by Bill Wilson in AA's *Big Book*. Wilson also suggested that anyone who wished to learn whether he or she was an alcoholic should try some controlled drinking.

By employing Moderation Management's drinking guidelines, many problem drinkers find that they can learn to moderate their drinking; others find the task mission impossible, and they are encouraged to try AA. As a result, MM has become a significant source of self-referrals to AA. Its address is: Moderation Management Network, Inc., P.O. Box 1752, Woodinville, Washington, 98072. Telephone: 888-561-9834. Web site: http://moderation.org

RATIONAL RECOVERY

Rational Recovery is also a self-help group for alcoholics who find much to object to in AA's approach to helping people stop drinking. Its address is: Rational Recovery, P.O. Box 800, Lotus, CA 95651. Telephone: 530-621-2667. Web site: http://rational.org/recovery

SECULAR ORGANIZATIONS FOR SOBRIETY (SOS)

A self-help group for people who have problems with AA centering around its religious aspects. Address: Secular Organizations for Sobriety (SOS), 5521 Grosvenor, Los Angeles, CA 90066. Telephone: 310-821-8430. Web site: http://www.secularhumanism.org/sos

SMART

SMART stands for Self-Management and Recovery Training, and it is a non-profit, abstinence-based program employing cognitive-behavioral techniques for coping with problem drinking along with a host of addictive/compulsive behaviors. Its address is: Self-Management and Recovery Training, 2400 Mercantile Road, Suite 11, Beachwood, OH 44122. Telephone: 216-292-0220. Web site: http://smartrecovery.org

WOMEN FOR SOBRIETY (WFS)

Women for Sobriety, Inc. is a non-profit organization dedicated to helping women overcome alcoholism and other addictions. Its address is: Women for Sobriety (WFS), P.O. Box 618, Quakertown, PA. Telephone: 800-333-1606. Web site: http://www.womenforsobriety.org

APPENDIX

THE TWELVE STEPS

1. We admitted we were powerless over alcohol—that our lives had become unmanageable.
2. Came to believe that a Power greater than ourselves could restore us to sanity.
3. Made a decision to turn our will and our lives over to the care of God as we understood Him.
4. Made a searching and fearless moral inventory of ourselves.
5. Admitted to God, to ourselves, and to another human being, the exact nature of our wrongs.
6. Were entirely ready to have God remove all these defects of character.
7. Humbly asked Him to remove our shortcomings.
8. Made a list of all the persons we had harmed, and became willing to make amends to them all.
9. Made direct amends to such people wherever possible, except when to do so would injure them or others.
10. Continued to take personal inventory and when we were wrong promptly admitted it.
11. Sought through prayer and meditation to improve our conscious contact with God as we understood Him, praying only for knowledge of His will for us and the power to carry that out.
12. Having had a spiritual awakening as the result of these steps, we tried to carry this message to alcoholics, and to practice these principles in all our affairs.

THE TWELVE TRADITIONS

1. Our common welfare should come first; personal recovery depends on AA unity.
2. For our group purpose there is but one ultimate authority—a loving God as He may express Himself in our group conscience. Our leaders are but trusted servants; they do not govern.
3. The only requirement for AA membership is a desire to stop drinking.
4. Each group should be autonomous except in matters affecting other groups or AA as a whole.
5. Each group has but one primary purpose—to carry its message to the alcoholic who still suffers.
6. An AA group ought never to endorse, finance, or lend the AA name to any related facility or outside enterprise, lest problems of money, property, and prestige divert us from our primary purpose.
7. Every AA group ought to be fully self-supporting, declining outside contributions.
8. Alcoholics Anonymous should remain forever nonprofesional, but our service centers may employ special workers.
9. AA, as such, ought never be organized; but we may create service boards or committees directly responsible to those they serve.
10. Alcoholics Anonymous has no opinion on outside issues; hence the AA name ought never be drawn into public controversy.
11. Our public relations policy is based on attraction rather than promotion; we need always maintain personal anonymity at the level of press, radio, and films.
12. Anonymity is the spiritual foundation of all our traditions, ever reminding us to place prinicples before personalities.

THE TWELVE CONCEPTS

1. The final responsibility and ultimate authority for AA World Services should always reside in the collective conscience of our whole Fellowship.
2. When, in 1955, the AA groups confirmed the permanent charter for their General Service Conference, they thereby delegated to the Conference complete authority for the active maintenance of our world services and thereby made the Conference—excepting for any change in the Twelve

Traditions or in Article 12 of the Conference Charter—the actual voice and the effective conscience for our whole Society.

3. As traditional means of creating and maintaining a clearly defined working relation between the groups, the Conference, the AA General Service Board and its several service corporations, staffs, committees, and executives, and of thus insuring their effective leadership, it is here suggested that we endow each of these elements of world service with a traditional "Right of Decision."

4. Throughout our Conference structure, we ought to maintain at all responsible levels a traditional "Rights of Participation", taking care that each classification or group of our world servants shall be allowed a voting representation in reasonable proportion to the responsibility that each must discharge.

5. Throughout our world service structure, a traditional "Right of Appeal" ought to prevail, thus assuring us that minority opinion will be heard and that petitions for the redress of personal grievances will be carefully considered.

6. On behalf of AA on a whole, our General Service Conference has the principal responsibility for the maintenance of our world services, and it traditionally has the final decision respecting large matters of general policy and finance. But the Conference also recognizes that the chief initiative and the active responsibility in most of these matters should be exercised primarily by the trustee members of the Conference when they act among themselves as the General Service Board of Alcoholics Anonymous.

7. The Conference recognizes that the Charter and the Bylaws of the General Service Board are legal instruments; that the trustees are thereby fully empowered to manage and conduct all of the world service affairs of Alcoholics Anonymous. It is further understood that the Conference Charter itself is not a legal document; that it relies instead upon the force of traditions and the power of the AA purse for its final effectiveness.

8. The trustees of the General Service Board act in two primary capacities: (a) With respect to the larger matters of overall policy and finance, they are the principal planners and administrators. They and their primary committees directly manage these affairs. (b) But with respect to our separately incorporated and constantly active services, the relation of the trustees is mainly that of full stock ownership and of custodial oversight which they exercise through their ability to elect all directors of these entities.

9. Good service leaders, together with sound and appropriate methods of choosing them, are at all levels indispensable for our future funcitoning and safety. The primary world service leadership, once exercised by the founders of AA, must necessarily be assumed by the trustees of the General Service Board of Alcoholics Anonymous.

10. Every service responsibility should be matched by an equal service authority—the scope of such authority to be always well defined whether by tradition, by resolution, by specific job description, or by appropriate charters and bylaws.

11. While the trustees hold final responsibility for AA's world service administration, they should always have the assurance of the best possible standing committees, corporate service directors, executives, staffs, and consultants. Therefore the composition of these underlying committees and service boards, the personal qualifications of their members, the manner of their induction into service, the systems of their rotation, the way in which they are related to each other, the special rights and duties of our executives, staffs, and consultants, together with a proper basis for the financial compensation of these special workers, will always be matter for serious care and concern.

12. General Warranties of the Conference: In all its proceedings, the General Service Conference shall observe the spirit of the AA Tradition, taking great care that the conference never becomes the seat of perilous wealth or power; that sufficient operating funds, plus an ample reserve, be its prudent financial principle; that none of the Conference members shall ever be placed in a position of unqualified authority over any of the others; that all important decisions be reached by discussion, vote, and whenever possible, by substantial unanimity; that no Conference action ever be personally punitive or an incitement to public controversy; that though the Conference may act for the service of Alcoholics Anonymous, it shall never perform any acts of government; and that like the Society of Alcoholics Anonymous which it serves, the Conference itself will always remain democratic in thought and action.

BIBLIOGRAPHY

BOOKS & PAMPHLETS

Anderson, Daniel J. *Perspectives on Treatment: The Minnesota Experience.* Center City, Minn.: Hazelden, 1981.

————. *Psychopathology of Denial.* Center City, Minn.: Hazelden, 1981.

B., Mel. "Bill W. and His Friends." Toledo, Ohio: unpublished manuscript, 1982.

————. *Ebby: The Man Who Sponsored Bill W.* Center City, Minn.: Hazelden, 1998.

————. *My Search for Bill Wilson.* Toledo, Ohio, 1991.

————. *New Wine: The Spiritual Roots of the Twelve Step Miracle.* Center City, Minn.: Hazelden, 1991.

Bailey, Margaret B., and Barry Leach. *Alcoholics Anonymous, Pathway to Recovery: A Study of 1,058 Members of the A.A. Fellowship in New York City.* New York: The National Council on Alcoholism, 1965.

Bean, Margaret. *Alcoholics Anonymous: A.A.* New York: Insight Communications, 1975.

Berg, Steven L., Dana Finnegan, and Emily McNally. *The NALGAP Annotated Bibliography: Alcoholism, Substance Abuse, and Lesbians-Gay Men.* Fort Wayne, Ind.: The National Association of Lesbian and Gay Alcoholism Professionals, 1987.

Berg, Steven L. *Spirituality and Addiction: A Bibliography.* Wheeling, W. Va.: The Bishop of Books, 1993.

Berryman, John. *Recovery.* New York: Farrar, Straus & Giroux, 1973.

Best of the Grapevine. New York: The AA Grapevine, 1985.

Best of the Grapevine, Vol. 2. New York: The AA Grapevine, 1986.

Best of the Grapevine, Vol. 3. New York: The AA Grapevine, 1998.

Bienvenu, Dudley. *I'm An Alcoholic: What's Your Excuse? An Alcoholic's View of Himself and His Illness.* New York: Vantage Press, 1982.

Bill Wilson & The Vitamin B-3 Therapy 1965–1971. Facsimile limited reprint. Wheeling, W. Va.: The Bishop of Books, 1993.

Bishop, Charles, Jr., and Bill Pittman. *The Annotated Bibliography of Alcoholics Anonymous.* Wheeling, W. Va.: The Bishop of Books, 1989.

Bishop, Charles, Jr., and William Pittman. *To Be Continued . . . The Alcoholics Anonymous World Biography 1935–1994.* Wheeling, W. Va.: The Bishop of Books, 1994.

Bishop, Charles, Jr., ed. *The Washingtonians & Alcoholics Anonymous: Three Classic Reprints Commemorating the 150th Anniversary of the 1842 Washingtonian Book.* Wheeling, W. Va.: The Bishop of Books, 1992.

Bissell, LeClair, M.D. *Alcoholism in the Professions.* New York: Oxford University Press, 1984.

————. and Watherwax, Richard. *The Cat Who Drank Too Much.* Bantam, Conn.: The Bibliophile Press, 1982.

————. "The Homosexual AA Member: A Descriptive Study." Unpublished presentation at National Conference on Alcoholism conference, Seattle, Wash., May, 1980.

Bufe, Charles. *Alcoholics Anonymous: Cult or Cure?* San Francisco: See Sharp Press, 1991.

Burns, John. *The Answer To Addiction: The Path to Recovery from Alcohol, Drug, Food and Sexual Dependencies.* New York: The Crossroads Publishing Company, 1990.

Came to Believe . . . New York: Alcoholics Anonymous World Services, 1973.

Cheever, Susan. *Home Before Dark.* Boston: Houghton Mifflin, 1984.

The Christopher D. Smithers Foundation, Inc., ed. *Understanding Alcoholism.* New York: Charles Scribner's Sons, 1968.

Darrah, Mary C. *Sister Ignatia, Angel of Alcoholics Anonymous.* Chicago: Loyola University Press, 1992.

Douglas, Ann. *Terrible Honesty.* New York: Farrar, Strauss & Giroux, 1995.

Dr. Bob and the Good Oldtimers, a Biography, with Recollections of Early A.A. in the Midwest. New York: Alcoholics Anonymous World Services, 1980.

East Ridge: A Laboratory for Living the Survivors Program—The Way Out When All Other Ways Have Failed. Hankins, N.Y.: East Ridge Press, 1999.

Ellis, Albert, and Emmett Velten. *When AA Doesn't Work for You. Rational Steps to Quitting Alcohol.* Fort Lee, N.J.: Barricade Books, 1992.

Fingarette, Herbert. *Heavy Drinking. The Myth of Alcoholism as a Disease.* Berkeley: University of California Press, 1988.

Fitzgerald, Robert. *The Soul of Sponsorship: the Friendship of Father Ed Dowling, S.J. and Bill Wilson in Letters.* Center City, Minn.: Hazelden, 1995.

Fosdick, Harry Emerson. *On Being a Real Person.* New York: Harper & Brothers, 1943.

Fox, Ruth, and Peter Lyon. *Alcoholism: Its Scope, Cause and Treatment.* New York: Random House, 1955.

Fox, Ruth, ed. *Alcoholism: Behavioral Research, Therapeutic Approaches.* New York: Springer, 1967.

Gallanter, Mark, ed. *Currents in Alcoholism.* New York: Grune & Stratton, 1979.

Harris, Irving. *Sam Shoemaker and the Story of Faith—at Work.* New York: Seabury Press, 1978.

————. *The Breeze of the Spirit.* New York: Seabury Press, 1978.

Hoffer, Abram, and Humphrey Osmund. *New Hope for Alcoholics.* New Hyde Park, N.Y.: University Books, 1968.

Huxley, Aldous. *Moksha.* Michael Horowitz & Cynthia Palmer, eds. Rochester, Vt.: Inner Traditions International, Limited, 1999.

James, William. *The Varieties of Religious Experience.* Garden City, New York: Image Books, 1978.

Jellinek, E. M., ed. *Alcohol Addiction and Chronic Alcoholism.* New Haven, Conn.: Yale University Press, 1942.

————. *The Disease Concept of Alcoholism.* New Haven, Conn.: College and University Press, in association with Hill House Press, 1960.

Jublilate: A History of the Zion Episcopal Church 1782–1982. North Adams, Mass.: Excelsior Printing Company, 1982.

Kirkpatrick, Jean. *W.F.S. & A.A.* Quakertown, Penn.: Women for Sobriety, 1976.

Klein, Mitchell. *How It Worked: the Story of Clarence H. Snyder and the Early Days of Alcoholics Anonymous in Cleveland, Ohio.* Washingtonville, Conn.: The AA Big Book Study Group, 1999.

Kurtz, Ernest. *Not God: A History of Alcoholics Anonymous.* Expanded ed. Center City, Minn.: Hazelden, 1991.

————. *Shame & Guilt: Characteristics of the Dependency Cycle (An Historical Perspective for Professionals.* Center City, Minn.: Hazelden, 1981.

————. *The Collected Ernie Kurtz.* Wheeling, W. Va.: The Bishop of Books, 1999.

Kurtz, Ernest, and Katherine Ketchum. *The Spirituality of Imperfection: Storytelling and the Journey to Wholeness.* New York: Bantam Books, 1992.

The Language of the Heart: Bill W.'s Grapevine Writings. New York: The AA Grapevine, Inc., 1988.

Leach, Barry. "Be a Double Winner." Center City, Minn.: Hazelden, 1985.

————. "Historical Perspective: Homosexual Men and Women in A.A." Unpublished presentation at the International A.A. Convention in Montreal, Quebec, Canada, 1985.

Levin, Jerome D. *Treatment of Alcoholism and Other Addictions. A Self-Psychology Approach*. Northvale, N.J.: Jason Aronson, 1987.

Living Sober. New York: Alcoholics Anonymous World Services, 1975.

Luks, Alan. *Will America Sober Up?* Boston: Beacon Press, 1983.

Mackay, Marianne. *Prisms*. New York: Fawcett Crest, 1983.

Mann, Marty. *New Primer on Alcoholism: How People Drink, How to Recognize Alcoholics, and What to Do About Them*. Rev. ed. New York: Holt, Rinehart & Winston, 1981.

Miller, Alice. *Prisoners of Childhood: the Drama of the Gifted Child: the Search for the True Self*. New York: Basic Books, 1981.

P., Wally. *But, for the Grace of God . . . How Intergroups and Central Offices Carried the Message of Alcoholics Anonymous in the 1940s*. Wheeling, W. Va.: The Bishop of Books, 1995.

"Pass It On," The Story of Bill Wilson and How the A.A. Message Reached the World. New York: Alcoholics Anonymous World Services, 1984.

Peabody, Richard. *The Common Sense of Drinking*. Boston: Little, Brown, 1931.

Peele, Stanton. *Diseasing of America: Addiction Treatment Out of Control*. Lexington, Mass.: Lexington Books, 1989.

Peele, Stanton, Archie Brodsky, and Mary Arnold. *The Truth About Addiction and Recovery*. New York: Simon & Schuster, 1991.

Pittman, Bill. *AA The Way It Began*. Seattle, Wash.: Glen Abbey Books, 1988.

———. *Stepping Stones to Recovery*. Seattle, Wash.: Glen Abbey Books, 1988.

Powers, Thomas E. *Death, and Then What?* Hankins, N.Y.: East Ridge Press, 1999.

———. *First Questions on the Life of the Spirit*. New York: Harper & Brothers, 1959.

———. *Invitation to a Great Experiment: Exploring the Possibility That God Can Be Known*. New York: The Crossroads Press, 1990.

Powers, Thomas P. *Great Books on the Way to Health*. Hankins, N.Y.: East Ridge Press, 1999.

———. *Great Books on the Way to God*. Fremont Center, N.Y.: East Ridge Press, 1998.

Practice These Principles and What Is the Oxford Group? Center City, Minn.: Hazelden, 1997.

Progoff, Ira. *Jung, Synchronicity and Human Destiny*. New York: Dell, 1973.

Robertson, Nan. *Getting Better, Inside Alcoholics Anonymous.* New York: William Morrow, 1988.

Shoemaker, Helen. *I Stand By the Door.* New York: Harper & Row, 1967.

Shoemaker, Samuel M., *Courage to Change: the Christian Roots of the 12-Step Movement,* compiled and edited by Bill Pittman and Dick B. Grand Rapids, Mich.: Fleming H. Revell, 1994.

Solberg, R. J. *The Dry Drunk Syndrome.* Center City, Minn.: Hazelden, 1970.

———. *The Dry Drunk Revisited.* Center City, Minn.: Hazelden, 1980.

Strachan, J. George. *Alcoholism: Treatable Illness. An honorable approach to man's alcoholism problem.* Vancouver, B.C.: Mitchell Press Limited, 1967.

Thomsen, Robert. *Bill W.* New York: Harper & Row, 1975.

V., Rachel [pseud.]. *Family Secrets: Life Stories of Adult Children of Alcoholics.* San Francisco, Calif.: Harper & Row, 1987.

———. *A Woman Like You. Life Stories of Women Recovering from Alcoholism and Addiction.* San Francisco: Harper & Row, 1985.

Vaillant, George E. *The Natural History of Alcoholism.* Cambridge, Mass.: Harvard University Press, 1983.

Wallace, John. *Alcoholism: New Light on the Disease.* Newport, R.I.: Edgehill Publications, 1985.

Walker, Richmond. *For Drunks Only: One Man's Reaction to Alcoholics Anonymous.* 3rd ed. Center City, Minn.: Hazelden, 1987.

Wegscheider, Sharon. *Another Chance: Hope and Health for the Alcoholic Family.* Palo Alto, Calif.: Science & Behavior Books, 1981.

White, William L. *Slaying the Dragon: The History of Addiction Treatment and Recovery in America.* Bloomington, Ill.: Chestnut Health Systems, 1998.

Wilson, Lois B. *Diary of Two Motorcycle Hobos.* Published by author for private distribution, 1973.

———. *Lois Remembers.* New York: The Al-Anon Family Group Headquarters, 1979.

Wilson, William G. *Alcoholics Anonymous Comes of Age.* New York: Alcoholics Anonymous World Services, 1957.

———. *Alcoholics Anonymous.* 3d ed. New York: Alcoholics Anonymous World Services, 1976.

———. *As Bill Sees It.* New York: Alcoholics Anonymous World Services, 1967.

————. *The A.A. Service Manual Combined with Twelve Concepts for World Service, 1989–1990 Edition.* New York: Alcoholics Anonymous World Services, 1989.

————. *Twelve Steps and Twelve Traditions.* New York: Alcoholics Anonymous World Services, 1953.

Wing, Nell. *Grateful to Have Been There: My 42 Years with Bill and Lois, and the Evolution of Alcoholics Anonymous.* Park Ridge, Ill.: Parkside Publishing Corporation, 1992.

ARTICLES

"Alcoholics Anonymous: Book Review." *American Medical Association Journal* 113, 9 (October 14, 1939): 1,513.

"Alcoholics Anonymous: Book Review." *Journal of Nervous and Mental Diseases* 92, 3 (September 1940): 399–400.

"Alcoholics Anonymous: Book Review." *Mental Health Bulletin* (November–December 1941).

Alexander, Jack. "Alcoholics Anonymous: Freed Slaves of Drink, Now They Free Others." *Saturday Evening Post* (March 1, 1941): 59–65.

————. "Drunkard's Best Friend." *Saturday Evening Post* (April 1, 1950): 17–18; 74–79.

————. "The Faith that Moves Drunks Can Move the World." *AA Grapevine* 7, no. 11 (April 1951): 3–4.

————. "Jack Alexander of Saturday Evening Post Fame Thought AA's Were Pulling His Leg." *AA Grapevine* 1, no. 2 (May 1945): 1, 8.

Anderson, Dwight. "Committee for Education on Alcoholism Historic Event, Says Dwight Anderson." *AA Grapevine* 1, no. 5 (October 1944): 1.

Apter, Julia T., and Carl C. Pfeiffer. "The Effect of the Hallucinogenic Drugs LSD-25 and Mescaline on the Electroretinogram." *Annals of the New York Academy of Sciences* 66, no. 3 (1957): 508–14.

Axelrod, Julius, Rosco O. Brady, Bernard Witkop, and Edward Evarts. "The Distribution and Metabolism of Lysergic Acid Diethylamide." *Annals of the New York Academy of Sciences* 66, no. 3 (1957): 435–44.

Bain, James A. "A Review of the Biochemical Effects *In Vitro* of Certain Psychotomimetic Agents." *Annals of the New York Academy of Sciences* 66, no. 3 (1957): 459–67.

Baker, Russell. "Bad News for the Old Booze School." *AA Grapevine* 22, no. 12 (May 1966): 17–19.

————. "The Drugcase Is Getting Heavier." *AA Grapevine* 23, no. 4 (1966): 12–14.

"Bill W." *Life* 13, no. 12 (Fall 1990): 66.

Block, Marvin A. "Alcoholism and Alcoholics Anonymous." *AA Grapevine* 30, no. 9 (February 1974): 12–14.

————. "The Doctor's View." *AA Grapevine* 10, no. 2 (June 1953): 19–21.

Bloom, Herbert. "A Rabbi Speaks." *AA Grapevine* 10, no. 10 (May 1954): 38–40.

Cain, Arthur H. "Alcoholics Anonymous: Cult or Cure?" *Harper's Magazine;* February, 1963; 226: pp. 48–52.

————. "Speaking Out: Alcoholics Can Be Cured Despite A.A." *Saturday Evening Post* 237 (September 19, 1964): 6.

Canavan, David I. "Impaired Physicians Program: Support Groups." *Journal of the Medical Society of New Jersey* 80, no. 12 (November 1983): 953–4.

Dole, Vincent P. "AA, Drug Addiction and Pills." *AA Grapevine* 29, no. 5 (October 1972): 2–4.

Douglas, Donald B., Eido Tai Shimano, and Roshi. "On Research in Zen." *American Journal of Psychiatry* 132, no. 12. (December 1975): 1300–02.

Dowling, Edward. "Three Dimensions of AA." *AA Grapevine* 12, no. 2 (July 1956): 26–28.

Ellison, Jerome. "Alcoholics Anonymous: Dangers of Success." *Nation* 198 no. 10 (March 2, 1964): 212–14.

Ester, D. N. "Alcoholics Anonymous: Book Review." *Mental Health Bulletin:* 20, no. 2; (November–December 1941): 8.

Evarts, Edward. "A Review of the Neurophysiological Effects of Lysergic Acid Diethylamide (LSD) and Other Psychotomimetic Agents." *Annals of the New York Academy of Sciences;* 1957; 66, no. 3 (1957): 479–95.

"Evidence on the Sleeping Pill Menace." *AA Grapevine* 2, no. 5 (October 1945): 1, 8.

Fox, Ruth. "Imagine Such a Disease . . ." *AA Grapevine* 23, no. 9 (February 1967): 23.

Gitlow, Stanley E. "A Pharmacological Approach to Alcoholism." *AA Grapevine* 24, no. 5 (October 1968): 12–27.

Haggard, H. W., and Jellinek, E. M. "Two Yale Savants Stress Alcoholism as a True Disease." *AA Grapevine* 1, no. 1 (June 1944): 1.

Heard, Gerald. "The Search for Ecstasy." *AA Grapevine* 14, no. 12 (May 1958): 15–17.

"Help for Drunkards." *Time* (October 23, 1944): 72–75.

"High Watch Farm, An AA Tradition in Jeopardy." *Alcoholism* 5, no. 4 (March–April 1985): 60.

Hoagland, Hudson. "A Review of Biochemical Changes Induced *In Vivo* by Lysergic Acid Diethylamide and Similar Drugs." *Annals of the New York Academy of Sciences* 66, no. 3 (1957): 445–58.

Hoffer, Abram, and Humphry Osmond. "Alcoholism and the Researcher." *AA Grapevine* 16, no. 8 (January 1960): 19–23.

Huxley, Aldous. "The History of Tension." *AA Grapevine* 14, no. 6 (November 1957): 17–23.

———. "Man and Reality." *AA Today.* (1960): 90–92.

Ignatia, Sister. "Care and Treatment of Alcoholics." *AA Grapevine* 26, no. 1 (June 1969); 5–8.

Hurtz, Ernest, and Linda Farris Kurtz. "The Social Thought of Alcoholics." *Journal of Drug Issues* (Winter 1985): 119–134.

Kurtz, Ernest. "Why A.A. Works: The Intellectual Significance of Alcoholics Anonymous." *Journal of Studies on Alcohol* 43, no. 1 (1982): 38–80.

L., Barry. "You Mean, Just Let Anybody In?" *AA Grapevine* (September 1976): 26–29.

"Living Sober: The 50th Anniversary of Alcoholics Anonymous." *Village Voice* (July 23, 1985): 63–74.

London, Jack. "Review of *John Barleycorn.*" *AA Grapevine* 4, no. 6 (November 1947): 8.

Macfarlane, Peter Clark. "The 'White Hope' of Drug Victims." *Collier's* (November 29, 1913): 16–17, 29–30.

Markey, Morris. "Alcoholics and God." *Liberty Magazine* 30 (September 30, 1939): 6+.

Marrazzi, Amedeo S. "The Effects of Certain Drugs on Cerebral Synapses." *Annals of the New York Academy of Sciences* 66, no. 3 (1957): 496–507.

Maxwell, Milton A. "Contemporary Utilizations of Professional Help by Alcoholics Anonymous Members." *Annals of the New York Academy of Sciences* 273 (1976): 436–41.

———. "The Washingtonian Movement." *Quarterly Journal of Alcohol Studies* 11 (1950): 410–51.

McCarthy, Katherine. "Early Alcoholism Treatment: The Emmanuel Movement and Richard Peabody." *Journal of Studies on Alcohol* (January 1984).

Maclean, J. Ross, D. C. MacDonald, Ulan P. Byrne, and A. M. Hubbard. "The Use of LSD-25 in the Treatment of Alcoholism and Other Psychiatric Problems." *Quarterly Journal of Studies on Alcohol* 22, no. 1 (March 1961): 34–45.

Menninger, Karl. "An A.A. Appraisal." *AA Today* (1960): 14–15.

Niebuhr, Reinhold. "Letter to AA from . . ." *AA Today.* (1960): 65.

———. "The Serenity Prayer . . . its origins traced . . ." *AA Grapevine* 6, no. 8 (January 1950): 6–7.

Norris, John L. "Acting within the Traditions." *AA Grapevine* 28, no. 9 (February 1972): 15–16.

———. "Bridging the Gap between Active Treatment and Normal AA Involvement." *Alcohol Health & Research World* 6, no. 4 (1982): 6–9.

———. "Doctors and AA." *AA Grapevine* 24, no. 5 (1968): 5.

———. "The General Service Board Proposals & Recommendations, 1965." *AA Grapevine* 22, no. 8 (January 1966): 3–7.

———. "Sponsor Your Doctor." *AA Grapevine* 32, no. 8 (January 1976): 8–9.

———. "Three Doctors Speak." *AA Grapevine* 10, no. 7 (December 1953): 6.

———. "What AA Can Offer Professional Schools and What It Cannot." *Annals of the New York Academy of Sciences* 178 (1971): 61–65.

Osmond, Humpry. "A Review of the Clinical Effects of Psychotomimetic Agents." *Annals of the New York Academy of Sciences* 66, no. 3 (1957): 418–34.

Oursler, Fulton. "Charming Is the Word for Alcoholics." *AA Grapevine* 1, no. 2 (July 1944): 1.

Paton, Alan. (untitled) *AA Grapevine* 16, no. 5 (October 1959): 9–11.

Peale, Norman Vincent. "Do You Yearn for Fellowship?" *AA Grapevine* 4, no. 5 (October 1947): 15.

Perelman, S. J. "The Meditations of Old Mr. Perelman on Dynamic Drunks." *AA Grapevine* 1, no. 6 (November 1944): 1.

"Philadelphia Alcoholics Anonymous." *Philadelphia Medicine* (February 12, 1942).

Potter, Milton G. "Alcoholism—A Challenge to the Medical Profession." *AA Grapevine* 5, no. 11 (April 1949): 5–7.

Potter, Milton G., M.D. moderator, panel discussion: "Chronic Alcoholism as a Medical Problem." Block, Marvin A., M.D. "Alcoholism—The General Practitioner's Viewpoint." Brightman, I. Jay, M.D. "Chronic Alcoholism as a Public Responsibility." Davis, C. Nelson, M.D. "Problems of Alcoholism—The Hospital Viewpoint." Smith, James J., M.D. "The Endocrine Basis and Hormonal Therapy of Alcoholism." Tiebout, Harry M., M.D. "Some Aspects of the Problem of Alcoholism." Wilson, William G. "Alcoholics Anonymous." *New York State Journal of Medicine;* July, 1950; pp. 1,697–1716.

Purpura, Dominick P. "Experimental Analysis of the Inhibitory Action of Lysergic Acid Diethylamide on Cortical Dendritic Activity." *Annals of the New York Academy of Sciences* 66, no. 3 (1957): 515–36.

Robertson, Nan. "The Changing World of Alcoholics Anonymous." *New York Times Magazine* 137 (February 21, 1988): 40.

Scott, Edward M. "The Technique of Psychotherapy with Alcoholics." *Quarterly Journal of Studies on Alcohol* 22, no. 1 (March 1961): 69–80.

Seiberling, Henrietta, and John F. Seiberling. "Origins of Alcoholics Anonymous." *Employee Assistance Quarterly* 1, no. 1 (1985): 33–39.

Seixas, Frank A. "My First Alcoholic Patient." *AA Grapevine* 31, no. 4 (September 1974): 2–5.

———. "Alcoholism Treatment: A Descriptive Guide." *Psychiatric Annals* 12, no. 4 (1982): 375–6, 381–5.

Shoemaker, Samuel M. "The Spiritual Angle." *AA Grapevine* 12, no. 5 (October 1955): 29–33.

———. "Those Twelve Steps as I Understand Them." *AA Grapevine* 20, no. 8 (January 1964): 26–34.

Silkworth, William D. "Doctor Calls 'Slip' More Normal than Alcoholic." *AA Grapevine* 3, no. 8 (January 1947): 1, 4–5.

———. "A Highly Successful Approach to the Alcoholic Problem." *Medical Record* 154, no. 3 (August 6, 1941): 105–7.

———. "A New Approach to Psychotherapy in Chronic Alcoholism." *The Journal-Lancet* 59, no. 7 (July 1939): 312–15.

———. "A Prescription for Sobriety." *AA Grapevine* 3, no. 8 (January 1947): 1, 8.

Sinclair, Upton. "Some Writers I Have Known." *AA Grapevine* 19, no. 12 (May 1963): 26–32.

Smith, Margaret Chase. "A Senator Evaluates the Steps and Traditions." *AA Today* (1960): 86–87.

Sokoloff, Louis, Seymous Perlin, Conan Kornetsky, and Seymour S. Kety. "The Effects of D-Lysergic Acid Diethylamide on Cerebral Circulation and Over-All Metabolism." *Annals of the New York Academy of Sciences* 66, no. 3 (1957): 418–34.

Strong, Jr., Leonard V. "On Anonymity." *AA Grapevine* 7, no. 7 (December 1950): 10–12.

Thurber, James, "The Bear Who Let It Alone." *AA Grapevine* 28, no. 1 (1971): 24–25.

Tiebout, Harry M. "AA is Bridge to Happy Living." *AA Grapevine* 4, no. 12 (May 1948): 1.

———. "The Act of Surrender in the Therapeutic Process." *AA Grapevine* 31, no. 1 (June 1974): 10–19.

———. "Alcoholics Anonymous: An Experiment of Nature." *Quarterly Journal of Studies on Alcohol* 22, no. 1 (March 1961): 52–68.

———. "Conversion as a Psychological Phenomenon in the Treatment of the Alcoholic." *AA Grapevine* 10, no. 10 (March 1954): 3–5.

———. "The Pink Cloud and After." *AA Grapevine* 12, no. 4 (September 1955): 2–7.

———. "Surrender versus Compliance in Therapy." *AA Grapevine* 10, no. 4 (September 1953): 3–8.

———. "The Therapeutic Mechanisms of Alcoholics Anonymous." *American Journal of Psychiatry* 100, no. 4 (January 1944): 468–73.

———. "Treating the Causes of Alcoholism." *AA Grapevine* 20, no. 6 (November 1963): 9–11.

———. "What Does Surrender Mean?" *AA Grapevine* 20, no. 11 (April 1963): 30–34.

———. "What Takes Place in an Alcoholic's 'Spiritual Awakening?'" *AA Grapevine* 10, no. 11 (April 1954): 30–35.

———. "When the Big 'I' Becomes Nobody." *AA Grapevine* 22, no. 4 (September 1965): 18–22.

———. "Why Psychiatrists Fail with Alcoholics." *AA Grapevine* 13, no. 4 (September 1956): 5–10.

———. "The Wiley Ego." *AA Grapevine* (December 1962).

Tunks, Walter F. "A.A. Is Religion with Feet on Ground." *AA Grapevine* 5, no. 2 (July 1948): 16.

———. "Eulogy of Dr. Bob." *AA Grapevine* 7, no. 8 (January 1951): 45–46.

Towns, Charles B. "The Physicians Guide for the Treatment of the Drug Habit and Alcoholism." 8-page pamphlet.

Wilson, Lois B. "Bill's Wife Remembers When He and She and the First AAs Were Very Young." *AA Grapevine* 1, no. 7 (December 1944): 1.

———. "How One AA Wife Lives the 12 Steps." *AA Grapevine* 10, no. 3 (August 1953): 40–42.

———. "Vignettes from the Past: Bill & Thomas Edison." *Parkside* 2, no. 2 (Winter/Spring 1990): 27.

Wilson, William G. "AA Is Not Big Business." *AA Grapevine* 7, no. 6 (November 1950): 24–26.

———. "AA's Tradition of Self-Support." *AA Grapevine* 24, no. 5 (October 1967): 8–9.

———. "Anne S." *AA Grapevine* 6, no. 2 (July 1949): 6.

———. "Basic Concepts of Alcoholics Anonymous." *New York State Journal of Medicine* 4, no. 16 (August 15, 1944): 1805–10.

———. "The Beginning of AA." *AA Grapevine* 22, no. 1 (June 1965); 2–9.

———. "Book Publication Proved Discouraging Venture." *AA Grapevine* 4, no. 2 (July 1947): 3.

———, James P. Timmins. "Speeches." *AA Grapevine* 19, no. 2 (July 1962): 2–3.

———. "The Book Is Born." *AA Grapevine* 2, no. 5 (October 1945): 2, 6.

———. "The Shape of Things to Come." *AA Grapevine* 1, no. 1 (June 1944): 3.

———. "The Society of Alcoholics Anonymous." *American Journal of Psychiatry* 106, no. 5 (November 1949): 370–75.

———. "Trustee Vote Fixes Policy on Gift Funds." *AA Grapevine* 3, no. 1 (June 1946): 2, 8.

———. "The Twelve Traditions: Our Keys to Survival and Growth." *AA Grapevine* 13, no. 6 (November 1956): 21.

———. "Who Is a Member of Alcoholics Anonymous?" *AA Grapevine* 3, no. 3 (August 1946): 3, 7.

———. "Will AA Ever Have a Personal Government?" *AA Grapevine* 3, no. 8 (January 1947): 3.

FILMS AND VIDEOS

Alcoholics Anonymous—An Inside View. New York: Alcoholics Anonymous World Services, 1992. 15 minutes. Videocassette.

Alcoholics Anonymous: GSO Today, Circles of Love & Service, [and] Markings of the Journey. New York: Alcoholics Anonymous World Services, Inc., 1987. 15 minutes each. Film on videocassette.

Bill Discusses the Twelve Traditions. New York: Alcoholics Anonymous World Services, Inc., 1969. 60 minutes. Film on videocassette. (For AA internal use only.)

Bill's Own Story. New York: Alcoholics Anonymous World Services, Inc., 1965. 60 minutes. Film on videocassette. (For AA internal use only.)

Can You Stop People from Drinking? NOVA. Boston, Mass.: NOVA, December 22, 1992. 60 minutes. Videocassette.

Dawn of Hope: The Founding of Alcoholics Anonymous: An Historical Perspective. Jack Glieck. Akron, Ohio: Cinemark, Inc., 1987. 30 minutes. Videocassette.

Days of Wine and Roses. Film, 118 minutes. Produced by Martin Manulis and directed by Blake Edwards. Burbank, Calif.: Warner Brothers, Inc., 1962.

I'll Cry Tomorrow. Film, 119 minutes. Produced by Lawrence Weingarten and directed by Daniel Mann. Hollywood, Calif.: MGM, 1955.

It Sure Beats Sitting in a Cell. New York: Alcoholics Anonymous World Services, Inc., 1987. 17 minutes. Videocassette.

Life of the Party: The Story of Beatrice. Film. 105 minutes. 1992.

Lost Weekend, The. Film, 102 minutes. Charles Bracket and Bill Wilder. Universal City Studios, Inc.: Paramount Pictures, 1945.

My Name Is Bill W. 120 minutes. James Garner, and Peter Duchow. Hallmark Hall of Fame: April 20, 1989.

Welcome to Akron, Birthplace of Alcoholics Anonymous. Video, 60 minutes. Chattanooga, Tenn.: Bill's Tapes, 1992.

We Never Talked About My Drinking, 56 minutes. Francis Hartigan, Hartford, Conn.: Connecticut Public Television and the Stepping Stones Foundation, June 24, 1990.

INDEX

CPSIA information can be obtained at www.ICGtesting.com
Printed in the USA
LVOW08s2053020616

490959LV00003B/470/P